Britain and
Soviet Communism

The Impact of a Revolution

F. S. NORTHEDGE
and
AUDREY WELLS

First published 1982 by
THE MACMILLAN PRESS LTD
London and Basingstoke
Companies and representatives throughout the world

ISBN 0 333 27192 0 (hc)
ISBN 0 333 27193 9 (pbk)

Filmset in 10/12pt Baskerville by
Reproduction Drawings Ltd., Sutton, Surrey
Printed in Hong Kong

Contents

Preface

FEW subjects which deeply affect our lives have had so little written about them as relations between Britain and the Soviet Union. Britain and Russia have been in diplomatic contact for over four hundred years, and each country has probably played a more sustained role in the other's international affairs over a long period than any other country. Since the revolution in Russia in 1917, the issues raised by Soviet communism have provoked as intense a debate in Britain as any in our history. It is also all too obvious today that our relations with the Soviet state, along with those of our allies, could go far to determine, not only the future of the human race, but whether there will be a future at all. And yet serious studies of Anglo-Soviet affairs are few.

One reason for this, of course, is the paucity of information available to Western scholars about the making of the external policy of the Soviet Union, and this was true to a large extent of Russian policy in Tsarist times, too. Moreover, the virtual absence of free contacts between the Soviet people and the world outside makes it difficult, if not impossible, for the non-Russian to assess what kind of impact the British have made on the Russians. We have therefore concentrated in this book, not on the two sides of the coin of Anglo-Soviet relations, as one might expect in a study of any other pair of countries, but on the British experience of the Soviet phenomenon since the revolution. We are concerned with what Britain has made of this great and strange force in world politics, Soviet communism, and how it has affected our life and thought.

The book is accordingly divided into two parts. Part I is devoted to the main themes in Britain's experience of the Soviet Union in war and peace during the past sixty-three years. Its object is to provide a broad account of what the Soviet state has meant for Britain in world political terms since 1917, and at the same time it formulates a judgement, or series of judgements, on how well British politicians and the British community as a whole have coped with this portent on the world scene. The story is presented in enough detail, it is hoped, to counteract partisan generalities which so often pass for considered opinions on British relations with Russia, while not losing sight of the main thread of events. In part II the impact of the revolution and its sequel in Russia on British affairs and thinking is considered in a somewhat broader sense, with attention paid to the extraordinary polarities of British reactions to things Russian, the switches from love to hate; to the profound effects of Soviet communism on the intellectual and academic community in Britain, both in the past and more recently; to the role played by the Soviet Union in the Labour and trade union movements in this country; and to the importance of the Soviet system at different times to the British economy, trade and employment.

Our principal argument is that the problem of how Britain is best to deal with the Soviet Union demands the most detached study of which we are capable, both because of the momentousness of the issues which now divide East and West, and because of the intense feelings in which so much of our thinking about Russia has been and continues to be steeped. British views about Russia have almost always violently oscillated from one extreme of emotion to another, owing partly to our ignorance of the other country (to which the Russians themselves, or their leaders, have systematically contributed), partly to the range and seriousness of the issues which the Soviet phenomenon has raised for us, and partly to the fact that our attitudes to Soviet communism are more often than not governed by our thoughts and feelings about things to which Soviet communism may be quite unrelated. This book is conceived as a modest contribution to the formation of more rational judgements.

The London School of Economics and   F. S. Northedge
Political Science   Audrey Wells
                                                                  May 1981

Part I

Neither Enemies nor Friends

1. Contact and Conflict

THE encounter between Britain and Russia has been of dominating importance to both countries for two hundred years. Throughout the nineteenth century, Russia was, for British Liberals, the incarnation of reaction, the suppressor of the Hungarians in 1849 and the Poles in 1830 and 1863. For British Conservatives, the Russian Bear was the most formidable threat to the Empire in its most brilliant sector, India, and to British sea power on the all-red route through the Mediterranean and the Indian Ocean to the Far East. With the coming of Bolshevism in 1917, Russia became a more searching challenge to British political assumptions and social stability than any in the country's modern history. Since the Second World War, Russia has presented the greatest and most puzzling threat to Britain's security, and not only Britain's, but that of the entire Western alliance.

For Russia herself, Britain has been perhaps the most momentous of all her international contacts, although since 1945 Britain's role as Russia's foremost adversary on the world stage has been inherited by the United States. In the century between the end of the Napoleonic wars in 1815 and the outbreak of the First World War, Britain was the major opponent of Russian expansion towards the high seas and into Asia and China. Britain stood, with 'the ships, the men, the money, too', as the Victorian music-hall jingle ran, across Russia's path into the Balkans, into Arab lands under Ottoman control in the Near East, into India and the Pacific. Wherever Russia moved, Britain was in the way. In 1905 Russia suffered her greatest reverse on land and sea at the hands of an ally of Britain, Japan.

After the Bolshevik seizure of power in November 1917, Britain represented, in the eyes of Lenin and his associates, the undoubted leader of the capitalist conspiracy to destroy the first communist state which the Marxist ideology postulated as a matter of course. Britain was not as intent as France on intervention in the civil war in Russia which followed the events of November 1917, nor as involved with

Poland in its struggle with the Red Army in 1920. But Britain was far and away the most influential capitalist Power of the day; if the bourgeois world was ever going to crush Soviet communism, it would be when London gave the signal, and many believed that signal was given in 1927, when Stanley Baldwin's government broke off diplomatic relations with the Soviets, thus inaugurating their greatest period of isolation between the civil war and Hitler's invasion in 1941. Again, when Russia was reviving after the Second World War, it was Britain, in Moscow's eyes, who seemed bent on recruiting a reluctant America, and the rest of the Western world as well, for a containment system aimed at placing obstacles in Russia's way at almost every point of the compass.

This long confrontation suggests that there must have been many times when the two states were actually at war. Both have considerable military traditions and have at one time or another fought with almost all their neighbours. But, strangely for world Powers, the British and Russians have fought only once since their first contacts in the sixteenth century, and that was during the Crimean war of 1854–56, really an intervention by Britain, France and Sardinia–Piedmont in a war between Russia and Turkey which had begun in October 1853. There is little dispute, at least among British historians, that the Crimean war was an illogical and unnecessary war, grossly mismanaged on both sides. The ostensible object of the allies was to combat Russian claims to guardianship of Christians in the Ottoman empire; behind this lay the long-standing British opposition to Russia's becoming the successor to the Ottoman Porte, Constantinople and the Straits. But it was not explained how this could be achieved by defeating the Russians in the Crimea. On the other hand, where were the allies going to fight, since Russia had evacuated and Austria had occupied the Danubian principalities (modern Rumania) where Russo-Turkish hostilities began in the first place? In the age of land armies, it was as much a problem for Britain and Russia to know where to fight as what to fight about.

Apart from the Crimean war, Britain and Russia, so far from fighting each other, have been allies, and allies desperately dependent on one another, in all the greatest wars each has fought in modern times. They were allies in the Napoleonic wars at the beginning of the nineteenth century. In 1812 Napoleon's Grand Army was defeated *in* Russia, if not precisely *by* Russia, and the Tsar, Alexander I, who, on a raft in the river Niemen at Tilsit in 1807 reached an agreement with the French Emperor comparable with Stalin's pact with Hitler in 1939, joined with the British as the two greatest victors of the war at the Congress of Vienna after Waterloo. The British and Russian governments fought an ideological war for the first half of the nineteenth century, when the Tsars used the Holy Alliance against constitutionalism in Europe, and Britain and France sided with liberal reform. In the second half of the century, conflict between London and St Petersburg over the moribund Ottoman empire brought them to the brink of war more than once. But hardly had the century ended when Britain, with France, was standing at Russia's side again, this time against the Central Powers in the First World War.

For the first three years of that war, the Russian army, at the cost of enormous casualties, saved the Western allies from defeat – the first battle of the Marne could not have been won without the Russian invasion of East Prussia – until it could stand the strain no longer. Again, in the Second World War, this time with far greater help from Britain and the United States, and with the benefit of Russia's industrial revolution in the 1930s, Soviet forces pounded the heart out of the German Wehrmacht as the two Anglo-Saxon Powers prepared for the assault on France on 6 June 1944. In these three struggles, against Napoleon, the Kaiser and Hitler, Russia acted as the stone of attrition while Britain and her allies planned their counterstroke.

Nor is the record of Anglo-Russian co-operation confined to wartime alliances. Even when, in peace-time, Russia and the West have been bitterly divided and war could not be ruled out, it was not seldom Britain who restrained her allies from going over the brink. Sometimes this occurred when British ministers took the initiative; sometimes when they responded to public opinion. In either case, Britain has a history of setting the pace for *détente* with Russia, especially since 1917. In the months between the Bolshevik seizure of power and the signing of the peace treaties with the Central Powers in June 1919, it was Britain, or rather the British Prime Minister, Lloyd George, who, of all the allies, and with the disapproval of some of them, argued the case for an understanding with Lenin. He continued to argue it until his fall from power in October 1922.[1] More especially in the period of the East–West Cold War after 1945, it was invariably the British who took the lead in movements in the West to come to terms with the Russians at summit meetings, until this role was taken over by the Kennedy administration in the United States after the 1962 Cuban missiles crisis. From Winston Churchill's pleas for opening up communications with Russia's new leaders after Stalin's death in March 1953 to Prime Minister Harold Macmillan's almost monotonous calls for top-level meetings with First Secretary Khrushchev in the later 1950s, British politicians were charged by the American, French and West German press with harbouring the 'English disease', an ailment with the symptom of persistent clamour for talks on easing tension with Soviet leaders. By the time President Nixon and Secretary of State Kissinger were making *détente* with Russia the centrepiece of their foreign policy, British ministers had tired the world with talking about it.

This intermittent congruence of the British and Russian outlook, reflected in wartime alliances and experiments in *détente*, could have had some basis in sympathy for the underdog, said to be common to both countries. True, Stalin's Russia became, for the British, a 'God that failed' after the Second World War,[2] but, after all, it had been a god; it had represented a more equal society, an image owing more to British desires than to the reality of the Soviet state. But the reasons for Anglo-Soviet co-operation are doubtless more earthy. They are that, whenever Europe has been threatened by some dominant power, Britain, a small island off its north-west coast, and Russia, an open land mass on its eastern marches, have in the end had to combine to defend their independence, and have done so with success. The words 'in the end' must be stressed because on each occasion, and especially before and even during the Second World War, almost insurmountable antipathies between the two countries prevented joint action until the last possible moment. After 1945, Germany, the chief threat to the European balance since its unification in 1871, ceased to play its role of bringing Britain and Russia together, owing to its total defeat and seemingly permanent division. Still, whenever fears of Germany revived in Britain, even after 1945, some of the old regard for Russia revived as well. For Britain, as for Russia, the division of Germany still makes a certain sort of sense.

Now, Britain and Russia are on opposite sides of the high fence of East–West conflict, Britain an important, though much diminished member of the various alliances for collective defence against the Soviet Union which the Western Powers have been forging since 1948, Russia the unchallenged leader of the group of East European states forming the Warsaw treaty organisation which have undergone communisation with her encouragement or at her command. With Russia's ascent to super-Power status comparable with that of the United States, and with the continuous decline in Britain's economic performance, Britain has long lost her primacy as Russia's partner and rival in the changing alignments of world politics. But the fact that Britain has often been ahead of her allies in reacting to Russia's policies, both with hostility and with friendship, and that they have generally come round to her point of view, may mean that she still has much to teach them about dealing with the Russian phenomenon.

II

It is not remarkable that Britain and Russia, in their four-hundred-year-old encounter with each other, have quarrelled from time to time, or that they have seen one another as their most redoubtable adversary. Few countries whose relations have been so important for world politics have differed as much as Britain and Russia, and any study of those relations must begin and end with the differences.

The British, in their small island off the coast of a politically turbulent continent, had to work hard to earn the means to pay for the imported food and raw materials needed for the industrialisation which turned them in the last two centuries from a mainly rural into a mainly urban people, but in practically every other respect they were smiled on by fortune. Their insular security, making them think that insecure people, like the French or Russians, must be paranoid; their political unity, which they took for granted while Europe was riddled with rival creeds; their location at the confluence of maritime highways leading to the world: these provided foundations for greatness as a world Power.

In almost every respect Russia, or the territories comprising the Russia that we know today, was equally *un*favoured. The first known communities which sprang up in western Russia in the Middle Ages – the trading city-states of Novgorod, Kiev, Smolensk, Ryazan, settled by the Varangians, or Vikings, from Scandinavia, and the Grand Duchy of Moscow, which sprang to pre-eminence in the fourteenth century – were advantaged in one particular: the system of rivers, navigable for hundreds of miles, connecting the Russia we know today with the Baltic to the north and the Black Sea to the south, and making Europe virtually an island. Russia's rivers, almost until the twentieth century, were the basic means of transport – as late as the mid-nineteenth century Russia had only 650 miles of railway in a country covering one sixth of the land surface of the globe. But the river system could be used as avenues of entry for invaders. And it led, in the north, to a Baltic Sea frozen in the winter and dominated until the time of Peter the Great (reigned 1689–1725) by powerful foreigners like the Swedes, Poles and Germans, and, in the south, to a Black Sea held by equally powerful nations, the Tatars and Mongols, the Byzantine empire and then the Ottoman Turks. The Russians lived in an empty land which was at the same time exposed and enclosed.

The Russian land, the land Moscow's rulers brought under their control between the fifteenth and nineteenth centuries, was rich in raw materials, but these, apart from timber, furs, hides and skins, tallow, gold and the grain from the rich black soil of the Ukraine, could not be much exploited with the technology available. The climate was varied, but in all habitable areas hot beyond endurance in the summer and cold beyond endurance in the endless winters. The greatest drawback of the Russian land, however, is its vulnerability to external attack, with its great navigable rivers and open plains, running for three thousand miles and more from western Europe to the easily crossed Urals and beyond into Siberia. Across the plains swept, until the consolidation of Muscovite power by the Romanovs from the accession of Michael in 1613, hordes of plundering armies year by year. This vulnerability was in fact an important element in the rise of Moscow, with its central location and the security provided for it by the endless northern forests. It was remote from the open steppe in the south and hence served as a refuge from marauding Tatars of the Golden Horde, the Grand Dukes of Moscow first serving as tax-gatherers for the invaders, and later, as their strength grew, leading excursions against the Tatars and driving them back to the Black Sea. The essence of this life until at least the Middle Ages was its harshness, isolation, insecurity, its need for strong government to protect the people and strong community spirit as a defence, both against the rulers of Moscow and their henchmen, the boyars, and against the foreign enemy.

England, too, was exposed to waves of invaders over a thousand years, the Romans, Angles, Saxons and Jutes from north Germany, the Vikings, Normans from northern France. But most of them brought a higher level of civilisation, certainly of technology, than that of the natives. In Russia's case, the impact which surrounding peoples made was worlds apart from the questioning European spirit for the most part; it was suppressive, conforming, symbolising force rather than the critical intelligence, authority rather than personal initiative. A typical episode in the life of Ivan III (1462–1505) was his effort to identify himself as the predestined successor to the Tatar hordes and the emperors of Byzantium after the fall of the latter to the Turks in 1453. He married a Byzantine princess, Zoe Palaeologus, the niece of the last Byzantine emperor, and took as his symbols of state the Tatar shapka, or cap, the Tatar knout, or scourge, and the two-headed Byzantine eagle of empire: tokens of power untouched with any suggestion of limitation or answerability. After 1453, the Russian Orthodox Church, more closely linked with the state than any Western church, embraced the notion of Moscow as the Third Rome, following ancient Rome and Byzantium, after which there would be no fourth. The monk Philoteus urged the idea on the rulers of Moscow in the fifteenth century, though it is not known how far it became official state doctrine. Of the three Romes, Moscow and Byzantium were most akin spiritually. The Rome of Cicero and Vergil were never much cultivated in Russia's universities, old or new. The preferred course was to blend Western technology with Byzantine and Tatar authority: in Lenin's words, Soviets plus electricity.

Besides the physical differences between the two countries, and the effects of outsiders on Britain's and Russia's development, there are the contrasts between their vital life experiences. In England, up to the eighteenth century, the dominant economic activity, apart from farming, was trade and on the basis of trade, carried on by merchant adventurers to India and China in the east and the Americas in the west, the British Empire began to be built up, ultimately to embrace a quarter of the land surface of the globe and a quarter of its population. The Empire was to provide much of the capital for the later industrialisation of Britain and wide-ranging markets for British exports. It furnished a schooling in government, the administration of justice, the use of military force, for Britain's ruling classes. But the Empire, strangely, also became a liberalising force in British politics, and the example of empire in North America is instructive in this respect. When the thirteen American colonies broke away from Britain in the late eighteenth century, they did so under the influence of ideas most of which came from Britain. The Declaration of

Independence might have been written by John Locke, with some French phrases. But the American Revolution, its exposure of the political ineptitude of George III and the men around him, and the democratic principles of the Founding Fathers, all fuelled the movement for reform in Britain, though it was checked for a time by the alarm created by Jacobinism in France.

For Russia, empire – like everything else – ran a different course. The Russian Empire, built up from its Muscovite core from the time of Peter the Great until the acquisition of the Liaotung peninsula from Japan (who had taken it from China) in 1898, was a land empire, extended continuously through two centuries, not by trade, but by military conquest, and not by roving merchants, but by generals of the Tsars and Tsarinas, leading substantial armies. The Russian Empire was a projection of the Russian state, not an appendix, like the British, capable of being discarded when its inhabitants came of age. The Russian Empire could hardly have been decolonised, as Britain has shed her colonial apanages, like ripe apples from the tree. Decolonising the Empire, Tsarist or communist, would be dismantling the Russian state.

The British Empire was won by soldiers and sailors who did their work for pay or adventure, or from a sense of duty, and press gangs made up deficiencies. The Tsar's armies, which created the Russian Empire, were a branch of serfdom, which was not abolished until 1861, and even then not completely. The Russian army, like the empire it appropriated, consolidated the monarchy, served the centralised state. The Empire, so unlike the British Empire, never liberalised the metropolitan government, but worked in the opposite direction. And because the Russian Empire was an extension of the Russian state, threats to it were regarded (and still are) as threats to the state. That is why, when Japan checked the spread of the Russian Empire into Korea and Manchuria in 1905, the Russian monarchy was shaken to its foundations, and continued to shake until 1917. When the British Empire was threatened by the American colonies in 1776, and, in the twentieth century, by African and Asian nationalism, the British political system was unaffected. It may even have been strengthened.

But perhaps the greatest difference in the life histories of Britain and Russia is their experience of industrialisation. Britain was the first country to pass through the Industrial Revolution, that is, the beginning of a process, about two centuries ago, of substituting mechanical energy for human muscles in the manufacture of objects and the moving of things. The British people became predominantly urban dwellers, their economic system was internationalised, and the social structure and political system were affected. By the time the Industrial Revolution began, that is, the 1760s, the battle for Parliamentary supremacy over the Crown had been fought and won a century before, but it was assured by the Industrial Revolution. The transformation of Britain from an agricultural into a manufacturing country was also a transfer of power from landlords who buttressed the monarchy to manufacturers, traders and financiers, whose new status was symbolised by the Reform Act of 1832. Men enriched by the coal and steam age joined forces and intermarried with lords and squires of the countryside as the masters of Britain. Their attitude towards the new working class of the towns and factories was not uniformly exploitative; often it was tempered by the spirit of welfare and charity of the old landed gentry, expressed in due course in factory legislation and local authority intervention in urban life. The treatment meted out to the poor in Victorian England now seems heartless, but compared, say, with the methods used against trade unions by American business in the same period, it was almost benign.

These circumstances help explain the moderation of the British trade union and labour movements which sprang from the Industrial Revolution. After the efforts to form a Grand National Consolidated Trade Union in the 1830s, with its revolutionary programme and plans for a general strike, British trade unions developed as orderly, almost bourgeois organisations, as real wages rose in the mid-century. With the onset of industrial depression in the 1880s, the unskilled began to form their own unions, like the dockers and matchworkers, with more militant leaders and policies. Nevertheless, the Trades Union Congress, founded in 1868, began and continued as a deeply conservative body, compared with similar organisations on the continent. When, in 1902, trade unions started to support the Labour Representation Committee, the forerunner of the Labour party, they chiefly wanted to use it to reform the law, especially the Taff Vale judgment of the House of Lords in 1901, which threatened them with financial ruin. If Keir Hardie had appealed for trade union support on the basis of a socialist programme, he would probably not have won it.

Industrialisation acclimatised British capitalists to the idea of social reform – it was surely better to have a contented than a discontented work-force – and it made British workers more patriotic, xenophobic, conservative. True, the First World War for a time exerted a strong influence in the opposite direction; combined with the long trade depression and mass unemployment left in its wake, the war aroused in British employers lively fears of social revolution, reflected in their hostility towards Soviet Russia, some effects of which will be considered in the next chapter. Even so, this never took on the extremist colour which it did in Belgium, France, Germany, Italy and elsewhere in Europe, except with a small minority. The British Union of Fascists in the 1930s was never more than a minor irritant, trying to make Olympia look like the Piazza Venezia. The war, too, stirred in working-class Britain disillusionment with the social system, with Parliament, politics, the Church, though not, it seems, the monarchy, and this was aggravated by unemployment and the dole. And yet the position of the Labour party, the chief political expression of working-class interests, was never seriously threatened by revolutionary factions, like the communists, the ILP, or the Socialist party of Great Britain. The rare militant Left-wing MP was treated with affection rather than distaste in the House, his mutterings against capitalism regarded as a relief from the serious business on the order paper.

When we turn back to Russia, we see how different was its experience of industrialisation, perhaps the most powerful agent of change in modern history. Russia had its Industrial Revolution, but a hundred years later than Britain. Until the 1860s, industry was still based on handicrafts and carried on mainly in the home; waterways were still the basic means of transport.[3] When mechanical industry came, it was confined to certain areas of the country, especially the Moscow region, St Petersburg, the Polish provinces, notably Lodz and Warsaw, and the Baltic lands; it never spread to the south.[4] It was also limited to certain industries, especially the railways, the metal trades and textiles. The state played a central role in the development of large-scale manufacturing enterprises, and these were the most typical forms that industrialisation took. Above all, the Industrial Revolution was to a large extent financed from abroad; under Alexander II (reigned 1855–81) Russia became the largest borrowing country in Europe, most of the public and private debt being held in France. In 1914, 80 per cent of government external debt was held in France. One third of all the issue stock of joint stock companies (apart from the banks) was estimated to be foreign-held; France had the major share, about one third, with Britain and Germany a close second and third respectively.[5] Two thirds of all pig iron enterprises were owned by French concerns, a half of coal mining. Germany was dominant in chemical manufacture and electrical engineering and Britain in oil extraction.

The Russian people were on the whole unaffected by the Industrial Revolution until Russia's forced industrialisation under the communists after the First World War. When that war began, only three million out of Russia's 170 million people worked in industry, though those who did were more densely massed in particular areas of the country and in big concerns than was the case in other countries. The work-force in industry generally consisted of large, closely knit groups in the manufacturing areas of Moscow and St Petersburg, cut off from the rest of the country and hence well adapted for mobilisation by revolutionary militants. The Russian people were never exposed to the liberalising effects of industrialism. The relatively small numbers who were drawn into the factories, mines and railways in the last three or four decades of the nineteenth century dealt either with government officials who were not answerable to any popularly elected body or, more often, with entrepreneurs for the most part foreign and remote. When Lenin in 1917 denounced the capitalist system, he was attacking something alien to the Russian people. The owners of manufacturing industry were for the most part invisible and had to be imagined, and Lenin had little difficulty in helping the people form an image of capitalists which suited his purposes.

In Britain, the Industrial Revolution made its contribution to Parliamentary democracy, representative government and ultimately to the reconciliation of social classes. In Russia, industrialism, in so far as it had any impact on the mass of the people, set them against the prevailing social order: it deepened the gulf between rich and poor. So far from stimulating national pride, it made Russia more like a colonial dominion, with much of the country's wealth and enterprise controlled from outside. Industry was external to society, not within it, and efforts to integrate it with growing social needs were tardy and ineffective. Hours of work and conditions of labour were not regulated until the 1880s, and even then the lack of efficient inspectors made regulation virtually non-existent. Trade unions came under criminal law until 1906. Strikes were illegal, even after the revolution of 1905, one aim of which was to give them legal status.

One might ask how, with the historical experience the British have had for over a thousand years, they could be other than a Parliamentary democracy today. How could they be other than deeply mistrustful towards dictatorship, the centralised state, the secret police, systematic indoctrination, the repression of dissent, a large standing army, and all the other features of the Russian state, Tsarist and communist, which have so provoked the British? And, in view of *their* historical experience, how could the Russians be other than an insecure, intensely xenophobic people, patriotic and submissive to government most of the time, though capable of kicking over the traces on occasion, with titanic results, deifying mechanical force and technological wizardry, while condemning the corruptions of wealth? It is as vain for the West to rail at Russia for not valuing the sort of things it would have valued had it had the West's kind of history, as it is for Russia's leaders to accuse the West of lacking the things it would have had if it had had Russia's kind of history.

III

We should now consider some of the ways in which the British and the Russians have been brought into each other's company over the centuries, the different areas in which their paths in history have intersected. There are at least four such places of encounter, some limited in duration, others more lasting.

The first, not in importance, but in time, is the commercial, the British (or rather English) discovery of Russia through trade. Characteristically the story begins with the merchant adventurers of the sixteenth century. The first successful English voyage to Russia was that of Richard Chancellor, who left London in May 1553, the last year of the reign of Edward VI, in the *Edward Bonaventure*, the only one to arrive of the three ships which set out. Chancellor landed at the port of Nenoksa, at the mouth of the river Dvina, and made his way to the court of Ivan IV, with whom diplomatic relations were established and ambassadors exchanged.[6] Within two years Queen Mary was granting a Charter to the Russia, or Muscovy, Company which Chancellor founded, and two more years saw Anthony Jenkinson taking out a new fleet of the Company to Russia, though he found trade prospects rather unpromising. In 1561–62 Jenkinson received permission from Moscow to travel to the Caspian Sea, then crossed into Persia and met the Shah at Kazvin. In 1566 an Act of Parliament gave the Muscovy Company the exclusive right to trade anywhere to the east, north-east and north-west of London.

Through all the vicissitudes of Anglo-Russian relations since these first contacts, commerce has remained a persistent interest. Countless British and Russian politicians and officials, in Tsarist and communist times, have looked to increased trade as the road to better political relations and the solvent of differences; in the twentieth century Right and Left in Britain have pressed for trade with Russia as a contribution to the reduction of unemployment. The fact remains, however, that constant and useful as Anglo-Russian trade has always been, it has never been more than small, even more so for Britain than for Russia, and on the whole unimportant for the economic health of either country. In the depressed 1930s, only about one per cent of British imports came from Russia, and only about one per cent of exports went to that country. In the early months of 1980, 1.6 per cent of British imports came from the USSR, about a half of the proportion coming from Denmark or Norway. One per cent of British exports went to Russia during the same period, about the same proportion as went to Denmark. In February 1975 Mr (now Sir) Harold Wilson went to Moscow as Prime Minister and concluded an agreement for the extension to Russia of the British Export Credits Guarantee scheme to a maximum amount of £950 million, but by 1980 only just over half of the guaranteed credit had been called upon. It is yet another peculiarity of Anglo-Russian relations that, just as the two countries have been at war with each other less than any other two major states, so economic relations between them have been fewer than between any other two major states. Whatever else one may say about the causes of Anglo-Soviet differences, economic conflicts have not been among them.

Of course, Russia, a great continental country, has always been less involved in international trade than an insular state like Britain; in the present century it has cultivated self-sufficiency as a matter of policy. Moreover, as far as Russia's imports were concerned, Britain was overtaken by Germany as a source of supply in the 1870s and Germany remained Russia's foremost trading partner until the First World War. Again, during Russia's industrialisation, from 1860 onwards, France, not Britain, was her predominant source of supply of foreign capital and industrial equipment, as well as Russia's leading export market for grain and raw materials. Then, in the period of intense industrialisation during the first Soviet five-year plan, initiated in 1928, a combination of circumstances prevented Anglo-Russian economic ties developing: Russia's state control of foreign trade; the conspiratorial climate of industrial management, reflected in the Metro-Vickers trial of British engineers in 1933;[7] the deadlock over compensation for assets confiscated in the revolution; Russia's endemic lack of foreign currency; and the endless difficulties of negotiating a loan in the London money market to finance trade.[8]

In the period since 1945, the Soviet Union has been increasingly in need of advanced technological equipment from the West, the search for which is often regarded as an important reason for her government's interest in *détente*, and certainly during these years British industry has not been embarrassed by a surfeit of orders from abroad. But, as it happens, the Russians have felt more inclined to shop for their needs in other Western countries, especially the United States and West Germany, though trade even with those countries has been hampered by NATO controls on the export of 'sensitive' equipment and materials to communist countries. Obviously, too, the increasing strength and consolidation of the Soviet bloc in themselves have tended to shut Russia off from economic relations with the West. The failure of the West and Russia to build up between themselves the economic association which might have given them a strong interest in resolving their political differences is not the least of the many missed opportunities in world politics this century. However, the whole subject of the economic aspect of Anglo-Soviet relations is dealt with more fully in a later chapter in this book.[9]

The second field in which Britain and Russia have found their paths in history crossing is the territorial, though this has declined with the decolonisation of the British Empire since 1945. From the end of the eighteenth and throughout the nineteenth centuries, the expanding empire of the Tsars came up against and clashed with the British Empire and its multitudinous apanages, protectorates, client kingdoms, buffer states and principalities, which straddled across the southern perimeter of the Russian domain, from the Balkans in the West to China and Tibet in the East. As, in the eighteenth century, Russian rulers stepped into the shoes of Mongols and Tatars along the northern shores of the Black Sea, Britain, as the dominant naval power in the Mediterranean, inevitably fell into its role as protector of the Ottoman Empire, with its capital at Constantinople and its control of the Dardanelles Strait leading, via the Sea of Marmora, from the Black Sea into the Aegean. Throughout the nineteenth century, Anglo-Russian relations in the eastern basin of the Mediterranean, or the Levant, and what was then known as the Near East, formed a branch of the Eastern Question, one of the most persistent and troublesome issues of Victorian diplomacy. It was the question of what was to happen to the territories governed from Constantinople, especially in South-East Europe and the Middle East, and to the Straits themselves, when Turkish power eventually collapsed, as it showed every prospect of doing from the beginning to the end of the nineteenth century. The powers of Europe discussed the Ottoman Porte like doctors round the bed of a sick patient; in reality, most of them were more interested in the terms of his will than in easing his last hours.

The Eastern Question might have served as a point of collaboration between London and St Petersburg in managing the demise of the Ottoman Empire: there were moments in 1844 and even as late as 1853 when that was not beyond the bounds of possibility. The British Government's traditional championship of Turkey against Russia was not uniformly popular, as Gladstone's campaign against Turkish atrocities in the 1880s showed. But in the Victorian age the British had all the fire-eating protectiveness towards their navy which they now find so alarming in the Russians, and the Russians experienced much the same feelings of irritation with Britain's assumption of a divine mission to rule the waves as affected William II of Germany in the first decade of the twentieth century. It is not surprising that the two countries clashed. The conflict brought them to the brink of war in 1878, when Britain, with Germany's mediatory assistance, forced the Russians to abandon their support for a big Bulgaria, which they wrongly assumed would be friendly to themselves, carved out of the Ottoman Empire and with a coast convenient for Russia's naval use on the Aegean Sea. The Congress of Berlin, which resolved the issue in Britain's favour, took place nine years after the opening of the Suez Canal, which the same British Prime Minister, Disraeli, who pushed the Russians out of the Aegean at Berlin, appropriated for Britain.

The crisis of 1878 was the most dangerous in Anglo–Russian relations in the nineteenth century; it touched matters much more fundamental than did the Crimean War. Yet the crisis was also a turning point in those relations, and that in a most characteristic way.

In the following year, 1879, the newly united Germany under Chancellor Bismarck entered into the Dual Alliance with Austria–Hungary, Russia's natural adversary in the Balkans. The Habsburg rulers of Austria–Hungary looked askance at Russia's defence of Balkan peoples, like the Bulgarians, Rumanians, Serbs, in their struggle against the Ottoman Porte. But they feared even more Russia's determination (if that is what it was) to act as the guardian, and also perhaps the stimulus to revolt, of the millions of Slavs within their own empire. At the Berlin Congress, Austria–Hungary was granted a virtual protectorate over the Slav provinces of Bosnia and Herzegovina, then still part of the Ottoman Empire in the Balkans, though without leave to annex them. This was a form of compensation to Vienna for having joined the bloc against Russia at Berlin for which Disraeli worked. Thirty years later, in 1908, Austria–Hungary did annex the two provinces and the stage was set for the struggle between the Habsburg determination to master the Slavs in South-East Europe and the Russian determination to protect them which formed an integral part of the tangle of conflicts which led up to the European war in August 1914. Events led in that fatal direction because, with the formation of the Dual Alliance in 1879, joined by Italy in 1882, Austria–Hungary had at her side the industrial and military might of Hohenzollern Germany, and Germany, after the fall of the circumspect Bismarck in 1890, had world power ambitions to pursue which did not necessarily square with restraining the fire-brands in Vienna. Russia, too, had her coadjutant after 1892, in the form of the redoubtable power of France, embittered by her defeat at Prussia's hands in 1871 and with many of her leaders dreaming of the coming day of *revanche*.

After the Congress of Berlin Britain tended to pass out of the Balkan scene owing to pressures on her imperial position elsewhere, which grew burdensome towards the end of the century. Her role as the opponent of Russia in South East Europe and at the Straits lessened, Austria–Hungary taking up the task. Britain's continuing naval rivalry with Russia, however, was reflected in her alliance with Japan in January 1902, though the Anglo–Japanese alliance is to be regarded more as a response to Britain's growing sense of isolation than as a move against Russia. Paradoxically, another such response to isolation was Britain's Entente with France in 1904, which inevitably brought her closer to Russia as the sense of strain with Germany grew. In 1907 came the Anglo–Russian convention, based

on the recognition of the spheres of interest of the two countries in
Persia, after many decades of competition and intrigue against each
other in that country. In August 1914 Britain definitely moved to
Russia's side in defence of Serbia against harassment by
Austria–Hungary in the crisis arising from the Sarajevo
assassination. When Turkey entered the war in November 1914 on
the Dual Alliance's side, Britain joined France and Russia in
agreements for the dismemberment of the Ottoman empire which she
had been supporting against Russia for more than a hundred years.
The core of these agreements was the proposed annexation by
Nicholas II of Constantinople and the Straits, described by the British
Foreign Secretary, Sir Edward Grey, as 'the richest prize of the entire
war'.[10]

The Constantinople agreement of May 1915 fell to the ground with
the Bolshevik seizure of power in 1917 and their publication of the
wartime secret treaties. After the signing of the Lausanne treaty in
July 1923, which the Allies, after five years' delay, negotiated with
the new Turkey of Kemal Ataturk, Turkey remained friendly
towards Britain throughout the inter-war period and correspondingly
cool towards Russia, after an early rapprochement between Kemal
and Lenin. Then, after the Second World War, in which Turkey was
neutral but not unhelpful towards the nations fighting the Axis, she
was again subjected to much the same kind of pressure from Russia as
she had experienced in the nineteenth century, expressed, as before,
in Russian demands for a share in control of the Straits. In February
1947 the British Labour government notified President Truman that
Britain was no longer in a position to support Greece or Turkey
against communist pressure from within and without. Through the
American response, formulated in the shape of the Truman Doctrine
on 12 March, the United States became the formal and public
guardian of the two countries. In 1951 they adhered to the North
Atlantic treaty through which, in April 1949, ten European countries,
including Britain, associated themselves with the United States and
Canada for joint defence in the North Atlantic area. In 1946 the
Turkish ambassador to the United States died. The Americans
conveyed his body back to his country in a battleship, intending to
symbolise the transfer to the United States of Britain's old role in the
Eastern Question.

Round the southern borders of the Russian empire in Asia in the
nineteenth century Britain pursued much the same policy of seeking

positions of strength against Russia as in South East Europe and the Near East, though without encouraging the movement to national self-determination of local peoples which Mr Gladstone saw as the most effective defence against Russian domination in the Balkans, and also with less risk of an armed confrontation between the two powers. In Afghanistan and Persia an elaborate Anglo–Russian game was played in the late Victorian era, in which the two powers vied with each other to win over local rulers to their side by the use of blandishments or force, as the prevailing situation demanded, and to oust the other from favour. In none of these side-shows was there any risk of serious confrontation. Contrary to the fears of Russophobes in London, whom Lord Salisbury at the end of the century advised to use large-scale maps in order to get the geographical dimensions of the problem right, the security of India and British power in the Indian sub-continent were never in any real danger, any more than they were after the First World War, when British Conservatives accused the Bolsheviks of trying to subvert Indian subjects from their loyalty to the Crown. Indian loyalty to the Crown was fading, even before the war, but the Russians had little to do with it. The Bolsheviks no doubt did try to subvert India, but India was too distant, its problems too huge and remote, for the Russians to do much damage, whether in the 1880s or the 1920s, try as they might. Then, in 1947, India became formally independent in the form of two separate states, a process in which the Russians had no hand, either through their propaganda or their much-dreaded subversion. By the 1950s, Pakistan, the Muslim two-part state whose people could not swallow the notion of unity with the Hindus, was firmly embedded in the Western camp, the member of as many Western-inspired collective defence arrangements as she was able to join. The other state, India, at least during Mr Nehru's long premiership, was too committed to non-alignment (of which Nehru was a joint exponent with Marshal Tito of Yugoslavia, whom the Russians had ousted from their camp) to prove susceptible to Moscow's designs, if such existed.

In the Far East, the collision of British and Russian policies, though sustained at arm's length, was potentially more dangerous. In the 1860s British Ministers watched with apprehension Russia's appropriation of the Amur river provinces from China, which gave her a footing on the Pacific coast at Vladivostok, although Britain's principal interest in China was financial and commercial and concentrated in the south. The inroads of Russia into Manchuria towards the end of the century were more disturbing, especially as they brought her strength to bear on the Far Eastern balance of forces with the building of the Trans-Siberian railway, opened in 1891. In 1898, she secured from Japan, who had wrested it from China three years before, the Liaotung peninsula which ended in the naval base of Port Arthur, known in the Russian navy as 'sacred Russian soil'. With the construction in these years of the Chinese Eastern Railway, which cut across the great salient of Manchuria and met the South Manchuria Railway running south to Port Arthur, Nicholas II succeeded in a few years in making Russia a first-class power to be reckoned with in Far Eastern affairs.

The object of the Anglo-Japanese treaty of January 1902 was to neutralise this Russian expansion. The idea of the treaty was that, if ever Britain were to fight Russia in the Pacific, and, in the circumstances of the time, that was the most likely place in which she would, Russia would not be joined by Japan; Japan would remain neutral. As it turned out, it was Japan who fought Russia and Britain who remained neutral. The ensuing total defeat by land and sea which the Japanese inflicted on the Russians in 1905 not only eliminated Russia as a Pacific Power for forty years, but rocked the political foundations of Tsarism itself, laying the basis for the great Russian upheaval in 1917. During the period of Britain's decline as a world power in the years between the two world wars, Russia was hardly of any importance in the Far East, at least for Britain.

The territorial encounter between Britain and Russia over the past two hundred years has been laden with tension and conflict, although the armed exchanges to which it gave rise were remarkably few. This stressful character of the Anglo-Russian territorial confrontation has been carried over into the period following the Second World War, with the United States and its forty or so allies taking Britain's place as the force confronting Russia along the rim of her expansion outwards. The Russian–American territorial encounter since 1945, like the Anglo-Russian territorial encounter, has been relatively free from armed conflict between the two principal adversaries. Where armed conflict has occurred, as in Korea and Vietnam, one side of it has generally been sustained by a proxy of one or the other super-power, especially the Soviet Union, rather than the super-power itself. This fact points to one important theme in Russia's external policies both before 1917 and afterwards, namely, Russia's persistent drive to expand into areas of weakness adjoining her central land mass, but always to ensure that the cost of doing so is the least possible, and that the risk of armed conflict with other great powers is the least possible, too. The Russians have striven from time immemorial to break out of their immense land into the world outside, but have never given much evidence of willingness to pay a very high price to do so.

When we come to the third area of the Anglo-Russian encounter, that is, that of the international balance of power, conflict has been somewhat less apparent, surprising as it seems, and on critical occasions Britain and Russia, perhaps to their own puzzlement, have found themselves on the same side of the fence, or in the same pan of the balance. In place of actual conflict, there have been, time and again, misunderstandings, differences in their interpretations of the prevailing state of the balance of power, doubt as to whether the other country would play its part in sustaining the balance, and hence a tendency for each side to compound with the common adversary so as to avoid being let down at the critical moment by the other. Thus, Alexander I temporarily came to a separate arrangement with Napoleon at Tilsit in 1807, and Stalin did the same with Hitler in August 1939, while, on the British side, not a few top-ranking people in the political hierarchy in the period between the two world wars flirted with the notion of joining forces with German Nazism in resistance to Soviet communism. Nevertheless, in the end, and until 1945, Britain and Russia came down on the same side of the political balance. If a triangular pattern of world power were to develop in the twenty-first century with the West, the Soviet Union and China as its poles, as many anticipate, it is by no means a foregone conclusion that the first and the third of these poles would always be found on the same side of the balance against the second.

The international balance of power, as an area of British and Russian relationship, was, for most of the life of that relationship, strictly a European affair. Since the French Revolution, Britain and Russia have had a strong common interest in defending their national security and independence against states which threatened to dominate central Europe, that is, first, Napoleonic France, and then Hohenzollern and Nazi Germany. It is unfortunate for long-term Anglo-Russian relations that it is when Europe had *not* been threatened by any indigenous power or combination of powers, that Britain and Russia have tended to get on with each other badly.

When it has been so threatened, they have tended to get on with each other well. That is why, in the 1980s, prospects for the foreseeable future in Anglo-Russian relations can hardly be visualised as hopeful. If Britain remains a member of the European Community, and if the Community develops into a well-integrated economic and military bloc (though it must be admitted that the prospects of that happening do not look good at present), British relations with Russia are likely to remain, at best, cool for some years to come. One possibility which might cause them to improve – namely, the emergence of a common interest between the West and Russia in controlling instability in intermediate areas such as overtook Iran in 1979 and the Gulf in 1980 – seem, for the moment, somewhat utopian.

Unfortunately in this perverse world states are not able to remain on good terms with all their neighbours all the time. Friendship between particular states has a way of breeding suspicion between those states and others, and such suspicion may create new friendships between those others, though these friendships in their turn are apt to wither when the suspicion fades. Such has been the story of Anglo-Russian relations.

The European balance of power, in which Britain and Russia periodically faced each other, has been swallowed up since 1945 in a world-wide balance in which Europe became merely one theatre, at first of prime importance, then, since the early 1960s, of declining importance. Since there is as yet no third power, with the possible exception of China, which could play a significant independent role in the world balance, the tension of the balance must run between Russia and its allies, at one extreme, to the United States and its allies, including Britain, at the other. The balance of power, therefore, which once brought Britain and Russia together in partnership, and on more than one occasion, now ranges them in opposition to each other and in camps armed with weapons more terrible than man has ever possessed before in all his terrible history. This has resulted, not so much from dislike of each other by British and Russians, or even from disagreements about systems of political values and types of social arrangements, but from the inexorable logic of the international system. When Britain and Russia were compelled by that logic to fight side by side against Nazi Germany during the Second World War, a Parliament full of Joseph McCarthys could not have dissuaded the British from embracing the Russians as comrades in arms. When the nightmare of Nazi Germany vanished with

Hitler's suicide and the rout of his armies in 1945, and a power vacuum opened up in central Europe, a million speeches by British crypto-communists could not have turned the country away from its American alliance.

The fourth and final area of historical encounter between Britain and Russia, the ideological, has certainly played its part, both in encouraging friendship between them and in entrenching differences. On the British side, admiration in the early 1940s, much of it painfully ill-informed, for Soviet economic planning and Soviet social services made Russia seem an ally worth having. When the tide of feeling turned with the onset of the Cold War, the grey totality of Soviet communism, its subordination of personal happiness to the state's needs, as interpreted by remote despots, its brutal treatment of other nations, like the Hungarians and the Czechs, could not but shock and frighten the British people, except in so far that some of them were so shocked and frightened by their own social and economic system during the 1930s that almost anything seemed preferable. But perhaps ideological factors, important as they undoubtedly were, have been exaggerated. Perhaps ideological attraction and repulsion have been as much the result of the state of relations between the two countries as the cause.

The revolution in Russia in 1917 was a vast upheaval in human affairs which challenged the existing forms of social and political order in many other countries. It set men and women thinking about their social systems and the governments ruling over them more searchingly than they had ever done since 1789. But, in the long run, it was other things, and especially the state of the international system as a whole, which determined, if not exactly how the British and Russian people should feel about each other, at least how they should act towards each other. The West is always tempted to dismiss the Russians from consideration owing to dislike of the ideological beliefs they accept or are forced to accept. This has proved disastrous to Western interests in the past and could prove disastrous in the future. Britons and Russians live on the same planet and within the same international system. Despite their mutual abhorrence, they must learn to manage both in peace.

2. Living with a Revolution

FOR Britain, the most important fact about the revolution in Russia in 1917 was that it occurred at the most critical stage of the great war waged by the Entente against the Central Powers. It swept away the Eastern front which Russia had held for more than three years and in doing so brought the Allies within an ace of defeat, despite being joined in April by the United States. The British army was pinned down in Flanders with monstrous losses rising day by day. The French suffered a shattering reverse in the Nivelle offensive on the Aisne in the spring, resulting in army mutinies so frightening that Haig, commanding British forces, dared not set the facts down on paper for fear of their becoming known to his men.[1] Italy was practically knocked out of the fighting by a combined Austrian and German thrust at Caporetto in November which opened the road to Venice to the enemy. The German submarine campaign almost starved Britain into surrender. All British reactions to the events in Russia – from the bread riots in Petrograd in February (March by the new calendar), which led to the monarchy's fall, to the Bolshevik seizure of power in October (November by the new calendar) – were dominated by the implications for the war.

At first, the fall of the Romanovs was regarded in London as helpful to the Allied cause, the March revolution being read as a protest against Tsarist mismanagement of the war. On 15 March, Bonar Law, a member of the War Cabinet, told the House of Commons that 'all our information leads us to believe that the movement . . . is not against the Government for carrying on the war, but against it for not carrying on the war with that efficiency and with that energy which the people expect'.[2] Though the Russian contribution to the Allied war effort in the first two years was immense, paid for at a staggering price in blood, by the winter of

1916–17 the ponderous Tsarist war machine was grinding to a halt. The British ambassador, Sir George Buchanan, had urged Nicholas II time and again to save the country from defeat by calling a national parliament with powers to deal with the crisis, only to be told that the Tsar would 'think it over'.[3] An Anglo-French mission, visiting Russia towards the end of 1916 to discuss supplies, were appalled by the mismanagement of all affairs, the corruption, undisguised German espionage at court and in departments of state, the wholesale inability of the regime to fight a total war and make it meaningful to the Russian millions who struggled with the Germans in the broad land.[4] That a highly patriotic people should want to fight more ;ctively sounded a natural inference in London.

By 1917, too, the war had taken on its full moralistic overtones. It was a war for democracy and against militarism. The United States had come into the conflict with a President apt to speak as though commissioned by the Almighty to bring justice into a wicked world, which included his own allies. If America was to throw its full weight into the scale, the moral rightfulness of the Allied cause must be placed in the forefront, and the collapse of despotism in Russia would make that easier.

With that was linked the whole subject of war aims. British ministers had never liked the massive territorial promises they and their French colleagues had been forced to make to Russia under the secret treaties of 1915 and 1916, especially Constantinople and the Straits, which British governments had defended against Russia throughout the nineteenth century. If the provisional government under Prince Lvov, which assumed responsibility from the Tsar's regime in March, was willing to reconsider the secret treaties, so much the better, always provided Britain's prospective gains were not affected. In a note to the provisional government on 8 June, the Cabinet welcomed the Russian acceptance of the Wilsonian principles of 'no annexations and no indemnities', and went on to say that Britain was 'prepared to examine, and, if need be, revise, wartime arrangements'.[5] But the Russian Liberals showed little interest. Nor did the White generals, Kolchak, Denikin and others, whom the Allies later supported against the Bolsheviks. Kolchak, for example, in replying to an Allied note of 26 May 1919 about Russia's future boundaries, denied that White leaders like himself had any authority to make promises about them, and asserted that decisions must rest with a future Constituent Assembly.[6] The odd thing was that the Bolsheviks, whom the Allies abominated, *were* in favour of revoking the secret treaties and all that they implied for Russia's future territorial shape. On the other hand, when they quit the war in March 1918, they had no option but to echo President Wilson's principles of self-abnegation.

Because British politicians, in their ignorance, looked to the Liberals to help them with the problems of the war, the seizure of power by the Leninists in November and their brutal dispersal of the Liberal regime came as a shock. It went far to determine the future of British relations with Soviet communism. In British ears, the word 'Liberal' was homely and Gladstonian, 'Bolshevik' a monstrous neologism. Members of Lloyd George's War Cabinet, like Bonar Law and Curzon, knew nothing of Lenin, Stalin, Trotsky, or their outlandish ideas. The press, in puzzlement, spoke of them as 'maximalists' or 'anarchists' for want of a better description, classifying them as outcrops of Russia's disordered history, eruptions of dark forces from her past. Lenin's rejection of annexations was admirable, but the alarming thing was his much publicised determination to make a separate peace with Germany and take Russia out of the war, if the Allies as a whole would not enter into peace negotiations. This was the first great rift between the Leninists and the West. Like Stalin's pact with Hitler twenty-two years later, it confirmed the view of Russia's new rulers as self-seeking fanatics who would not hesitate to cut their dearest friends' throats if it suited their purposes.

Only slowly did British Ministers reconcile themselves to the bleak conclusion that Lenin meant to make peace with Germany, as he did at Brest–Litovsk on 3 March 1918. The failure of the intense Kerensky, who succeeded Prince Lvov as chief Minister on 16 July, to revitalise the Russian war machine should have been a warning. So, too, should the unavailing efforts of General Brusilov to wrest a victory in the Carpathians in the summer. Even so, it was never clear until the end that Lenin would have no alternative, if he was to keep the power the Bolsheviks seized in November, but to endorse the army's decision to end the war and 'vote for freedom with their feet', whatever the cost in territorial terms. Throughout the long negotiations at Brest–Litovsk, he repeatedly urged Trotsky, the new Foreign Minister, to break off and resume the fighting rather than accept the disastrous German terms. But the essential condition for that was that Russian forces would continue to fight, and it was plain that they would not. When the stomachs of the Bukharinites turned at the German peace terms, Lenin's reply was: 'give me an army of 100,000 men, an army which will not tremble before the enemy, and I will not sign this peace. Can you raise an army? Can you give me anything but prattle and the drawing up of paste-board figures?'[7] Lenin was almost alone among the Bolsheviks in realising that the Russian soldier's refusal to continue fighting was the only condition on which power could be held. It was the most important fact in Russia's position.

Intermittent talks in Petrograd between Lenin and three semi-official Allied intermediaries – Lloyd George's agent, Bruce Lockhart, Sadoul, a member of the French military mission to Russia, and Raymond Robins, of the American Red Cross, whose reports went back to the White House – failed to secure a resumption of the war, ostensibly because Allied assistance could not be assured on a scale large enough to satisfy the Bolsheviks, and because the Allies would not undertake to call off Japanese intervention in Russia's Far Eastern provinces. On the evening of 16 March, when Lenin heard that neither Lockhart nor Robins had heard from their governments, he told Robins, 'I shall speak for the peace. It will be ratified'.[8] But the overriding fact was that the Russian army would no longer fight. The resulting Bolshevik decision to quit the war was frightful for the Allies. Even if the Germans kept the curious promise they gave at Brest–Litovsk not to transfer their forces to the West after making peace with Russia, nothing could prevent them using the now quiet Eastern front to refresh their forces before the final German offensive in the West, which came on 21 March and brought the Kaiser within an ace of victory. This circumstance laid the basis for the ill-fated Allied intervention in Russia in 1918. As the European Left never tired of reminding the world later, the Great War ended, not in Berlin, but in Archangel.

Allied intervention in Russia in 1918 and 1919 was ill-fated in that none of its ostensible objectives were realised, and, in return for not inconsiderable costs in life and money, the Allies gained nothing but the permanent hostility of the Russian communists. In intervention was born the legend that the Allies had only one motive for their actions, and that was to switch the war against the Central Powers into a war to uproot the Leninist regime and turn the clock in Russia back to the brief Liberal experiment which followed the fall of the monarchy. And it is true that some British and French leaders did wish to replace the Leninists by White substitutes, though those they were able to find turned out to be no inferior to the Bolsheviks in lust for power and contempt for democracy as understood in the West. Churchill relates at the beginning of the final volume of *The World Crisis, 1911–1918* how he proposed for the night of 11 November 1918, when he was Minister of Munitions, an 'armistice dream', in which a great European army would be formed, to include the just defeated Germans, having for its object 'the liberation of Russia and the rebuilding of Eastern Europe'.[9] Churchill made his own contribution to this enterprise in April 1919 by slipping over to Paris, where the peace conference was in progress, when the Prime Minister, Lloyd George, had returned to Westminster to still the fears of Conservative MPs about reparations. Churchill tried and failed to talk the peace-makers into realising his 'dream'.

Such interludes could only be brief. Once the Germans laid down their arms in November 1918, there was no going back to the trenches for British soldiers. Even the Councils of Action which sprang up in Britain in protest against the government's support for the Poles in their war with Russia owed their existence to war weariness, rather than to sympathy with the Bolsheviks. As one British communist, later an MP, Walter Newbold, put it, workers and soldiers were 'tired of the whole business of the war . . . there was no desire to follow Russia'.[10] In a speech in the Commons on 16 April 1919, while Churchill was busy with his designs in Paris, the Prime Minister sought to restrict Allied action in Russia to arresting 'the devastating flow of lava so that it shall not scorch other lands'. He was adamant that 'when she is sane, calm and normal, we shall make peace with Russia . . . we have had quite enough bloodshed'.[11]

The original aim behind intervention on the British side, at least, was entirely different from the legend, though that did not mitigate the consequences for later Anglo-Soviet relations. It was to support by all available means everyone in Russia willing to go on fighting the Germans and make things difficult for all those wanting to make peace: and to prevent supplies the Allies had sent to Russia falling into German hands. The Germans themselves helped Lenin return to Russia from his Swiss exile by furnishing him with the famous 'sealed train' (actually a coach in a train) to travel home through Germany, their hope being that he would smoothe Russia's way out of the war. The Allies felt justified in doing all they could to aid and succour

Russians who wished to do the opposite. But there was no future for that kind of thing after Germany's defeat.

No-one understood this better than Lloyd George. Once the peace conference assembled in Paris , in January 1919, he worked unstintingly to break the deadlock in Soviet Russia's relations with the West by angling for a Bolshevik delegation to come to the conference to discuss, above all else, the economic reconstruction of Europe, in which Britain had such an enormous stake. He failed, but it was not for want of trying. It is a curious fact that the economist J. M. Keynes resigned from a comparatively junior position on the staff of the Treasury which went to Paris with the British delegation on the ground that, as he wrote later in *The Economic Consequences of the Peace*, published in 1919, 'the fundamental economic problem of a Europe starving and disintegrating before their eyes, was the one question in which it was impossible to arouse the interest of the Four.'[12] And yet the British Empire team at the conference was led (or rather, dominated) by a Prime Minister who harped monotonously on the need to think less about frontiers and security and more about getting the European economy moving again. In doing so, he called for a 'truce of God', in which the Bolsheviks would join the Paris talks on economic reconstruction and the revival of trade.[13] The French Premier, Georges Clemenceau, would not hear of it. He called the Bolsheviks a 'colony of lepers', who would contaminate revolution-prone Paris with their infections. If Lloyd George must proceed with his schemes, he suggested a meeting place on the island of Prinkipo in the Sea of Marmora, which the Turks used as a refuge for lost dogs. The Bolsheviks, though never officially informed of the Prinkipo idea, got to hear of it and agreed to go. The White groups in Siberia, Archangel and southern Russia, with their spokesmen under French patronage in Paris, did not and the whole idea went into limbo.[14]

Accordingly, the Bolsheviks were never associated with the peace treaties of 1919 with Austria, Bulgaria, Germany and Hungary. They *were* invited to the Lausanne conference which made a belated peace with Turkey in July 1923, but only to the section of the conference which dealt with the Straits. The resulting Straits convention was the first multilateral agreement to be signed by the Soviet government, though in the event they did not ratify it since it did not, as they had hoped at Lausanne, close the Straits, and hence the Black Sea, to foreign warships. Strangely enough, Soviet Russia was charged by British politicians in the 1930s with being equivocal and insincere in the professions she made of willingness to defend the 1919 peace settlement when it was threatened by Hitler, even though that settlement was made without her consent and greatly to her disadvantage.

The Prinkipo affair was not the end of Lloyd George's efforts to rid Europe of the tangle of war debts and reparation claims, and to do so by drawing the Bolsheviks into one or other of the international meetings at Mediterranean resorts in the 1920s which characterised the Prime Minister's diplomacy and shocked some of his puritanical fellow-countrymen. The conference at which a Soviet delegation, led by Foreign Minister Georgi Vasilievich Chicherin, eventually put in an appearance, thanks to Lloyd George's efforts, was the international economic conference at Genoa in April and May 1922. The invitation was inspired by the Welshman's illusion that Lenin's New Economic Policy, which provided for a limited return to the market economy, represented the final abandonment of communism and a reversion to 'business as usual'. In the event, nothing was achieved at Genoa by way of reintegrating Russia into the economic life of the rest of Europe. Mutual suspicions were too strong, as was also the conflict between Allied bondholders' claims for compensation for property confiscated during the revolution and Soviet counter-claims arising from damage done in Russia by Allied forces during intervention. Chicherin argued that there could be no question of compensating the bondholders without external economic help for Russia's recovery, and the Entente side would not talk about a loan except on the condition that Russia was virtually restored to private enterprise and the book of communism closed.

The Russians did, however, bring off something of a *coup* by going off with members of the German delegation at the Easter week-end to Rapallo, a resort twenty miles from Genoa, and there provided a spectacle of how two pariah nations could bury the hatchet between them in the face of the world's unfriendliness. Otherwise, the Genoa conference only put the retort into French mouths that if you act reasonably towards the Germans, they reply by making deals with the communists to harass you. Nevertheless, the conference underlined the point, which is a permanent truth for Britain, that the country, with its immense stake in international trade, cannot benefit from the shutting off of a great power like Russia behind an impenetrable *cordon sanitaire*. Admittedly, Lloyd George was naive in his assumption that trade was a never-failing cure for the bizarre ideas foreigners sometimes acquire. He tried to reassure one Parliamentary critic by saying that he would find, 'by and by', that Lenin was a man 'after his own heart' if he 'did a little business with him'.[15] But that was a typically British illusion.

II

The Soviet regime slowly emerged from isolation, partly self-imposed, partly enforced from outside. As soon as the Bolsheviks had defeated their internal enemies and made peace of a highly disadvantageous sort with their immediate neighbours, the dilemma which has held every Russian government in its grip from that day to this made its appearance. Were they to give priority to fomenting revolutions abroad, or should they build up a strong domestic base, entering into normal relations with suitable capitalist states and biding their time? The answer would depend upon international circumstances and on the sort of men who came to the top in the Soviet hierarchy.

As to the international circumstances, for a time the immediate post-war strains of recovery in the capitalist world, the slumps, the unemployment and business failures clouding the early years of peace, seemed to portend the arrival on the horizon of the great leap forward into socialism. The angry quarrels between Britain and France over Germany, culminating in the Franco-Belgian occupation of the Ruhr in 1923 and the renewed threat of war, together with the altercations over war debts and reparations, looked to Marxists like the final lurchings of the bourgeois world towards disaster. But then, with the Dawes plan of 1924, the stabilisation of the German mark, the reconciliation of France and Germany through the Locarno treaties of 1925 and the friendship between the French and German Foreign Ministers, Aristide Briand and Gustav Stresemann, capitalism seemed to be given a new lease of life.

In the duel between Stalin and Trotsky which followed the death of Lenin in 1924 – not the only, but certainly the most important, battle between his heirs – these external circumstances were of critical effect. Stalin seemed to represent the Slavophil legacy in Marxist thought: inward-looking, intensely suspicious of the world outside Russia, certain that the country could raise itself to pinnacles of achievement far beyond the debased West. His rival, Trotsky, evidently embodied the Westernising strand in Russia's history, the notion that Russia had been given the chance, owing to historical accident, to realise herself through social revolution, but that in any long run she would be left far behind as Western countries like Germany and the United States went into a future of boundless progress as a result of the communist revolution. In the ensuing debate, Stalin had the logic of events working on his side. In the years 1925 to 1927, when the two men struggled for mastery and Stalin won by securing Trotsky's expulsion from the party, along with that of Zinoviev, in November 1927, the tenth anniversary of the Bolshevik seizure of power, the regime passed through its worst period of isolation since the civil war. It underlined Stalin's argument that, if Russia pursued world revolution and neglected her national defences, she would be annihilated within a ring of foes.

In those two years, Germany, the first country to recognise the Soviets, was passing from being a pariah nation, linked at Rapallo with the other pariah nation, Russia, into a widely acclaimed friendship with the other two leading capitalist states in Europe, Britain and France. The Locarno treaties, signed on 16 October 1925, which symbolised this, had a distinctly anti-Soviet significance, whether or not that was the intention behind them. They were almost an advertisement to German nationalists that Britain would not necessarily object even to a forceful revision of Germany's eastern borders, which Britain refused to guarantee at Locarno, provided the status quo in the West, which Britain did guarantee, was respected. Germany received a further accolade of respectability in 1926, when she was welcomed into the League of Nations, blackballed by the Soviets as a 'league of robber states'. In the same year, the general strike in Britain brought charges in London against Soviet interference to a pitch of frenzy, and was followed a year later by the momentous breach of diplomatic relations with Russia. In that year, too, Generalissimo Chiang Kai-shek, leader of the nationalist revolution in China and successor to Dr Sun Yat-sen, Lenin's friend and father of Chinese nationalism, began to persecute Chinese communists, expelled the Soviet political and military missions, which Lenin had sent in agreement with Dr Sun, and closed Soviet consulates. It was hard for anyone in beleaguered Russia not to agree with Stalin that to brandish the revolutionary sword at such a time of isolation, as Trotsky proposed, was to condemn the Soviet regime to extinction. Stalin had few, if any, humane qualities; compared with the brilliant Trotsky, he was boorish and dull. But his grasp of international realities was far superior.

British ministers, whatever their party, were not much concerned with doctrinal or personal conflicts raging within the citadel of Bolshevism. Their sole consideration was the implacable hostility of Lenin's successors to the capitalist world. The interlude of dreaming that Russia's leaders might discard their odious dogmas if fair trading terms were offered ended at the Genoa conference and the Rapallo agreement. Thereafter, British grievances against the Bolsheviks focused on two issues: their confiscation of foreign property, public and private, without much said about compensation, and their evident determination, despite all promises to the contrary, to bring the bourgeois world to its knees by propaganda and subversion.

The satisfaction of foreign bondholders was a more serious matter for the French than the British, one reason why the French authorities were more unforgiving towards the Bolsheviks during the peace conference, and more committed to building a containment belt against them in eastern Europe. Russia's industrial growth in the late nineteenth century, after all, had proceeded on the basis of large-scale imports of French capital. Nevertheless, the fact that British businessmen who lost money in Russia during the revolution feared to lose more when they opened their newspapers in the 1920s and read of rising discontent among the unemployed did not dispose them to take the nationalisation of foreign property lying down. But here was a dilemma. There was virtually only one way, short of using force, of recovering any part of the sequestrated wealth, and that was meeting and talking with the Bolsheviks about terms of settlement. That in itself was repulsive. When it was realised that it might mean lending the Bolsheviks still more money, so that they could use it to earn the wherewithal to repay the money they had stolen, the spirit recoiled in horror.

The problem of dealing with Bolshevik propaganda and subversion was, if anything, even more elusive. It is easy to deride British politicians of the 1920s, with their strange phobias of 'red' plots to dislodge the newly independent Irish government and set up a Soviet state on Britain's doorstep, and their measures to stop the Russian circulation in India of 1000-rouble notes with the slogan 'Workers of the world, unite!' printed on them in nine languages.[16] Lord Curzon, the Foreign Secretary in the last years of Lloyd George's coalition government, was driven to collect the most doubtful stories, many manufactured by an agency in Berlin which made a fair profit out of them, to fill his accusing notes to Moscow. After one of his charge-sheets had been effectively answered by the Russians and he was at loss how to reply, his advisers said he should simply 'reassert the truth of our charges, without however producing any evidence (because we have not got it)'. Curzon doubted whether any reply were possible, in which case, he wrote, there would be 'nothing left for me but to bear the odium of having made public charges which I cannot sustain'.[17] But Britain was under pressure, with troubles in Ireland (until independence in 1921), India and Egypt, with rising unemployment which mocked the promises of a better Britain that rang from recruiting platforms during the war, depressed areas and slumped basic industries, in a world sunk in economic depression and also a mindless frivolity shaming the sacrifices of the dead in the Great War. Crowning all this, the new leaders in Russia summoned working men and women in capitalist states to revolt and financed nationalists in Africa and Asia to pull their empires down about their ears.

The difficulty about countering communist subversion was that, while the Soviet government might be told they could expect no financial help from bourgeois states unless they adhered to the normal rules of international relations, and while they signed solemn undertakings to do so, there was practically nothing the British, or any other, government could do to ensure the fulfilment of such undertakings. By the first commercial agreement signed by Britain and Russia on 16 March 1921, which accorded *de facto* recognition to the Soviet regime, both sides undertook to refrain from 'hostile acts and propaganda' against each other, and Russia further pledged not to encourage Afghanistan or India in 'hostile action' against Britain.[18] But when charged by the British authorities in the 1920s with repeated violations of the agreement, the Russians either blandly denied the charges or justified themselves by the thousand-and-one excuses available to governments in such circumstances, as for instance that the propaganda activities complained of were simply innocent expressions of opinion by ordinary Russian workers. One of the most irritating and baffling of these excuses was that the propaganda in question, if such it was, emanated from Comintern, or the Third International, which had given no undertaking to refrain from propaganda, not from the Soviet government, which had. Foreign Minister Maxim Litvinov argued the point as follows:

The mere facts of the Third International having for obvious reasons chosen Russia as the seat of its executive committee as the only land which allows full freedom to the spreading of communist ideas and personal freedom to communists, and of some members of the Soviet government in their individual capacity belonging to the executive committee, give no more justification for identifying the Third International with the Russian government than that the Second International, having its seat in Brussels and counting among the members of its executive committee M. Vandervelde, a Belgian Minister, gave justification for rendering identical the Second International with the Belgian government.[19]

The Russians seemed to count on having their cake and eating it. On the one hand, they had the benefits of a commercial treaty with the world's most important trading nation, with which their accounts were invariably in surplus, and a British undertaking not to make propaganda against them. On the other hand, they could make as much propaganda as they liked against Britain, the British Empire and the whole British social system from the unassailable rostrum of the Third International in Moscow, not that that propaganda was ever as effective as British Conservatives made out.

These matters came to a head in January 1924, with the formation of the first Labour government in Britain with James Ramsay MacDonald as Prime Minister, after an election in December in which the Conservatives lost 88 seats and Labour gained 50. The government, reliant on Liberal support, was to survive for nine months and ended in a way closely connected with Russia and fear of a revolution on the Russian model in Britain. This occurred when the government decided to drop the prosecution under an Act of 1797 against J. R. Campbell, then the acting editor of the *Workers' Weekly* for publishing an article on 25 July urging soldiers not to use their weapons 'in a class or military war'. The Campbell case was used by the Conservative Opposition (and Liberals in the Commons supporting the government largely acquiesced) to press their long-standing argument that the Labour party was 'soft' on communism and would open the floodgates to revolution if entrusted with power. The government were defeated on a censure motion at the end of September by a Commons vote of 364 to 191. The fact that the Campbell case did destroy the Labour government, and that the so-called Zinoviev letter – an alleged instruction from the Third

International to the British communists about subversion – helped to defeat Labour's prospects in the ensuing general election, showed that any British government which sought to regularise its relations with the Soviet regime would have a hard time.

The short-lived Conservative administrations under Bonar Law and Stanley Baldwin (who succeeded Law on 21 May 1923) which preceded MacDonald's Cabinet had had no strong incentive to accord *de iure* recognition to Moscow. The Bolsheviks were still far from disenchanted with the prospects of world revolution and British Conservatives had no wish to give their morale a boost. The Bonar Law government moreover had been formed when the Conservatives withdrew their support from Lloyd George's coalition in October 1922, and one of Lloyd George's many sins in Conservative eyes was that he had worked hard to restore the new Russia to the international family. A leading figure in Bonar Law's team was Curzon, with his almost mystical veneration for the Indian empire, of which he had been Viceroy before the war. India, Curzon believed, was marked out as the most important object in the Bolshevik campaign against the British empire. But Curzon represented an older strand in Conservative tradition, with roots in land ownership and imperial service, one which began to give way after the war to newer business groups rather less frightened by the new Russia and more interested in trade prospects with it. Baldwin, Curzon's rival for leadership of the Conservatives after Bonar Law's death, reflected these newer business interests. He beat Curzon in the leadership race partly because Curzon was in the Lords, and that was unacceptable in a twentieth-century Prime Minister, partly because he spoke the language of business interests and Curzon did not. The men who supported Baldwin had all Curzon's aversion for Soviet communism, but were willing to give it a trial and see whether there was business to be done with it. In August 1923, a delegation of British businessmen, including representatives of 80 engineering firms, had visited Russia and returned with a favourable opinion about recognition.[20]

On the Labour side, *de iure* recognition of the Soviets was included in the party manifesto at the 1923 election, the Conservatives being silent on the question. The Labour party had scarcely anything in common with the Bolsheviks, but many of its members thought they should at least be given a chance; there was also the grim unemployment situation to be taken into account. Curzon's bullying had failed to soften Soviet communism: perhaps recognition and more trade would have a better effect. Labour, too, like the Conservatives, had changed after the war. With the opening of the party to individual members when the new constitution was adopted in February 1918, radical intellectuals, many of them former Liberals, entered its ranks, men like Charles Roden Buxton, Charles Trevelyan, E. D. Morel, Norman Angell and Arthur Ponsonby, and these considered recognition a rational act of policy. Besides, *de iure* recognition, which MacDonald's government granted on 1 February 1924, after enough delay to underline his lack of sympathy with the Bolsheviks, was fully in accord with British practice of acknowledging foreign governments, whatever their ideology, provided they are in effective occupation of the national territory. MacDonald told the Labour party's annual conference in 1924 that the Soviet government had been recognised 'for exactly the same reason that Christian Foreign Secretaries have recognised Mohammedans and people whose religious persuasions were of somewhat more doubtful quality even than that'.[21]

But that was about as far as the Prime Minister would go with the Soviets. Recognition, he had written in 1923, 'in no way meant that our Labour movement agreed with the Soviet government'. On the contrary, 'the Second International had borne the brunt of the fight against Bolshevism in its young, vigorous days . . . only by a continuation of the same policy could the noxious weed be cleaned out'.[22] He insisted that the two countries should be represented in each other's capitals only at the level of chargés d'affaires; ambassadors were not exchanged until 1929. His coolness was again shown in April, when, after putting in an appearance at the opening of talks with a Soviet delegation under Khristian Georgiyevich Rakovsky to discuss outstanding financial questions on the 14th, he pointedly stressed the differences between the British and Russian brands of socialism. He then left the proceedings in the hands of his Under-Secretary, Arthur Ponsonby, and did practically nothing to defend the two treaties which emerged in August from the talks, after the most tortuous negotiations, when they came before the House of Commons and were defeated in October.

Much fun has been made, especially by British sympathisers with Soviet Russia, of MacDonald and his Cabinet colleagues on account of the ridiculous Court dress and other regalia of a bygone age which they allowed to smother their early socialist beliefs. When King George V complained about the singing of the 'Red Flag' at a Labour victory rally at the Albert Hall in 1924, MacDonald apparently excused the incident by saying 'they had got into the way of singing this song and it will be by degrees that he hoped to break down this habit'.[23] But the fact was that if the Labour party was ever to win for itself a secure place in British life, to move in and out of office without the electorate thinking the country was being given over to red ruin, it had to merge into the staid background of the British scene. The differentiation of British socialism (if that is what the Labour party really stood for) from the Soviet variety was an essential means of doing so. To this end MacDonald devoted himself with brilliant success. Perhaps his greatest achievement was to make moderate socialist reformism by parliamentary means acceptable in conservative Britain, to rob it of all revolutionary associations and clothe it in respectability. 'It was the weakness of the Labour party', he wrote, 'that it represented a "Red Terror" to the minds of large masses of people who knew little about it.'[24] Without MacDonald, it is doubtful whether there could have been an Attlee government in Britain in 1945, whether the welfare state, in all its strength and weakness, could have become the established order after the Second World War. The irony of it is that MacDonald, the most reviled leader the Labour party ever had, did more than any other of its leaders to put the party on the map, and did so by making it bourgeois, which is what most of its members really wanted. In its 1922 manifesto the party described itself truthfully as the 'best bulwark against violent upheaval and class war'.[25]

Whatever sympathies with the Bolsheviks might exist in a handful of rebel Labour MPs from the Clyde, MacDonald and his colleagues knew they must above all else shun infection with the Soviet plague. Recognition and trade, according to Philip Snowden, Chancellor of the Exchequer in MacDonald's first Cabinet, was a way of *ending* Russian communism, not of strengthening it. The more Russia trades with other countries, he argued in the Commons in 1922, 'the more it would approximate the Russian system to that of other countries'.[26] The Zinoviev letter, exploding in October 1924 and consolidating Labour's defeat in the election, showed the realism of this strategy of the Labour leadership. It also explains MacDonald's detachment during the Parliamentary debates on the two treaties with Russia. For the first Labour Prime Minister, dependent on Liberal support in the Chamber, which was withdrawn in October on the issue of alleged communist influence on Labour Ministers in the

Campbell case, openly to identify himself with the defence of agreements with Russia would have been fatal. Another explanation was put forward by the government, namely that in August, when the treaties were complete and ready for Parliamentary approval, the Prime Minister was involved in the more important negotiations in London which led to the adoption of the Dawes plan and the revival of the German economy. On the other hand, he had kept the Foreign Office to himself when forming his government in January, and leaving an important transaction with the Soviets to a junior Minister could hardly have been other than deliberate. It set a precedent for that persistent belittling of Russia which proved so disastrous in the next decade.

In the negotiations with Rakovsky which began in April, the focus was twofold: the assurances the Soviet team could give that the old pledges of abstention from propaganda and subversion would be honoured in the new agreements, and a formula for the settlement of British bondholders' claims for compensation together with Soviet counter-claims. Unless agreed formulas could be worked out on these questions, financial assistance from Britain to Russia would be out of the question, and it was that which the Soviet delegation were chiefly interested in. It was not a matter of a British government loan to Russia: no-one had the audacity to suggest that. It was a case of a British government guarantee of a loan which the Russians were seeking from finance houses in the City. In the end, it was the City which would have to decide whether the terms the Russians were offering as compensation for the nationalised property were acceptable. In order to construct a form of words to express the extent of agreement on this point, a group of backbench Labour MPs worked might and main with Ponsonby and the Soviet delegates, and their efforts were successful in that a formula was devised to the satisfaction of a majority of the bondholders and the treaties were signed and presented to Parliament for ratification.[27]

All that MacDonald would say about the treaties when he turned up at the Commons debate on them on 7 August was that the British signature on the treaties implied no more than the government's willingness to lay them before Parliament for acceptance or rejection, in itself a most unusual view to be taken by a Minister in charge of important negotiations with another country.[28] Not surprisingly, the treaties suffered a decisive defeat in the ensuing debate, concentrated, not so much on the commercial agreement, which accorded Russia

most-favoured-nation treatment, the benefits of the Export Credits
Guarantee scheme and diplomatic immunity for members of the
Soviet trade mission, but on the general treaty, which concerned the
contentious issue of compensation to the bondholders. It is doubtful,
however, whether any amount of re-drafting could have overcome
the basic difficulty: the rooted aversion of most British politicians for
doing business with the Bolsheviks.

To the ordinary MP, leader-writer or businessman, Russia's
leaders were murderers and appropriators of other people's property.
A few 'agitators', intellectuals in Bloomsbury bookshops, spongers
who lined the dole-queues, might think otherwise, but that did not
affect the general opinion. A figure who helped shape this sort of
consensus was David Lloyd George. Now consigned to what looked
like permanent exclusion from power, widely mistrusted as devious
and untruthful, he had nevertheless been the great war leader and still
wielded vast prestige. He had sympathised with the Bolsheviks during
their early years of power, wanted them called to the Paris peace
conference, fought successfully against Churchill's campaign for a
war against Bolshevism. He had headed a government which
concluded the first British trade agreement with the Soviets and
worked tirelessly to restore economic relations with them until his fall
from power in October 1922. Yet, almost singlehandedly, and almost
by a single speech in the House of Commons, Lloyd George
destroyed the treaties with Russia which the Labour team had so
painfully negotiated. He called them, 'a fake . . . a thoroughly
grotesque agreement'. This was rendered credible by an act of gross
misrepresentation, that is, the suggestion that the funds which would
go to Russia by the loan agreement (which, incidentally, would not
have been effective unless the bondholders were satisfied with the
actual terms of compensation) would come, not from financiers, who
expected to make a profit on any deal they undertook, but from the
unsuspecting taxpayer, who was required to subsidise red terror in
Russia.[29]

Lloyd George's famed mercurial temperament might have been
responsible for this extraordinary *volte-face*. But he was enough of a
politician to know that, in the prevailing climate of opinion, there was
little to be gained by showing sympathy for the Russian communists,
and probably a good deal to be lost. When the Parliamentary Liberal
party discussed the two treaties on 1 October, only two MPs voted in
their favour, and a week later, when the MacDonald government fell

on the issue of the Campbell case, no more than a handful of Liberal members voted in the government lobby.

The two treaties died without honour. All that remained of Labour's efforts to normalise relations with the Soviet government was the act of *de iure* recognition. It is impossible to say whether, if the treaties had been ratified and gone into effect, trade between Britain and Russia, which it was their most important object to promote, would have flourished. Even had it done so, the effects on Britain's employment prospects would have been slight: during the 1920s Britain's trade with Russia was never much above one per cent of her total trade, and it was always in Russia's favour. But the demise of the treaties, when the moment seemed propitious to dissipate the venom between the two countries since the revolution, gave a further stimulus to Russia's isolation when it was already severe. When eventually the first five-year plan for economic reconstruction was adopted in Russia in 1928, the country had to reconcile itself to rising to its feet by its own bootstraps.

Had Soviet industrialisation begun on the basis of substantial economic co-operation with the West, Western countries might have been in a position to exercise some influence on Soviet affairs during those crucial years when Russia's future was in the melting pot. The fact that the Soviets went without economic assistance from outside and were forced to raise capital by starving the population of consumer goods and many necessities of life no doubt helped to make the iron communist dictatorship harsher than it might have been. On the other hand, when the Great Depression struck in the early 1930s and pulled down linked Western societies like so many houses of cards, the Russians might have congratulated themselves on having escaped involvement in the bourgeois world in the 1920s when they so sedulously sought it.

III

The affair of the Zinoviev letter, which helped to rob MacDonald of victory in the general election in 1924, began with the interception by the Foreign Office and the *Daily Mail* newspaper of an alleged message from the Third International's headquarters in Moscow to the British Communist party inciting it to acts of subversion. Strictly speaking, it had nothing to do with the Labour party, but its publication in the *Mail* on 25 October satisfied many voters that

Soviet Russia was a pernicious influence in British life; that it exerted a malign spell over British Left-wing politicians, the distinction, if there was one, between communists and social democrats being regarded as abstract and irrelevant; and that no political organisation which sympathised with the Soviet regime should ever again be entrusted with power in Britain even if a mistake of that kind had been committed in respect of the MacDonaldites in 1923. Whether the letter was a forgery, fabricated in the election campaign to sink the Labour boat, was almost irrelevant, though the internal evidence that it was is formidable. The Foreign Secretary in the incoming Baldwin government, Austen Chamberlain, wrote bluntly to Rakovsky on 21 November that 'the information in the possession of His Majesty's Government leaves no doubt whatsoever in their mind of the authenticity of M. Zinoviev's letter and His Majesty's Government are therefore not prepared to discuss the letter'.[30] And that was that. Nevertheless, it was the sort of message Comintern habitually sent to their correspondents abroad, and Comintern leaders never made any concealment of their aim to destroy bourgeois society and its institutions by any means available, fair or foul. The important thing about the Zinoviev affair was that it testified to the deep suspicions about the Bolsheviks and all their works which prevailed in Britain. As such, it set the tone of British attitudes towards Russia for the next decade.

They were years of unrelenting hostility, culminating in the breach of diplomatic relations by Britain, which was communicated to the Soviet mission by Chamberlain on 27 May 1927. Relations were not restored until the advent of the second Labour government, again with Ramsay MacDonald as Prime Minister, though this time with Arthur Henderson at the Foreign Office, in 1929.[31] Not surprisingly, these years of stress in Anglo–Soviet relations coincided with a Conservative government, whose attitude towards Russia can be imagined, though Chamberlain himself fought a running battle on the issue with his more rabid Cabinet colleagues and backbench Conservative MPs. In the end, the Foreign Secretary (of whom Birkenhead said he 'always played the game and always lost it') succumbed. Probably he would not have opted for the diplomatic breach had it been left to him to decide.

The 1927 breach arose from the government's allegation that the Soviet trade agency in London, Arcos, operating from 49 Moorgate, was being used for espionage and subversion. No definite evidence that this was so seems to have been in the hands of the Home Office when a raid by 200 policemen was carried out on the agency's premises on 12 May. Moreover, though the raid was conducted with the greatest thoroughness, not to say ruthlessness, no incriminating documents came to hand, or rather none that the British authorities admitted the existence of or saw fit to publish. No prosecution was ever mounted against any British or Soviet nationals for offences against the law of the land, though the charges alleged certainly were such offences. On the face of it, it seems most unlikely that the Soviet authorities, who were at that time making the most strenuous efforts to increase their trade with Britain, would have chosen a trade agency in London, of all places, to carry out their designs against Western capitalism. Such designs certainly existed, but the struggle between Stalin and Trotsky, which ended in Trotsky's defeat and exile in the year of the breach, turned precisely on the question of whether the Bolsheviks should put the campaign against Western capitalism first, as Trotsky wished, or subordinate it to Russia's own national interests, as Stalin wished.

But the British Conservative leaders, men like Churchill, Birkenhead, Joynson-Hicks, Hoare and Worthington-Evans, who worked for the Arcos raid and the break with Russia, knew little and cared little about what was going on inside the Soviet state. They wanted the Reds out of Britain and did not mind how they did it. They had had a fright the year before in the shape of the nine-day General Strike and the seven-month miners' strike which touched it off. They conceived Russia's leaders as exploiting industrial strife as a means of paving the way for a Bolshevik-type seizure of power by their dupes, a minority of misguided or corrupt trouble-makers, while the mass of ordinary British workers inertly followed, too stupid to realise how they were being used. It was a picture of the industrial situation in Britain false in almost every respect. The big men in Russia certainly welcomed the General Strike, like every other symptom of working-class unrest in the capitalist world, especially after so much disappointment over the failure of general revolution to break out in Europe at the end of the war. They sent a certain amount of money for strikers' families, said to have been collected through the Soviet trade unions. No doubt they ferreted out all the information they could about the class war in Britain. But there is no hard evidence that it went any further. The General Strike was not masterminded from Moscow. The titanic struggle between the

Stalinists and the Trotskyites, followed by Stalin's assaults on the Bolshevik Right-wing, to say nothing of the stricken state of the country after the civil war, placed other things on the Soviet agenda.

On the British side, the trade union leaders in the General Strike – though this was not so true of the mineworkers' leaders – had every appearance of being frightened men, terrified of the whirlwind they had unleashed, or rather which had been unleashed by history for them. The notion, so dear to ministers who ordered the Arcos raid, that these nervous, eminently respectable Labour men, many of them Sunday-school teachers and lay preachers, were so debauched with 'Moscow gold' as to be ready to act as firebrands for the Kremlin, while watching their union members play football with the police during the strike, was too laughable to be taken seriously. Yet it was so taken by the Right in Britain, or sufficiently so that the Arcos raid and the diplomatic breach, for which the raid served as a pretext, were staged by the government with the wholehearted support of the party it led in the two Houses of Parliament, while Chamberlain disapproved, though in silence.

The breach with Russia did no good to anybody. Britain was not much freer from industrial conflict after 1927 than it was before. If it was, this was due to reasons which had nothing to do with Anglo-Soviet relations. British capitalism was no healthier. It might even be said that Britain's failure to build up trade with Russia in the years 1927 to 1929, when diplomatic relations were restored, during which time the country was undergoing intense industrialisation, if anything aggravated the decline in foreign trade which helped to produce mass unemployment in the 1930s. To which should be added the fact that the diplomatic breach shut Britain off from its listening post in Moscow for two vital years in which the Soviet regime was embarking on radically new courses in home and foreign affairs. Diplomatic breaches are sometimes justified as providing relief for pent-up feelings. If so, that is about the only benefit Britain derived from the affair, to offset the considerable harm it suffered.

For Russia, the breach was little short of a disaster. In the Far East, there occurred in the same year as the breach with Britain the rupture by Chiang Kai-shek of the link between revolutionary Russia and revolutionary China which Lenin and Sun Yat-sen had forged. In Europe, Russia lost her only friend, Germany. Although the Soviet-German Rapallo agreement of 1922 was renewed by the Treaty of Berlin in 1926, the Weimar Republic had now made its choice, and that was to settle its differences with France at Locarno, with the help of a highly satisfied Britain, to join the League of Nations and to re-establish itself within the Western world's financial system through first, the Dawes plan and later, in 1930, the Young plan.

The ring of the capitalist world was closing round Russia in 1927. This could not fail to make Stalin's point for him – that in Russia's besieged situation she could not afford decadent Western freedoms; that, as far ahead as one could see, there could be no future in Russia for the Marxist idea of the 'withering away of the state' so long as enemies thronged the gate; and that Stalin's iron rule, so far from being allowed to mellow as the years elapsed, must be strengthened and made harder. For on that iron rule depended all Russia's hopes of surviving the combined attack from the capitalist world which the events of 1927, and especially the breach with Britain, had shown to be not textbook logic but a practical certainty. It is hard, then, to think of the British government's decision in 1927 to sever relations with Russia other than, at best a huge irrelevance, inspired by fear and prejudice, at worst a disastrous set-back to the normalisation of relations with this strange new state. The breach did nothing to solve the problem of how those relations were to become normal. It is with us still.

IV

What happened in Russia in 1917 was that an old, virtually changeless autocracy took the shock of the most violent war in history, and collapsed, though later than might have been reasonably expected. That was not surprising; the war rocked to their foundations all the societies in all the states involved in it, and not a few which were not. In the ensuing turmoil in Russia, the Bolshevik section of the Marxist faction came to the top, not only because of their ruthlessness and superb organising ability, but because they were the only political group in the country at that time willing to accept the decision of the masses to have done with the war and go home, and to make that decision the basis of their policy. Lenin was about the only leader, even among the Bolsheviks, who grasped the fact that the army had had enough of fighting and would not fight again. This the Allies did not understand, and they paid for their lack of understanding by condemning the forces in Russia they relied upon, the Liberals of the March revolution, Kerensky and the White generals, to extinction.

Inevitably, the men who unceremoniously seized power in Petrograd in November 1917 were not the moderate, God-fearing Labour leaders in cloth caps who shuffled into the House of Commons in increasing numbers as the twentieth century wore on, nor the sober, middle-class reformers who joined their ranks, determined to make a new world, but to make it slowly, through committees and voting on resolutions and amendments. They were wild men, with wild ideas, offspring of a hard, tyrannical country, conspirators who had spent their lives on the run from the police, or had sat it out in cheap rooms in Brussels, Geneva or Paris, arguing endless points of doctrine and dreaming of the long night of vengeance to come. To expect such people at once to don the habits of Westminster or the City of London when they came to power, as many British politicians seemed to do, and then to be outraged when they did not, was to fly in the face of all the obvious facts of history. British politicians, or enough of them to drown the more cautious voices of men like Austen Chamberlain, thought they could deal with the Russian problem – and their own inability to understand it – by an act of banishment, just as Clemenceau had tried to do in 1919 and as their own successors were to attempt to do, with disastrous results, in the 1930s. In the 1920s, Britain was still such a great power, and Russsia such a weak one, though the weakness could only be temporary, that such ideas were perhaps not wholly irrational. But Britain's power was declining, and errors of judgment like these are more than a declining power can afford.

The Russian revolution took place at a time when the social order in all the countries which passed through the First World War was being called into question. The Russian Bolsheviks were not responsible for this, as many of their opponents in Britain, like Churchill, seemed to believe. To suppose that, by banishing the Bolsheviks from Britain, or even from Russia, one could somehow banish the social problem, which the First World War had written into the agenda of nations, without being its cause, was yet another of the illusions which the revolution engendered in Britain. In reality, so far from the Leninist regime in Russia being the cause of social unrest in Britain after the war, it helped prevent that unrest taking on a revolutionary form. The Bolsheviks frightened British Conservatives, but not more than they frightened British Labour leaders. Men like

Ramsay MacDonald, Philip Snowden, J. R. Clynes were the official opposition to the Tories, but they could not feel more opposed to the Tories than they felt to the Bolsheviks. And the fact that the Bolsheviks had brought off a revolution in Russia made such men determined not to countenance a revolution of that sort, or indeed of any sort, in Britain. When Labour men and women called for more trade with Russia, they did so, not out of any sense of community with Soviet communism, but in order to destroy it. Churchill and men like him had not succeeded in crushing Bolshevism by force. Perhaps it was time, Clynes suggested, 'to try some other method'. Other Labour MPs said the same. 'If they were to save the country . . . to remove unrest and discontent and prevent the social revolution', they argued, 'Anglo-Soviet trade must be restored.'[32]

The fact that there had been a violent revolution in Russia in 1917 helped, paradoxically, to prevent a repetition of it in Britain. For that, the British people and their governments should have been grateful. Instead, by some defect of logic, they embarked on a sterile and inconsequential feud with the very people in Russia who had shown them how not to overcome the social upheavals of the times.

3. Our Fatal Choices

I

BRITAIN and Russia were allies for three quarters of the First World War and the struggle cost them dear. They were allies again in the Second World War and once more the price was heavy. For Britain, the political cost alone was almost fatal, though Russia was restored to the pinnacle of power by her victory over Germany. Both countries had the strongest interest in averting a second world war; their failure to do so made that war practically inevitable. When the war came, in 1939 for Britain, in 1941 for Russia, neither could emerge victorious, or perhaps survive, without the other's help. Why then could the two not work together in the 1930s?

The outlook for Anglo-Soviet relations was sombre but not hopeless at the close of the 1920s, with weariness in Britain over the diplomatic breach in 1927 and demands on the Left for ending it, though more for commercial than political reasons. Labour became the largest party in the House of Commons as a result of the general election in May 1929 (288 seats as against 260 Conservatives) and formed a government with the support of the 59 Liberal members, and with MacDonald as Prime Minister for the second time. The party's election manifesto, *Labour's Appeal to the Nation*, pledged it to resume diplomatic and trade relations with Russia; the Conservatives were silent on the issue. On 15 July, however, MacDonald told the Commons that there would be no exchange of ambassadors with Moscow without Parliamentary approval, an unusual procedure which annoyed his Foreign Secretary, Arthur Henderson, since it would rule out a full resumption until the next Parliamentary session, which began in October.[1] MacDonald needed to make his usual point about contacts with Moscow.

Henderson told Valerian Dovgalevsky, the Soviet ambassador to Paris, who had been sent to London in July to represent Russia in the talks, that the interval before October could be spent settling disputed questions, such as the hoary issues of propaganda and public and private debts. The Russians bridled at this and eventually had their way through the British acceptance of a curious formula which 'confirmed' article 16 of the unratified Anglo-Soviet agreement of 1924 concerning propaganda, and the deferment of other issues until later. The documents were signed by Henderson and Dovgalevsky at Lewes (conveniently near Labour's annual conference at Brighton) on 3 October, and the exchange of ambassadors was approved by the Commons on 5 November by a vote of 374 to 199. The Lords dissented by a vote of 43 to 21, but they could be ignored since no legislation was needed. Sir Esmond Ovey went to Moscow for Britain and Gregory Sokolnikov came to London.[2] The King refused to shake hands with him and he had to be content with the Prince of Wales. In the following year, however, anti-British propaganda from Moscow increased and a serious dispute sprang up with the trial in Moscow of certain Soviet officials who incriminated Britain and France in their confessions of guilt. 'For my own part', wrote Henderson to Ovey in December 1930, 'I am bitterly disappointed with the results of one year's renewed relations with the Soviet government, whose actions seem designed deliberately to play into the hands of opponents of continued Anglo-Russian relations.'[3]

Nevertheless, the ending of the diplomatic breach with Britain was genuinely welcomed in Russia. It lessened the chilling isolation of the late 1920s, and moreover the breach with Britain had cost Russia dear in foreign exchange. Anglo-Soviet trade was never large, but it was heavily weighted in Russia's favour, the Soviets exporting to Britain in 1925, for instance, £25 million worth of goods and buying from Britain only £6 million worth. Trade was seriously affected by the diplomatic breach, falling to £21 million worth of Soviet exports to Britain in 1928, and then, with the diplomatic resumption, rising to £34 million in 1930, though this was halved at the bottom of the world economic recession in 1933.[4] In the early 1930s, Britain was taking 33 per cent of Russia's exports, as compared with 16 per cent for Germany, the next biggest customer, and a mere 3 per cent for the United States. For a country in Soviet Russia's parlous economic state in 1929 and 1930, as the first five-year plan moved uncertainly forward, foreign exchange from Britain, even on such a modest scale, could not be ignored.[5]

On 16 April and 12 May 1930 respectively temporary trade and fisheries agreements were signed by Henderson and Sokolnikov, though these were to be bedevilled by old problems of debts and new

British charges against Russia of dumping surplus products on saturated Western markets. Moreover, the Ottawa agreements of 1932 for the protection of British Empire trade had adverse effects on business with Russia, as also did a bilateral agreement signed by Britain with Canada at the Ottawa conference, article 21 of which prevented goods entering either country from a third state if their export prices were 'maintained by state action', and if such trade jeopardised the Ottawa agreements. Acting under this arrangement, the National Government formed in Britain in August 1931 denounced the temporary Anglo-Soviet commercial agreement on 16 October 1932, and a new treaty was not signed until 16 February 1934, which was approved by the House of Commons without a division on 1 March.[6] For all that, Britain remained in the forefront of Russia's trading partners for the rest of the 1930s, taking 16.6 per cent of her exports in 1934, rising to 23.5 per cent in 1935 and 32.7 per cent in 1937, when she supplied between one fifth and one sixth of Russia's external needs. These figures must be read, however, against the general decline in world trade in the 1930s.[7]

Politically, too, despite the distaste for the Soviets of the predominantly Conservative National Government, the outlook for better Anglo-Soviet relations in the thirties was not unfavourable. Britain and her friends in the League of Nations had proved themselves powerless before the Japanese conquest of Manchuria in 1931–32, with all its implications for Soviet security. The world disarmament conference, too, which opened in Geneva in February 1932 and stumbled on by stops and starts until its liquidation in 1934, was not marked by any close Anglo-Soviet accord. Nevertheless, Britain, like the rest of the capitalist world, was too shaken by the world economic crisis to have much time or inclination to take up again the old anti-Soviet vendettas of the 1920s.

On the Soviet side, the 1930s wrought a transformation in foreign policy, though this took some time to complete. Until the 1930s, Soviet leaders regarded, or professed to regard, the capitalist world as a single undifferentiated enemy, propelled by internal contradictions towards endless internecine warfare, but united in its determination to destroy the Soviet state. With the accession to the Chancellorship in Germany of Adolf Hitler on 30 January 1933, this image began to give way to another. It was now evident to Moscow that, while the capitalist system remained implacably hostile, the German Nazis were most immediately so, no doubt because monopoly capitalism had reached its most advanced stage of development in Germany. In any case, Germany was the nearest powerful capitalist state to Russia. All this was clear from undisguised pronouncements by Nazi leaders, as for instance that of the Minister for Economic Affairs, the German industrialist, Alfred Hugenberg, who, at the World Economic Conference in London in June 1933, proposed a mandate for Germany 'to use her constructive and creative energies' to 'reorganise' Russia.[8] Stalin also seems to have thought (though in this he was wrong) that other capitalist states, such as Britain and France, could not remain indifferent to what had happened in Germany in 1933, and that they must in their own interest join forces with countries, even including the despised Russia, that were now coming within the range of Germany's new guns. Later, when the German threat had been dealt with, Russia would no doubt have to return to her posture of vigilance against all her capitalist enemies. But that was for the future. The immediate need was to forge links with all the capitalist states threatened by the new forces in Germany. Franklin Roosevelt's recognition of the Soviet regime in March 1933 was perhaps a beginning.

Accordingly, on France's initiative Russia applied for and in September 1934 was granted membership of the League of Nations, an organisation she had consistently denounced from its birth. Collective security became Russia's watchword: she gave full support to the League sanctions policy against Italian aggression in Abyssinia and called for a strengthening of the League Covenant to deal with future breaches of the peace.[9] For the time being, it was necessary to put the policy of world revolution – if Stalin ever really believed in it – on ice. At the same time, it was essential, as threats to the international order mounted, to discourage capitalist states from joining the new Germany against Russia, or acquiescing in German moves against the Soviets. This was the logic behind Soviet Foreign Minister Maxim Litvinov's shibboleth: the indivisibility of peace. It meant that Germany's campaign against Russia was a campaign against all the European states, and that none of them had anything to gain from sympathising with it.

Stalin also returned to the principle of a Franco-Soviet alliance intended to hold Germany in a vice from east and west. The alliance, signed on 2 May 1935, was never more than a pale reflection of the great axis formed in the 1890s by Paris and Moscow against the Dual Alliance of Germany and Austria–Hungary. The ideological gulf

between France and Russia in the 1930s, the fear of communism on
the French Right, ensured that. Besides, since 1919 France's security
system had involved ties with the successor states of Eastern Europe,
such as Poland and Rumania, against which Russia had irredentist
claims. Nevertheless, the Franco-Soviet alliance, apart from
neutralising communist party opposition to rearmament in France,
made all but the most extreme Right-wing politicians in France aware
of Russia's importance in any future arrangements for defence
against Hitler.

The Soviets also began to bid for British friendship. Ivan Maisky,
sent as Soviet ambassador to London in October 1932, recalls in his
memoirs the insults he and his entourage were greeted with on his
arrival, and then, for a brief spell in 1934 and 1935, the mild 'thaw'
as British politicians and officials, notably Churchill and the
Permanent Under-Secretary of Stated at the Foreign Office,
Vansittart, sensed the new threat from Germany and Britain's
common interest with Russia in opposing it.[10] Vansittart talked with
Maisky about the French proposals for an Eastern Locarno and other
devices for strengthening the status quo.[11] And, in Moscow the
authorities there played their part. After arresting twenty-five
employees of Metropolitan-Vickers Electrical Co. Ltd, including six
British engineers, on charges of espionage and wrecking on 11 and 12
March 1933, the Soviet authorities acquitted one of the British team,
expelled three and sentenced the other two to three and two years'
imprisonment respectively, by no means harsh treatment considering
the offences. The Russians then released the two engineers on 1
July.[12] The Soviet intention was presumably to encourage the lifting
of a British trade embargo imposed by the Privy Council in
retaliation against the arrests on 18 April, and to secure a resumption
of the trade negotiations, which were broken off on 20 March and
resumed on 3 July. But it must also have been intended to ease the
task of those in Britain who wanted closer relations with Russia.

One of these was Anthony Eden, who became Lord Privy Seal on 1
January 1934 and then Minister for League of Nations Affairs in
June 1935, when Sir Samuel Hoare was appointed Foreign
Secretary, a post he was to hold for only six months. In March 1935
Eden accompanied Sir John Simon, Hoare's predecessor at the
Foreign Office, to Berlin for two days' talks with Hitler. The visit had
been postponed for a few days by the German Chancellor as a rebuff
to the British statement on defence on 4 March, which announced

increased spending. Between that statement and Simon's and Eden's visit to Berlin on 25 and 26 March, came the announcement of conscription in Germany in violation of the Versailles Treaty. It is a remarkable indication of the National Government's attitude to Germany and Russia respectively at that time that it was not deterred from sending the Foreign Secretary and his assistant to Berlin by Germany's breach of the treaty, or from concluding an agreement with Hitler in June which condoned Germany's naval rearmament, again in defiance of the Versailles Treaty. There was no suggestion, however, that a senior minister should go to Moscow.

Eden accordingly went on to the Soviet capital from Berlin on 27 March, the first British minister to do so since the revolution. He talked with Stalin and Foreign Minister Litvinov, ate iced pudding inscribed with the words 'Peace is indivisible', and gave an account of the talks Simon and he had had in Berlin. Eden regarded his Moscow visit as a step in the right direction.

> To me [he wrote] the passage in our joint statement that there was at present no conflict of interest between the two governments on any of the main issues . . . expressed what I believed should be the true nature of relations between our two countries at that time. I thought that we ought to try to bring this influence to bear with good effect in Europe, where dangers were every day more threatening.[13]

Other members of the government took little interest in Eden's Soviet venture. Simon, only five days after Hitler announced his intention of setting aside Part V of the Versailles Treaty, achieved after the most inhuman sacrifices by millions in the First World War, which committed Germany to disarmament, almost congratulated the German leader in a speech in the House of Commons on 21 March (the seventeenth anniversary of the last German offensive in 1918!), which included the words,

> The object of British policy has been . . . to help bring this great state back into the councils and comity of Europe on terms which are just to her and which are fair and secure for all of us, so that she, with her great talents and resources, may contribute with a full sense of equal status and dignity to the task which every good European who wants peace has got to share, and that is the task of

sustaining and strengthening general peace by good relations and by co-operation between neighbours.[14]

II

In the 1930s the central issue for Russia and her sympathisers was the conflict between Fascism, embodied in the German and Italian dictatorships, and ordinary men and women – the 'good and true people' – everywhere. The conflict was symbolised by the Italian invasion of Abyssinia, in which the British and French governments acquiesced, with some show of support for League sanctions while Russia's support for sanctions was undeviating, and Hitler's reoccupation of the Rhineland on 7 March 1936, to which Britain and France offered no effective resistance while Russia called for action, even though they were bound to oppose Hitler's move by the Versailles Treaty and the Locarno treaties of 1925 and she was not; but especially by the civil war in Spain, which began with an uprising in Spanish Morocco of so-called Nationalist forces led by General Francisco Franco on 17 July 1936 and strongly backed, though in different ways, by Hitler and Mussolini, and which ended in victory for Franco in March 1939. The Spanish civil war, with the popularly elected Republican government in Madrid supported by Soviet Russia and the forces of the Left in Europe, on one side, and the Nationalists, symbolising Fascism and supported by Nazi Germany and Fascist Italy and their clients all over Europe, on the other, took on the image of the international system in miniature. The admirers of Hitler and Mussolini saw in Franco's cause the hopes of European civilisation against communist barbarism. The admirers of Stalin saw in it a portent of the end of the ordinary person's freedom unless an effective anti-Fascist front was forged in time.

There were a few – almost to be counted on the fingers of one hand – on the political Right in Britain at that time who enrolled themselves in the struggle, if not against Fascism, certainly against the German resurgence. Pre-eminently there was Winston Churchill. He had been a life-long opponent of communism. The man marked out by fate to lead Britain into partnership with Russia during the Second World War had done his utmost to strangle the Bolshevik system at its birth; had exerted himself to persuade the Allies in 1918 to turn the war against Germany into a war against communism; had congratulated Mussolini on saving Italy from communism; and drew no distinction between Hitlerism and communism except that during his own moment of power in 1940 the former happened to be more dangerous to his country 'than the latter. That record made it impossible for this lonely Conservative to lead and instruct the confused legions of the Left in the ideological divide of the times.

Admittedly, the government of the day in Britain in the middle and late 1930s, the ruling few who ran the country and decided its foreign policy, could hardly take the simplified 'democracy versus Fascism' view of the world scene. It was not merely that they were the social elect and felt no community with a 'clothcap' country like Russia; or that, if there had to be a choice, they preferred high-ranking Nazis and Fascists, who lived their kind of life and talked their kind of talk, to boot-faced Russian commissars. But, such considerations aside, anyone in Britain in the 1930s who had to do with the making of foreign policy must have had difficulty in accepting the Left's image of the diplomatic situation, and in striving for accord with Moscow as a result.

For British decision-makers, 'Fascism' was not the single, integral evil, to be fought by an alliance of all good men and true, of the Left Book Club stereotype. In reality, Fascism embodied itself in three different totalitarian regimes, the German, Italian and Japanese, all of them threats to British interests and to peace, but each a different sort of threat, of a different order of magnitude. No British politician could, with the allies likely to be available, contemplate taking on all three at the same time. The Minister for the Co-ordination of Defence, Sir Thomas Inskip, was not exaggerating when he told the Cabinet in February 1938 that,

> The plain fact which cannot be obscured is that it is beyond the resources of this country to make proper provision in peace for the defence of the British Empire against three powers in three different theatres of war.[15]

The likely allies did not, of course, at any time in the 1930s include the United States, whose assistance was essential to the defeat of the Central Powers in the First World War, and without whose fleet coercive action against Japan in the 1930s would have been impossible. American public opinion at that time was so solidly opposed to participation in any international effort to check the dictators that it was unmoved by Hitler's conquest of Western

Europe in 1940 and only agreed to fight when America's own fleet
and territory came under attack.

Italy and Japan, Britain's allies in the hard-fought First World
War, were as good as in the enemy camp. Nor could the Dominions,
the self-governing countries of the British Empire – Australia,
Canada, New Zealand, South Africa – be counted upon
automatically to join Britain in war. In 1914 Britain had called them
to arms without asking their opinion, and they had come. Now, as a
result of the Statute of Westminster of 1931 and other enactments,
they made their own decisions, and all of them had made clear since
1918 that, if they ever fought again, it would have to be because *their*
vital interests, and not merely Britain's, were at stake, and because
there was no alternative. None of them were satisfied about either
condition in the 1930s until quite late in the day.

Winston Churchill, in his call for a grand coalition, led by Britain,
with French and Soviet support, against the aggressors, was, of
course, thinking about Germany as the adversary. He had no interest
in taking on Italy – Hoare, the Foreign Secretary when Italy attacked
Abyssinia in October 1935, was justified, Churchill said, 'in going as
far with the League against Italy as he could carry France', but no
further.[16] He said practically nothing about Japan. The National
government could not afford to be so single-minded. Italian
aggression against Abyssinia was a vital matter to them because it
stirred public opinion deeply, though not for long, and general
elections and by-elections Baldwin had to win, and Churchill did not.
Baldwin's Cabinet was forced to take part in, and lead, League
sanctions against Italy in the teeth of the better judgement of all its
members (except Eden) and of Churchill himself. The form of Italian
aggression against Abyssinia, too, was so unabashed and primitive
that it could not be ignored. The same was almost true of Japan's
expansion at China's expense, in Manchuria in 1931 and in China
proper in 1937. Churchill was practically silent. He could afford to
concentrate on Hitler's evil deeds.

The band of democratic nations which Churchill conjured up in his
imagination had all the marks of an optical illusion. In the end, only
France and Russia counted as Britain's partners against Germany,
Italy and Japan. Whether France had the national unity to stand a
struggle to the death with German forces, only time would and did
show. The international civil war between Left and Right in Europe
which erupted so cruelly in Spain might erupt in France, too. Could

the French Right, which cried 'better Hitler than Blum', fight another Marne, another Verdun, with the communists as their allies? Even if France had the unity for war, what sort of war would the French fight? A war against Germany, perhaps, but a defensive war, fought for the soil of France, and from the shelter of the Maginot line. Not a war against Italy or Japan. In France, Britain had a dubious ally. But there was Russia, at least a potential ally, and one in company with which Britain was in the next few years to fight and win a war against all her adversaries.

III

There was a brief period after Hitler's accession to power in January 1933 when the Russians made known what *Izvestia* in an article on 6 May called their 'wish to live at peace with Germany', words which since 1945 have been cited as a reproach against them, as though from 1933 right through until 1939 the British and French governments did not persistently thrust such wishes upon the Nazi regime.[17] But, after that interlude, Soviet calls for collective defence against Hitler through the League and outside it were consistent and unvaried. It is true that, in making such calls, Stalin acted in the narrowly conceived interests of his own country, indeed in the interests of his own power as master of Russia. But such is the law of life in the international system, and if united action in defence of peace was in Russia's interest, it was assuredly in that of Britain and France, too. Britain was more to blame for sacrificing realism to political prejudice when she ignored this fact than France. At least, the French, at the risk of stoking up the fires between Right and Left at home, made their alliance with Russia in 1935. Repeatedly, as the bastions in Hitler's path fell, French ministers begged their British colleagues to enter into commitments with as many status-quo states as possible, including Russia. Each time the reply from London was negative.

In March 1936, when Germany remilitarised the Rhineland and there was a flurry of activity among the Western Powers intended, in the famous words of *The Times* in a leader on 9 March, to 'rebuild' on the site lately occupied by the Versailles Treaty, no suggestion was heard in London that Russia should be brought into the deliberations. After all, Russia was not a signatory of the Locarno agreements of October 1925, which, in British eyes, Hitler had violated even more grossly than the Versailles Treaty by his Rhineland *coup*. Indeed, the Locarno agreements, by excluding any guarantee of Germany's eastern borders to parallel the guarantee in the west, were all but a signal to Berlin that any plans it had for revising its eastern frontiers – or, in other words, for moving in Russia's direction – would not necessarily be opposed by the West.

Again, Hitler's annexation of Austria in March 1938 did not move Britain to discuss the situation with Russia, and another Soviet appeal on 14 March for an international conference was rejected. Russia, it could be argued – though the British government did not even think it necessary to argue the point – was technically ineligible to be consulted: she was not a signatory to the treaties of Versailles or St Germain of 1919, or the League of Nations agreements in the 1920s for financial assistance to Austria, all of which guaranteed Austria's independence and were infringed by Hitler's action. On the other hand, Austria was a central European state, and the Anschluss at once put in jeopardy another central, or east, European state, Czechoslovakia. Germany's armed might was inexorably moving towards the Soviet homeland. Moreover, Russia had grappled with the combined forces of Austria and Germany in the First World War and had given many lives to make possible the peace settlements which the Nazi government in Germany was now in the process of tearing down. But when Austria and Germany were forcibly yoked together by Hitler, with far-reaching consequences for the balance of power in Eastern Europe, the Russians were not asked for an opinion.

In his speech in the Reichstag on 20 February 1938, the German Chancellor had announced his intention of protecting the 10 million Germans (he should have said German-speaking people) living outside the Reich.[18] Once the Austrian bastion, with its six and a half millions, fell in March, the spotlight moved to Czechoslovakia and its three and a half million German-speaking Sudeten population inhabiting the western rim of the Bohemian plateau bordering the Reich. Thereafter, 1938 unfolded its inexorable length through the different phases of the tragedy, in which Hitler, while egging on the Sudeten German leader, Konrad Henlein, to make increasingly impossible demands for autonomy on the Czechs, fulminated about German demands for justice for kith and kin across the border, which he said he could not much longer hold in check, and Britain took the lead over France in pressing the Czechs to cede the disputed territories to Berlin and in urging Hitler to accept them peacefully. The tragedy culminated in the oft-told climax of the Munich conference on 29 September, at which the Sudeten territories were assigned to the Reich by agreement between Britain, France, Germany and Italy. The Czechoslovak rump was guaranteed by the four, but the guarantee was shown to be worthless when German armoured columns swept into Bohemia with impunity on 15 March of the following year. Bohemia became a German protectorate and its sister state, Slovakia, a puppet state of the Reich – that is, after the jackals, Hungary and Poland, had also dined, by Hitler's invitation, on the body of the Czech state. Nothing now stood between Germany and Poland.

There will continue for years to come controversy as to whether the Russians really intended to come to Czechoslovakia's assistance, had she been attacked by Germany in 1938, and had not Britain and France forestalled them by capitulating to Hitler at Munich. They were bound by a treaty signed on 16 May 1935 – shortly after Russia joined the League of Nations – to help Czechoslovakia against aggression, but this pledge was only operative if France, bound to Czechoslovakia by a mutual security treaty since 1921, came to her assistance first, and, throughout 1938, no-one, not even the French themselves, knew whether they would. Repeatedly during 1938 the Russians said they would assist Czechoslovakia if it was attacked, but only in co-operation with France. Lord Chilston, the British ambassador to Moscow, heard this undertaking from Potemkin, a Soviet Deputy Foreign Minister, on 8 September.[19] On 24 September, Mr R. A. Butler and Earl de la Warr had an interview in Geneva with the Soviet Foreign Minister, Maxim Litvinov, and he told the same story, which he had repeated the day before at the Political Committee of the League Assembly.[20]

Of course, at that time, though not today, Russia had no common border with Czechoslovakia: her forces would have to pass through Poland or Rumania, or their air space, to join the Czechs in action against Germany. Doubt persisted throughout the year whether the Poles or Rumanians would allow them to do so. For this reason, the Russians said, they could take no action without a supporting resolution from the League Council, which they seemed to think would induce Poland and Rumania to co-operate. They intended, as they put it, to 'refer the matter to the Council', if called upon to honour their obligations to Czechoslovakia. The French, in passing on to London what they heard about their Soviet ally's intentions, always emphasised this aspect of the matter. The British ambassador to Paris, Sir Eric Phipps, for instance, told the Foreign Office on 8 September that his hosts informed him that this was Russia's purpose, and that Poland and Rumania would not allow Soviet aircraft to overfly their territory.[21] Bonnet, the French Foreign Minister, notoriously anxious to avoid war with Germany over the Sudeten question, had a strong interest in throwing doubt on Soviet sincerity. British politicians, like the Conservative MP, Robert Boothby, who talked with Litvinov in Geneva, came away with a different impression.[22]

There was also doubt whether the Czech authorities themselves could have accepted Soviet forces on their soil, or any form of co-operation with the Bolshevik state. In a broadcast from Prague on the evening of 30 September, after the territorial surgery in Munich that day, M. Vavrecka, the Czech Minister of Propaganda, said:

> We had to consider that it would take the Russian army weeks to come to our aid, perhaps too late . . . . It was even more important to consider that our war by the side of Soviet Russia would have been not only a fight against Germany, but it would have been interpreted as a fight on the side of Bolshevism. And then perhaps all of Europe would have been drawn into the war against us and Russia.[23]

M. Vavrecka seemed to be making the extraordinary suggestion that Britain and France, rather than see Czechoslovakia saved by the Russians, would join Nazi Germany in attacking it if the Czechs called on Moscow for help. As for President Benes, only in the extreme of desperation did he inquire of the Russians what their attitude would be if the Czechs resisted, and that was on 19 September, when he was pressed by the British and French governments to agree to the immediate transfer to Germany of the Sudeten districts before Chamberlain went to his second meeting with Hitler at Bad Godesberg. He was told that Russia would honour her obligations if France played her part.[24]

The Soviet position in the Czech crisis was therefore ambiguous. About the only evidence of definite Soviet intentions was Moscow's note to Poland of 23 September warning that any crossing of the Czech frontier by Polish forces would mean a Soviet denunciation of the Soviet-Polish non-aggression pact signed in July 1932, and the reported movement of 30 Soviet infantry divisions to the vicinity of Russia's western borders.[25] But, if Soviet policy during the crisis was enigmatic – and, after all, British and French policies, too, were shifting and uncertain from beginning to end – there was hardly any disposition in London or Paris to probe it, to discover at the highest level of government what the Russians meant to do, and how they meant to do it, in different kinds of contingencies. Britain and France relied on reports from their ambassadors in Moscow (and neither of these seems to have had any serious interview with Stalin throughout the crisis, nor was he instructed to); on talks with Litvinov in Geneva; and on discussions with Soviet ambassadors in London and Paris. Whereas, during Neville Chamberlain's colloquies with Hitler in September, French ministers and their Chiefs of Staff came repeatedly to London to co-ordinate every step of the two countries' approach, no suggestion ever seems to have been made that a senior British or French minister or military officer should visit Moscow or that Soviet political or service chiefs be invited to London. The subject of Russia was in fact excluded from debates in the British Cabinet throughout the crisis until, in March 1939, the rickety structure of Munich fell to the ground.[26]

But perhaps the most remarkable instance of this sullen cold-shouldering of Russia by Britain and France during the Czech crisis was the handling by the two countries of the proposed guarantee to Czechoslovakia in the event of the Sudeten provinces being eventually ceded to Germany. When Mr Chamberlain went on the first of his two visits in September to see Hitler – that is, the flight to Berchtesgaden on the 15th – he took with him a proposal for a guarantee of the rump state by Britain, France, Germany, *and Russia*. The guarantee was approved by the Cabinet on 14 September, but not a word of it, or of Chamberlain's general intentions when he saw Hitler, was conveyed to Moscow.[27] As it happened, the Prime Minister did not bring up the question of the guarantee in that form at the Berchtesgaden talks, but before his next meeting with Hitler, that is, at Godesberg on 22 September, the Cabinet specifically charged him to insist upon Soviet participation in the guarantee, though, once again, without any consultation with Russia.[28] Once more, with a strange forgetfulness, Chamberlain overlooked the matter of Soviet participation when he talked with the Chancellor at Godesberg, and when Mr Duff Cooper, the First Lord of the

Admiralty, and the only Cabinet member to attach any importance to Russia, asked about this omission, he received no answer.[29]

At Munich at the end of September, the Prime Minister never mentioned the possibility of the Russians being party to the guarantee. He did not tell Russia about this, nor that he had undertaken in Cabinet to insist on Russia being a party, though, in that instance, too, he had not bothered to ask the Russians whether they agreed! To crown it all, when the British authorities took the strongest action they permitted themselves throughout the crisis and issued the famous Foreign Office communiqué on 26 September, when war seemed inevitable, stating that 'if, in spite of all the efforts made by the British Prime Minister, a German attack is made on Czechoslovakia, the immediate result must be that France will be bound to come to her assistance and Great Britain and Russia will certainly stand by France', there is no evidence of consultation with Russia even being suggested.[30] Incredible as it sounds, after this contemptuous treatment of a Russia willing since 1933 to join a common defence against Nazi aggression, Sir Alexander Cadogan, the Permanent Under-Secretary of State, could introduce a major review of the Czech crisis in mid-October with the words:

> What follows is based on the assumption that there will be no sensational changes in Europe, that Germany will continue on her present course, that there will be no collapse in Italy, that Russia will continue as aloof and unhelpful as she is now.[31]

IV

In February 1939, Sir William Seeds, at the British embassy in Moscow, concluded that Churchill was right in thinking that Britain, by her thoughtless behaviour, had made co-operation with Russia virtually impossible. 'The Soviet government and people', he wrote, 'see no sign whatever that France and Great Britain would do anything but continue to capitulate.' 'The Soviet Union', Seeds thought, 'would therefore keep aloof, all the more readily as their interests are not directly threatened.'[32]

But the charge-sheet against British policy-makers in the months leading up to the outbreak of the Second World War extends to more than merely the cold-shouldering of Russia, the only state capable of halting Germany's advance in Eastern Europe; more than the exclusion of Russia from Anglo-French exchanges on the crisis and the rejection of Russian appeals for a four-Power conference on the grounds that it might deter Hitler from co-operation; more even than the unseemly last-minute turn to Russia when all else had failed, and Britain and France, through their own thoughtlessness, were left to face the German war machine alone. Going further than all this, what Britain and France would have liked to do, had Hitler been willing to join them, was to break all Russia's alliances with states in central and western Europe, to drive her back into Asia, and build up a 'civilised' Christian Europe as a barrier against Russia in the West. The French Prime Minister, Daladier, told Welczeck, the German ambassador in Paris, in May 1938 that, 'speaking frankly as a French ex-serviceman', he dreaded a European war and the destruction of European civilisation because 'into the battle zones, devastated and denuded of men, Cossack and Mongol hordes would then pour, bringing to Europe a new "culture"'. This must be prevented, he went on, 'even if it entailed great sacrifices'.[33] It was strange language for the Prime Minister of a country which had signed an alliance with Russia only three years before, and to the representative of the country against which that alliance was directed.

That alliance, together with all Russia's alliances with western countries, was to be destroyed if the Chamberlain Cabinet had its way. In June 1938, the Foreign Secretary, Lord Halifax, prepared a plan, for which he sought French support, for 'remodelling' Czechoslovakia's treaty relations in order to cut it off from Russia, and even from France itself:

> By reducing what Germany professes to regard as provocative elements in the Czech system of treaties, [the plan would] tend to promote stability in Central Europe and lessen the chances of France being called upon to fulfil her obligations to Czechoslovakia in possibly unfavourable circumstances . . . . The easiest and least disturbing course would be to invite Czechoslovakia to remodel her treaty relations.[34]

By the same logic, since Germany 'professed to regard as provocative' the Franco-Soviet alliance of 1935 (Hitler had used it as a pretext for the reoccupation of the Rhineland), presumably that treaty was next on the list for 'remodelling'.

The argument for the isolation of Russia was restated in a carefully compiled Foreign Office memorandum drawn up in October which reviewed the balance-sheet after Munich. It amounted to a recommendation that Hitler be given *carte blanche* in Central and Eastern Europe while building up British and French defensive strength so that Hitler would be discouraged from striking out in their direction.[35] The comment of a British historian on this paper is that 'there is evidence here to justify the Soviet charge that Britain planned to set Germany at war with Russia in the hope that the result would be "the lasting balance of power" '.[36]

In the British government's mind there were three objections to collaboration with the Russians: that Russia was military a nonentity; that its political regime was insufferable and unreliable; and that any suggestion of collaboration with Moscow would put an end to all the hopes that Chamberlain and his colleagues entertained that, one day, once Germany's grievances had been attended to, Hitler would settle down and become a respectable member of the international community.

On Russia's military strength, there was no disagreement among the government's advisers: all were unanimous and all were wrong. Lord Chilston, the British ambassador in Moscow, reported home on 19 April 1938 the opinion of his military attaché, Colonel Firebrace, that Stalin's purges in 1936 and 1937 had affected 65 per cent of senior Red Army officers. He concluded that the Soviet Union 'must for the time being be counted out of European politics in so far as the exercise of a decisive influence one way or the other is concerned'.[37] That remained the view of the War Office at least until Munich.[38] Even after the fall of Bohemia to Nazi Germany in the following year, the Chiefs of Staff clung to the notion that Russia was militarily insignificant.[39] Russia's vast reserves of manpower, her performance for three bloody years in the First World War, her industrial revolution since then, all counted for nothing.

This assessment reinforced the political objections to dealings with Moscow. Russia was fundamentally unreliable, far more so than Hitler or Mussolini. Hitler's word on the piece of paper Chamberlain brought back from Munich could be taken with some seriousness; not so Stalin's. To Chamberlain, the Russians were 'stealthily and cunningly pulling the strings behind the scenes to get us involved in war with Germany'; he knew this, he wrote, because 'our Secret Service doesn't spend all of its time looking out of the window', though no Secret Service document has ever been produced giving evidence of this allegation.[40] For Alexander Cadogan, Permanent Under-Secretary at the Foreign Office in 1938, the Russian aim was 'to precipitate confusion and war in Europe', a strange charge if Russia was really as weak as Cadogan, and most of his friends, believed.[41]

Moreover, the argument ran, if Britain talked with Russia about security in Europe, Hitler would not like it, and the main objective of British policy in the late 1930s was to come to a *modus vivendi* with Hitler. Halifax considered, in discusions in the Cabinet's Foreign Policy Committee in March 1938, that the more Britain linked herself to France and Russia, the more Germany would feel encircled and reject a 'real settlement'.[42] Above all, in the government's view, Russia wanted action to stop German aggression and the government were unwilling to contemplate that, at least until 15 March 1939, and perhaps not even then. Chamberlain explained the government's approach in the House of Commons on 24 March and dismissed Litvinov's suggestion of 17 March of a five-Power conference in Bucharest (Britain, France, Poland, Rumania and Russia) with the frank words:

> [The Soviet] proposal would appear to involve less a consultation with a view to settlement than a concerting of action against an eventuality that has not yet arisen. Its object would appear to be to negotiate such mutual undertakings in advance to resist aggression as I have referred to, which, for reasons I have already given, HMG for their part are unwilling to accept.[43]

It is an extraordinary fact that, even after the total collapse of Chamberlain's policy on 15 March 1939, when Germany invaded Bohemia amid the ruins of the Munich agreement, and the Prime Minister, by 20 March, had finally decided that, if Germany took the offensive once again, 'we must take steps to stop her by attacking her on all points in order to pull down the bully', he nevertheless refused to follow up a suggestion of Lord Chatfield, Minister for the Co-ordination of Defence, that staff conversations with France should be immediately extended to Russia.[44] Instead, he made the fatal choice of giving guarantees to Poland and Rumania, without a word to Moscow about them, or about how they could possibly be implemented without prior agreement with the Russians. His thought, if we may employ Chamberlain's own form of words, would appear to have been: we will not talk to the Russians unless and until we are really in trouble; in any case, they are good for nothing. It is worth reflecting how this behaviour must have struck the Russians as they pondered what they should do as the curtain rose on that fateful year, 1939.

V

If Chamberlain and other politicians of his generation had reached the conclusion after the First World War – into which many said that ordinary people had been railroaded by politicians and businessmen – that the people would have to railroad politicians and businessmen into the next war, if they wanted one, they came near to seeing their wishes fulfilled in the spring of 1939. The immediate reaction, expressed most sharply in the House of Commons, to the events of 15 March was that Ministers must get up and do something, it hardly mattered what, to show that Germany would not be allowed to commit further acts of force. Many nodded in agreement in the Commons on 15 March with Godfrey Nicholson when he said:

> We should feel heavy responsibility for our surprise today over what has happened, for our weakness, for our anxiety for the future. I frankly admit that I feel that I, as an MP, have failed in my duty, and that every MP, without distinction of party, has failed in his duty.[45]

Now the National government was being pushed into the trenches and over the top, while the ordinary people, or rather their Parliamentary spokesmen, sat in the chateaux behind the lines cheering them on.

The Chamberlain government's reaction *was* (after two days' delay) to do something, more by way of demonstrating shock than as premeditated policy. This was, on 31 March and 13 April, to give the celebrated guarantees to Poland, Rumania and Greece. The substance of the guarantees (France was already bound by treaty to Poland and Rumania) was that if those countries were attacked and felt it necessary to resist with their national forces, Britain would come to their assistance. The informing spirit behind the pledges was correct, if belated, but the government's grasp of their implications was lamentable. And lamentable in two senses. First, the guarantees were a blank cheque on which the recipients could draw unlimited credit for the sort of reckless diplomacy for which they were notorious. That Britain, of all countries, which had fought so hard since 1918 to avoid open-ended commitments it might have to honour in unknown circumstances, should have handed over the right to make war to governments over which it had no control, and which for twenty years had shown little prudence in their foreign policies, is remarkable. But in March 1939, it could be argued, the Chamberlain government had no option. Parliament demanded action, and Chamberlain was forced to look for something or somebody to guarantee. Poland and Rumania were next in the firing line, and that placed them in the strongest position vis-à-vis Britain and France.

Instead of being suppliants seeking help, they, or rather Poland, found themselves in a sellers' market. They had something to trade, their own guaranteeability, and the British government was ready to pay the highest price any sovereign state can pay, namely, its right to go to war at times and over issues of its own choosing. If Britain had no option but to accept Polish and Rumanian terms for the guarantees, and if, as the Polish Foreign Minister, Colonel Beck, made clear on his visit to London on 4 April, Poland would in no circumstances have Russia involved in the guarantee and reserved the right to conduct her own negotiations with Germany, that was a measure of the dead end which the British government had worked themselves into in the six years since Hitler came to power.[46]

The other sense in which the guarantees to Poland and Rumania demonstrated the greatest poverty of imagination on the British side concerns the relation of the guarantees to the Soviet Union. It is fascinating to speculate what Stalin must have made of the political scene in Western Europe in the early months of 1939. The situation was that the Munich agreement, on which the British Prime Minister had set such store, and from which Russia had been excluded, though it concerned her as much as it did Britain and France, had tumbled to the ground, and the two Western democracies, in their anxiety to find some solid ground, now turned to Poland and Rumania. To these they gave guarantees against aggression which they had not the least notion how they were going to fulfil, and on terms – especially the exclusion of Russia, the only country which could ensure the implementation of the guarantees – dictated by the guaranteed. Halifax expressed the self-contradiction of the British position when he wrote to Lindsay, the ambassador in Washington: 'our attempts to consolidate the situation will be frustrated if the Soviet Union is openly associated with the initiation of the scheme'.[47] Stalin could have been forgiven for thinking that British and French affairs must be run by men who, if not positively malicious, were so devoid of business sense as to be hardly worth entering into serious transactions with.

The pledges to Poland, Rumania and Greece, though binding Britain and France to go to war, if need be, in defence of the status quo on or near Russia's borders, were effected, like all major acts of British policy in the 1930s, without consulting Moscow. The Germans, supposed to be the trouble-makers, were actually reassured that the guarantees had no aggressive intent towards them, but no word of explanation was vouchsafed to Russia. As the Russians must have perceived the guarantees, Britain and France might still go back on their word if Germany attacked one or other or all the guaranteed states: after all, this is precisely what they did in regard to the guarantee they gave Czechoslovakia at Munich when the Germans invaded Bohemia in March 1939. Yet, in April 1939, after rejecting a Soviet proposal for a three-Power pact against aggression, to include Britain, France and Russia, the British government naively asked the Russians to follow the British and French example and give unilateral guarantees to Poland and Rumania, but only if these states wanted Soviet assistance when the moment came, and all signs pointed to the probability that they would not.[48] This meant that if, as was by no means unlikely, Britain and France reneged on their guarantees and the Germans attacked, the Russians would be left to grapple with the aggressor alone, and if, as was even more likely, Poland or Rumania or both refused Soviet offers of help, the Russians would be expected to remain within their own frontiers until the Germans had mopped up Poland and Rumania before turning to them. This extraordinary British proposal was made *after* Stalin said at the 18th Congress of the Soviet Communist party in Moscow on 10 March that, while Russia was willing to defend countries threatened by aggression, it had no intention of 'pulling chestnuts out of the fire' for other people.[49]

The French, with greater realism, urged Britain to accept the idea of a tripartite pact which Russia wanted, involving reciprocal pledges to come to each other's assistance if hostilities occurred out of the defence of the status quo in Central and Eastern Europe. In reality, the British Prime Minister did not much care whether Russia was interested or not in the contemptible role he was casting her for; 'I am so sceptical of the value of Russia's help', he wrote later in the year, 'that I should not feel our position was greatly worsened if we had to do without them'.[50] The story of the rest of the negotiations with Moscow was one of the progressive abandonment by the British of that absurd opinion, and of their realisation that, without Russia, they must stand and watch Poland being swallowed up into the German empire. By that time the Russians had had enough of Western contempt.

The British position had to change, as could have been seen from the outset. By 24 May the Cabinet agreed, and perhaps influenced Chamberlain to agree, to the idea of an alliance which Russia had pressed for all along.[51] But it could not have done so with greater loathing. 'The decision had been taken tardily and grudgingly', Vansittart observed.[52] Oliver Harvey, Halifax's private secretary, described Chamberlain as wanting the decision 'to be covered up as much as possible by introducing it into the League machinery'. 'The wheel has come full circle', he went on, 'when we have the PM, who has done more than any responsible statesman to sidetrack Geneva, trying to cover himself with Geneva clothes in order to hide the shame of direct agreement with Soviet Russia'.[53] Reality, nevertheless, was thrusting its way in, in the form, first, of the utter impossibility of implementing the Polish guarantee without an agreement with Russia, and, secondly, of the reports now reaching the Foreign Office almost daily of Russia and Germany groping towards an understanding. One of the most impressive of the latter was that by Erich Kordt, a senior counsellor in Ribbentrop's office in Berlin, who visited London in mid-June and 'stated definitely that the Germans and Russians are in contact as a result of an approach made by Ribbentrop to the Soviet ambassador in Berlin'. Kordt's conclusion, as reported by Vansittart, was that 'if we want an agreement with Russia, we had better be quick about it'.[54]

Hence, at last, the decision to send a mission to Moscow to accelerate the exchanges through ambassadors. But, even at this desperate hour, there was no suggestion of a senior figure, like Eden, leading the mission. The choice fell upon William Strang, an able but subordinate civil servant, then head of the Foreign Office's Central Department. The Germans could send their Foreign Minister in August to entice the Russians into the Nazi-Soviet Pact, but not the British.

Strang found himself sitting in Moscow with the ambassador,

Seeds, and the French envoy, Naggiar, facing Molotov (he replaced Litvinov, ominously, as Soviet Foreign Minister on 3 May), who sat at a desk before them, on what seemed a raised dais. The scene symbolised the supplicatory character of the Anglo-French position, and this was further reflected in the spate of concessions which Britain, taking the lead from France, was now compelled to make. First, the British reference to the League in their draft agreement had to go; then the guaranteed states had to be increased in number, from Poland and Rumania, to the Baltic states, Estonia and Latvia, and Finland, although all three protested their unwillingness to be associated in any defence arrangement with Russia; then, although Russia consented to the inclusion of Belgium, Greece, Luxembourg and Turkey among the guaranteed states, Britain had to agree to the omission of Holland and Switzerland, which she wished to see included; then Britain agreed to the naming of the guaranteed states, though in a secret annex, not in the public treaty; then she had to accept the idea of the agreement coming into force in a case of indirect, as well as direct, aggression, that is, when a guaranteed state was forced to comply with the aggressor's will, as Slovakia was in March 1939, without actually being invaded, though in the end the British had their way in insisting that the definition of indirect aggression should not be capable of being used by a guarantor to interfere in a guaranteed state's internal affairs. The Russians, on their side, made few concessions; they agreed to guarantee states in western Europe, and that the guaranteed states should not be publicly named. But otherwise the running was all in their direction, and this was inevitable. Britain and France had initiated the negotiations, and did so because they realised, late in the day, that their guarantees to Poland and Rumania could not be implemented without Soviet help.

But how were the pledges to the guaranteed states now being negotiated in Moscow to be implemented in the event of an armed clash between them and Germany? The British had not thought of that. It hardly seems that British ministers in 1938 and 1939 really thought that things would ever reach that pass; even when war came in September 1939, they had 'no real belief that the state of war need be turned into a war of steel and blood'.[55] The Russians wanted to know the practical arrangements. They intended to contribute not far short of 200 divisions in the event of war; they wanted to hear what the Western contribution would be. Plainly, it would not be impressive. For the French, there was the Maginot line; it had been built to sit in, and that was that. When it came to war in 1939, the French put a toe in the water, then withdrew it. As for the British, never have her ministers proposed to do more than send two or three divisions to the continent at the outbreak of a major war. The initial shock would be taken by Britain's allies and only after two or three years would the full weight of Britain's effort begin to tell.

The Russians wanted to know where they stood and insisted that British and French military missions be sent to Moscow to negotiate a military convention, which must be signed before the political agreement came into effect. The British were worried. Would it mean that military secrets would pass to Moscow before it was known that the alliance would be concluded? But the inexorable logic of their position left them with no alternative. All they could do was to see to it that the military missions went about their work so half-heartedly that the Russians would realise they did not mean business. Owing to the difficulties of going through Germany by train and the aversion of the French head of mission, General Doumenc, to air travel, the two teams – the British were led by an able admiral, with the Gilbertian name of Sir Reginald Aylmer Ranfurly Plunkett-Ernle-Erle-Drax-went to Leningrad by a slow chartered ship, *The City of Exeter*, arriving on 11 August, seventeen days after Molotov made it clear that the Russians would not continue the negotiations without military discussions.

However, when the military talks began on 12 August it was clear that it was on a political issue that they would founder, the same issue which had dogged progress towards an understanding in Moscow from the beginning. It was stated by Seeds on 15 August, when he reported to London that the Soviet military chief, Voroshilov, had raised 'the fundamental problem on which the talks will succeed or fail, and which has indeed been at the bottom of all our difficulties since the very beginning of the political conversations, namely how to reach any useful agreement with the Soviet Union so long as this country's neighbours maintain a sort of boycott which is only to be broken . . . when it is too late'.[56] In blunt terms, would the Poles (for they were the people who really stood in the line of German fire) allow Soviet forces into their territory to deal with a Nazi attack? Colonel Beck's answer, given to the British ambassador, Sir Howard Kennard, on 19 August, was the same as ever: no. All he would add was that the case might be different some day, if and when the Germans attacked and the Poles were fighting for their lives.[57] The

French made their gloss on this reply, in passing it on to the Russians, by saying that the Poles did not object 'in principle' to Soviet assistance. The British said they 'assumed' the Poles would have the 'right attitude' when the moment arrived. But by that time Russia was in the final stages of her pact with Germany, which Molotov signed with Ribbentrop on 23 August. Voroshilov told the Anglo-French military missions that he now had other work to do and that in any case he saw no point in carrying on the talks until the political situation was clearer.[58]

Colonel Beck's objections were not without reason. He protested that once Soviet forces entered Poland, they would in all likelihood never leave, and that prophecy proved correct in the years after the Second World War. But the effect of Beck's refusal was that, later that year, Poland had to endure invasion from two countries, not one, and that, when eventually freed from German forces in 1945, it was to suffer indefinitely from the Soviet domination which Beck thought he could avoid in 1939; whereas an Anglo-French-Soviet alliance, had Polish agreement made it possible, might have deterred the German attack of 1 September 1939. The truth was that in the 1930s Poland and other East European states had no means of preserving the independence they won in 1919: either they must submit to Germany, or to Russia, or to both. The only hope for them was that Britain and France, which were able to negotiate with Russia the terms of a three-Power pact against Germany, might help decide with Russia, as they could never do with Germany, the terms of Poland's and Rumania's inevitably limited freedom of action in the future.

That hope the Poles themselves destroyed. Because of the nature and circumstances of the guarantees they had given, Britain and France were compelled to acquiesce in Beck's illusion that Poland could continue to enjoy its independence entirely on its own terms; that it could be defended if attacked by Germany without Soviet help, and even if attacked by Germany and Russia combined; and that, even if it were overrun, it could be liberated by its guarantors and restored to a quite unqualified independence. In humouring these hallucinations, Britain and France not only sacrificed the alliance with Russia which alone could have averted war in these last desperate days of peace; they began to dig the vast divide between themselves and Russia which appalled the world after the struggle against Germany was eventually won.

VI

There is bound to be dispute over whether Stalin served the cause even of his own country by his pact with Hitler in August 1939. With that agreement began the long disenchantment with Soviet communism which thereafter increasingly swept the world. In that one act Stalin seemed to erase from the slate the record for wisdom and realism he had earned for his foreign policy throughout the 1930s. For the moment, at least, and for some people for all time, he placed Russia on Hitler's level for violation of treaties, unprovoked aggression, the plunder and despoliation of innocent people's land and homes. There was also the cost in national advantage, offsetting Russia's territorial gains in eastern Poland and the Baltic states. As a result of Soviet neutrality during the lifetime of the pact, Hitler was free to subjugate western Europe and a large part of south east Europe, too. When he finally turned against Russia on 22 June 1941, France was spent and Britain just managing to hold on. About the only consolation Stalin had then was that, when the German attack came, Soviet forces, as a result of the pact, were in foreign territory, away from their own frontiers, though to these they were soon thrust back.

Yet, as we have seen, the alternatives with which Stalin was faced in the summer of 1939, and the balance of advantage, which, as he saw it, lay on the side of signing the pact with Hitler, were to a large extent created by the mismanagement of Britain and France. The two Western Powers had tried to satisfy Germany by concessions at the expense of East European states which threatened Russia's security, and in doing so took no account of Russia's interest or feelings. When that policy, against which Russia had advised, failed, they turned to Russia as a disagreeable last resort, and made proposals for action against Hitler which were bound to throw the greatest burden upon her. She would pay the greatest price for the arrangements they were proposing, and in a war for which even Britain's war-time leader, Winston Churchill, was later to write that the 'English-speaking peoples' bore the greatest responsibility by 'allowing the wicked to rearm', as the motto of his memoirs of the war has it. In negotiating that price, Britain and France showed that they had more respect for Poland's wishes than for Russia's, even though, when the war with Germany finally came, Poland counted for nothing and Russia for everything. It was some indication of how they would regard Poland

and her wishes later, when Russia had borne most of the brunt of defeating Germany.

As if this were not enough, the British and French governments, and the teams they sent to Moscow in 1939 to negotiate the alliance which might have saved the peace, had no expectation that Russia could stand the strain of war. To many powerful people in London and Paris, the Moscow negotiations were a ritualistic exercise which had to be staged in order to prove to tiresome critics in Parliament and the press that the Russians were useless and unreliable.

The conclusion which Stalin, or any intelligent Soviet leader, must have drawn was that the two Western Powers neither understood serious business nor had any intention of transacting it, and that he must seek out people who did. Alexander Cadogan, reading his diary of these last months of the peace towards the end of his life, wrote that British policy-makers 'left the impression of a number of amateurs fumbling about with insoluble problems'.[59] On any showing, negotiations with men of this kind could hardly fail to convince any moderately reasonable Soviet man or woman that Russia could not afford to consult any other interest but her own. Soviet foreign policy since 1917 had never been conspicuously altruistic; nor had that of any other state. But there can be no doubt that in the 1930s, at least as far as European security was concerned, Russia's interests were parallel with those of Britain, France and many other threatened states. Russia's leaders worked to the utmost to bring this home to British and French politicians, and the reaction of the latter was such as to convince the Soviet government by 1939 that they had failed. Finally, after a terrible war which was bound to be frightful for Russia whatever the circumstances in which it began, the Soviet Union emerged as one of the two strongest powers in the world, after having contributed notably to the cause of her allies. The choice Stalin made in August 1939, morally shocking though it was, cannot have been all that mistaken. But the circumstances in which he felt compelled to make it must have planted in his mind a deep suspicion of the two Western Powers. The conclusion was inescapable in the light of all that had happened since Hitler's accession to power in 1933: either they lacked elementary competence in the management of their foreign policies, and hence could be a risk to all they chose to cultivate as allies; or they were actuated by a sullen will to injure the Soviet state and people. Or both.

4. The Wartime Alliance

I

WHEN Britain and France went to war on 3 September 1939 after the expiry of their ultimatum to Germany, Russia remained neutral under the Nazi-Soviet pact until Hitler's attack – Operation Barbarossa – on 22 June 1941. During those twenty-two months Russia's name was abominated in Britain as a fellow aggressor with Germany and the charge-sheet was long: Russia's annexation of eastern Poland, which her forces attacked on 17 September; her invasion of Finland on 30 November; her absorption of the Baltic states, Estonia, Latvia and Lithuania, and her seizure of Northern Bukowina and Bessarabia from Rumania in June 1940. Stalin and Hitler were depicted by British cartoonists as virtually the same person. It was bad enough that Russia stood aside when Nazi forces overran western Europe in 1940; she went further and helped Germany with war supplies, though not nearly on the scale that the United States helped Britain and France.

The charge was made, notably by Winston Churchill, that Stalin, besides being a knave, was a fool as well, in that, up to the eve of the German attack on Russia in 1941, he shut his ears to British warnings of Hitler's intentions, and, by allowing western Europe to be overrun in 1940, removed the Second Front which he so desperately called for once Hitler struck at him. In Churchill's words, Stalin was 'at once a callous, a crafty and an ill-informed giant'.[1]

From January to March 1941 the Foreign Office in London passed on to Moscow reports it received of the coming German attack on Russia. As late as 3 April Churchill wrote to Stalin through Sir Stafford Cripps, who went to Moscow as ambassador in June 1940, that the invasion was imminent. As it happened, Cripps delayed handing over the message until 22 April, to the Prime Minister's intense annoyance.[2] The Soviet reply was given to Foreign Secretary Anthony Eden by Maisky on 13 June, only nine days before the blow fell, and stated that Germany had no intention of attacking Russia, though it is hard to reconcile this with Cripps' explanation of why he did not at once forward Churchill's message to the Russians, namely, that it dealt with 'facts of which they are certainly well aware'.[3]

Nevertheless, it requires some imagination to accuse Stalin, of all people, of blindness to Russia's interests, whatever the morality of the means he chose for promoting them. Britain and France had taken Hitler's assurances at their face value in the 1930s when Stalin would not; it is hard to understand why he could have become so credulous once the war had begun. Grigore Gafencu, the pre-war Foreign Minister of Rumania, shows in his book, *Prelude to the Russian Campaign*, how little trust there was between Germany and Russia, at least in the Balkans in the years between 1939 and 1941.[4] As for the argument that Russia made her position in 1941 worse by letting the whole of western Europe, excluding Britain, fall to Hitler while she was neutral, it is true that the Soviet government were dumbfounded by the French collapse in 1940, though they were not alone in that. It is impossible to say how Stalin would have acted in 1939 had he known that France was as weak as she proved to be. What is clear is that, in the first nine months of the war, Britain and France had little or no intention of taking on Germany in the west, as by their pledges to Poland they were bound to do, and of this Stalin must have been aware when he rejected their proposals for an alliance in the summer of 1939. Churchill visited French frontier defences on the eve of the war and wrote,

> What was remarkable about all I learned on my visit was the complete acceptance of the defensive which dominated my most responsible French hosts and imposed itself irresistibly on me. In talking to all these highly competent French officers one had the sense that the Germans were the stronger, and that France no longer had the life thrust to mount a great offensive. She would fight for her existence – *voilà tout!*

Churchill added: 'in my own bones, too, there was the horror of the Somme and Passchendaele offensives'.[5]

The British government claimed that the Munich agreement in September 1938 'bought time' to prepare for the coming struggle. Whatever the truth in that, we cannot deny the Russians the right to make the same claim for their time of neutrality. No-one in the west knows how Russia spent those twenty-two months. But, when invasion came, their war machine acquitted itself well, though at enormous cost. It worked better than it did in the Winter War in

Finland in 1939–40, better than any British military expert thought it would, better than the German invaders thought it would. Churchill wrote: 'by indifference to the fate of others [the Russians] had gained time, and when their hour of trial struck on June 22, 1941, they were far stronger than Hitler imagined'.[6]

The period of Soviet neutrality was notable, not only for Stalin's intense unpopularity in Britain, but also because, for one hilarious moment, Britain and France almost went to war with him. The incident arose, partly from the Allies' wish to stop the supply of Swedish iron ore to Germany (it went by rail to the Norwegian port of Narvik and also south to the Gulf of Bothnia, which, like the Baltic as a whole, is normally frozen in the winter), and partly from the crusading fervour stirred in Britain and France by the Soviet invasion of Finland in November 1939. Once Poland had been swallowed up, the two democracies felt they should strike somewhere at Germany, and possibly at Russia, too, if only as a way of showing some spark of activity. The idea was (to say it was toyed with is about as far as one can go) to combine an expedition landed at Norwegian ports and aimed at seizing the Swedish mines, with a force (incredible as it sounds) of British and French 'volunteers', modelled on the Axis forces in Spain during the civil war, to help the Finns against the Russians.

The enterprise was feather-brained in conception, confused in execution. Landings in Norway were designed, then cancelled, brought out again and revised for application in quite different places, cancelled again without commanding officers being informed, then put in train again and starting orders issued. The consent of the Norwegian and Swedish governments was assumed; then, when in January they were invited to authorise the passage of Anglo-French forces through their territory, they refused. Nevertheless, on 3 February the Supreme War Council went as far as to offer Finland 100,000 heavily armed troops. A British historian has written that 'the only charitable conclusion is to assume that the British and French governments had taken leave of their senses'.[7] On 12 March, the Finnish government acceded to Soviet territorial demands (they comprised the withdrawal of the Finnish frontier in the Karelian isthmus some hundred miles north of Leningrad, territory in the Petsamo area in the north, and a lease of the naval and air base at Hangö) and made peace. A month later, on 9 April, the Germans put an end to Anglo-French drollery in Scandinavia by invading

Denmark and Norway. British forces were withdrawn from the Norwegian ports of Namsos and Andalsnes on 2 May and from Narvik on 8 June. The only benefit Britain derived from the affair was the fall of the Chamberlain government on 10 May and the formation of a coalition, with Labour and Liberal leaders, under the eventual architect of victory, Churchill. By an odd coincidence, Churchill himself, as First Lord of the Admiralty, had been responsible, in part at least, for framing the plans for the Norwegian fiasco, the failure of which catapulted him into power.

II

In May and June 1940 came the lightning German conquest of western Europe. The diplomatic counterpart to that event was the signature of the Tripartite Pact between Germany, Italy and Japan on 27 September, which committed the three to the creation of a new order in Europe and the Far East. Russia's role was left undefined. On his visit to Berlin on 12 November, Foreign Minister Molotov inquired about this aspect of the arrangement and was told that Russia would benefit to the south 'in the direction of the Persian Gulf and the Arabian Sea', and at the expense of the British empire.[8] But this did little to deter Hitler from pushing eastwards into the Balkans, with scant regard for the Soviets. On 12 October 2500 German 'instructors' entered Rumania. At the same time, Rumania was compelled by the Vienna Award to cede two thirds of Transylvania to Hungary and Southern Dobrudja to Bulgaria. Hitler then gave a guarantee to Rumania, and this seemed intended, not so much as a consolation to King Carol, but as a warning to Russia, which by this time had taken Bessarabia and Northern Bukowina from the Rumanians.

On 6 April 1941 German forces entered Yugoslavia. The implications for the Russians were disturbing, though Stalin made no move. The Nazi invasion was referred to in Churchill's letter to Stalin, mentioned above, which Cripps handed over on 22 April. It pointed out that German troops, then moving into southern Poland in readiness for an attack on Russia, had been halted and sent to Yugoslavia because of a *coup* in that country directed against Prince Paul's policy of collaboration with Germany. Churchill was no doubt seeking to show Stalin that resistance to Germany paid, and that Russia should join the small but growing band of Hitler's opponents.

Vyshinsky replied on Stalin's behalf that the 'prerequisites for a wide political discussion' on Anglo-Soviet co-operation did not exist. Stalin evidently concluded that in the final resort Russia must rely upon herself alone and await what was to befall her alone.

The German attack on Russia on 22 June 1941, planned the previous November and launched with 160 divisions, 20 of them armoured, and with four-fifths of the German air force, changed all that and created the opportunity for a better future for Anglo-Soviet relations. Churchill, broadcasting in London on that fateful Sunday evening, welcomed Russia at last into the alliance against the Axis, concluding with the words, 'the Russian danger is our danger and the danger of the United States', the last words indicating where his real hopes lay. At the same time, according to the official historian of British foreign policy during the Second World War, 'the British government did not rate highly the chances of a successful Russian defence against the German attack'. Churchill himself was not quite so pessimistic, but the Foreign Office and Service departments thought Germany would win. The Ministry of Economic Warfare did not believe she would have to pay a high price for victory.[9]

As the 1200-mile eastern front sprang into flame from Finland to the Black Sea, Britain was seized with boundless admiration for the heroic deeds of the Red Army, especially the glory of Stalingrad. For the next four years, it was almost impossible to speak a word of criticism in public of our Soviet ally in the Great Patriotic War; utterances of politicians were scanned for evidence of anti-Soviet feeling. Mrs Churchill danced to the tune of 'My lovely Russian rose' with Soviet diplomats. This was a people's war now, the saying went, and Russia was showing that only the people could win it.

But that was the public face of things. No-one in the know believed that the Prime Minister, or perhaps any of his War Cabinet colleagues, had changed in any important respect their life-long hostility towards all that the Soviet state stood for, or that they would not resume their struggle against it, once the common enemy, Germany, had been overcome. Churchill's reply to his private secretary, Colville, when asked how he could possibly work with communist Russia – 'if Hitler invaded Hell, I would find something complimentary to say about the Devil in the House of Commons' – sufficiently indicated the temporary character of the tie with Moscow. Russia was still 'Hell' and her government 'devils', and that was that. He welcomed 'our new ally', but Hitler's attack on

Russia was 'no more than a prelude to an attempted invasion of the British Isles'. For the rest of the war, there was to be between Churchill and Stalin the link between two wolves, joined together for the moment against the hunter of both.

With the United States it was entirely different. As soon as America entered the war after the Japanese attack on Pearl Harbour on 7 December 1941, the Prime Minister could not get to Washington soon enough. Leaving London five days later, he stayed three weeks in the White House with Roosevelt in the press of all his wartime work: 'we saw each other for several hours every day and lunched always together'. 'The President's heart seemed to respond to many of the impulses that stirred my own'. At Christmas, Churchill spoke to the crowds in the White House gardens about 'the two great peoples who speak the same language, who kneel at the same altars, and to a very large extent pursue the same ideals'.[10]

It was the same at all levels, from the base to the summit. For all practical purposes, Britain and America were almost federated for the struggle against the Axis Powers, however much Roosevelt might wish on occasion to flee from the Churchillian embrace and talk to the Soviet leader for a change. Churchill did his best to ensure that he did not. The war operations were jointly planned by the staffs of the two countries and jointly executed. War supplies, war production, the war's social problems, were the subject of combined Anglo-American endeavours. The war's larger purposes were spelled out in joint declarations like the Atlantic Charter, signed by Churchill and Roosevelt on 14 August 1941 – even before America entered the war – which Stalin was later asked to sign, even though the two western leaders knew that much of it was inconsistent with Soviet ideals and policies. Churchill and his colleagues turned aside from all this unwillingly to the problems created by 'our new ally – surly, snarly, grasping'.

These feelings were reciprocated on the Soviet side. For Stalin, the Anglo-Soviet alliance which began on 22 June 1941 and was joined by the United States on 7 December was nothing more than a convenience, unmixed with gratitude or trust on either side, a makeshift arrangement reached with deadly foes and likely to last only so long as Hitler lived. Co-operation with the West was limited to essentials – and essentials for Russia's survival – and at all times and all levels steeped in mutual mistrust. From the moment of the Nazi invasion, Stalin's undivided concern for Russia's national interest as he saw it dominated all his thinking. His aims in his relations with Britain seemed to be two: to get her, and, after Pearl Harbour, the United States, involved in the war up to the hilt, and, second, to extract from London and Washington the fullest possible support for Russia's post-war territorial claims.

The former was embodied in the long, angry Soviet campaign for a Second Front, echoed by the British Communist party, which, until 22 June 1941, had denounced the struggle against Hitler as an 'imperialist war'. The Second Front Campaign, and Churchill's stubborn resistance to it, formed an intricate blend of military necessity and political emotion on both sides. It was sustained intermittently, varying with the changing fortunes of war on the eastern front, from the moment German forces plunged into Russia until the Anglo-American assault on Hitler's Europe, OVERLORD, on 6 June 1944, when, ironically, the British and American leaders began anxiously to question the Russians about *their* contribution to the enemy's defeat. For Stalin, it did not matter much where the Western allies hit Germany, though he thought there was no real substitute for an attack through France. The first Soviet appeal to London, suggesting northern France or the Arctic as the location for a Second Front, came on 18 July.[11] It was followed on 14 September by a desperate call for 25 or 30 British divisions to be sent to the eastern front itself, which Cripps dismissed as a 'physical absurdity', and Churchill agreed with him. In October, when Soviet forces were reeling back and Moscow was being evacuated, Stalin appealed again to Churchill with the same result.[12]

When the spring and summer fighting in Russia was resumed in 1942, Molotov came to London in May to sign the 20-year Anglo-Soviet treaty; the Second Front again dominated the agenda. Churchill was once more opposed, but then heard the news that the Soviet Foreign Minister, during a visit to Washington which he paid during his stay in Britain, had extracted from Roosevelt a statement saying that his talks with Molotov had ended in 'full understanding with regard to the urgent tasks of creating a second front in Europe in 1942'. Churchill protested that this statement could not be regarded as a 'promise'; it was, however, issued in the name of all three Powers on 11 June. When the Prime Minister visited Moscow for the first time in August of that year, he had to tell the Soviet leader that there would be no invasion of France in 1942, but a landing in North Africa (TORCH) in November, and, vaguely, another, 'very large'

Anglo-American operation in 1943.[13] Later Churchill wrote, 'I am sure now that . . . the attempt to cross the Channel in 1943 would have led to a bloody defeat of the first magnitude with measureless reactions upon the results of the war'.[14]

When given an account of the meeting of Churchill and Roosevelt at Casablanca in January 1943, after the consolidation of the North African landings of the previous November, Stalin again inquired about a cross-Channel attack. He complained that Russia was holding down 185 German divisions and that since December Germany had transferred 27 divisions to the eastern front owing to the slackening of the fighting in Tunis.[15] Stalin was told that it was to be hoped the attack on France might be in August or September, but that a landing in Sicily had been decided upon first. He exploded that this was no substitute for the promised assault on France and on 15 March sent a warning to Roosevelt of the 'serious danger of any further delay in the opening of a second front in France'.[16] Such words stirred fears, especially in America, that, unless help came soon, the Russians would make a separate peace. By July, contact between Moscow and the two western capitals almost ceased because of the tension over the Second Front and, possibly as a mark of Soviet displeasure, Maisky was withdrawn from the London embassy and Litvinov from the Soviet embassy in Washington.

On 2 June Stalin had been told of the decision reached by Churchill and Roosevelt at their TRIDENT meeting in Washington in May that the cross-Channel invasion would take place on 1 May 1944. But presumably he was sceptical about this, after so many earlier disappointments, especially since it was also agreed at the TRIDENT meeting that Italy must be cleared of Axis forces first, which the Russian leader seemed to consider an irrelevance. To some extent Stalin's suspicions were confirmed when, at the three-Power Foreign Ministers' conference in Moscow that October (1943), Secretary of State Cordell Hull and British Foreign Secretary Anthony Eden were pressed by Stalin and Voroshilov for further assurances about OVERLORD, and they replied that 'an unqualified promise was not to be had'. Only at the Teheran conference between 28 November and 1 December, when Churchill, Roosevelt and Stalin met together for the first time, did the Soviet Prime Minister seem entirely reassured about the cross-Channel invasion and the accompanying attack on southern France, ANVIL, which was to be 'on the largest possible scale'.

The fact that the intensity of Soviet pressure for the Second Front varied with German military successes and Soviet setbacks on the long eastern front shows that the campaign for the Second Front was based in the first instance on genuine Soviet concern that Britain and America should share the burden of the war. No doubt Stalin was urged by his military commanders to importune his western partners for help. Moreover, the fact that in 1942 and 1943 Britain was compelled to postpone until the winter months convoys shipping vital war supplies to the Soviet ports of Archangel and Murmansk, owing to devastating German U-boat attacks during the perpetual summer daylight in the Arctic, was an added grievance for the Russians. On the British side, there was no less resentment that the Russians did not seem to appreciate the sacrifices British sailors were making to ensure that the supplies got through, when in reality all that Britain had promised was to make them available at her own ports. The invidious comparisons the Russians, Stalin included, drew between their own courage and that of the British in face of the enemy did not improve matters. Perhaps the Russians could not forget the 'phony' war which followed Hitler's conquest of western Poland, when Britain and France, having declared war, showed no zeal to wage it.

Britain's argument with Stalin about the Second Front was all the more difficult to sustain because the Soviet leader had an ally in Roosevelt and most of his military advisers. The Americans were not as burdened as the British with memories of trench warfare in the 1914–18 conflict. They did not share Churchill's obsessions about Soviet post-war domination of Europe, which they inclined to regard as designed to inveigle the United States into shoring up Britain's international position and empire. Their main desire was to put politics aside for the duration, to smash Hitler, not by indirect blows, but in a head-on collision, and then to mop up Japan and go home. Churchill had to spend almost as much time convincing the Americans as he did the Russians that a Second Front could not come this year but might come next.

Stalin suspected that British prevarications about the Second Front were a cover for secret parleys with the Axis about a separate peace. He hinted at this again and again. One event stirring these suspicions was the flight to Britain on 10 May 1941 of Hitler's deputy, Rudolf Hess, followed by the long silence the British authorities kept about it, even when Britain and Russia became allies in June. The Russians immediately pressed for an international tribunal for the trial of war criminals like Hess who fell into Allied hands. On 19 October, the

Soviet newspaper *Pravda* went as far as to describe Britain as rapidly becoming 'a refuge for Nazi gangsters'. Eden vehemently rejected the allegations in the Commons on 21 October and Stalin put an end to the argument for the time being by assuring Britain that 'Hess is not worth all these charges'. But on 12 November came another note from Moscow making the same accusations, to which Britain replied on 11 December.[17] The Hess affair was never really cleared up; perhaps the Soviet refusal, maintained for over thirty years after the war, to agree to Hess's release from Spandau jail, in which he was incarcerated by the International Military Tribunal at Nuremberg in 1945, has its roots in Soviet suspicions of British double-dealing during the Great Patriotic War.

Some alleviation of Soviet fears of Britain making a separate peace with Germany was afforded by the agreement Cripps signed with the Russians in Moscow on 12 July 1941, committing the two countries to combine their efforts against the common enemy and to make no unilateral peace. In the 20-year treaty of alliance which Britain and Russia signed on 26 May 1942, the same pledge was reaffirmed to fight the struggle against Hitler to the end and unite against any renewed German aggression after the war. The idea played its part, too, though there were other considerations, in the agreement reached by Churchill and Roosevelt on the principle of the Unconditional Surrender of the Axis Powers, and somewhat unexpectedly announced by the President at his meeting with the British at Casablanca on 24 January 1943.

This took place in the midst of yet another storm over the politics of the alliance. When the British and Americans made their landings in North Africa in November 1942, the Commander-in-Chief, General Eisenhower, for a short time employed the services of Admiral Jean-François Darlan (he was assassinated on 24 December) in securing the co-operation of local French forces and administrators, to the great disgust of the Free French leader in London, General de Gaulle, many liberal-minded people in the West, and the Soviet government. From February 1941 until April 1942, Darlan had been Vice-Premier and Foreign Minister in the puppet regime created at Vichy after the Franco-German armistice in June 1940. He happened to be in Algiers when Anglo-American forces landed. Eisenhower's explanation was that Darlan was capable of ensuring local French co-operation with Allied forces, but to the ever-suspicious Russians the incident was further proof of Anglo-American tenderness towards fascism.

Then, in July 1943, as British and American troops forced their way up the leg of Italy, came the fall of Mussolini, the formation of a new government in Rome under Marshal Badoglio and its application to surrender. The tortured negotiations for an armistice which followed marked one of the most strained periods of Russia's relations with the Western Powers during the war, arising out of Stalin's charges that he was being elbowed out of peace negotiations with a major Axis Power. At their QUADRANT conference in Quebec in August 1943, Churchill and Roosevelt received a message from the Soviet leader on the subject 'which made them both mad'. 'Until now', Stalin wrote, 'the matter stood as follows: the United States and Great Britain made agreements, but the Soviet Union received information about the results of the agreements between the two countries just as a passive third observer'. 'I have to tell you', he concluded, 'that it is impossible to tolerate this situation any longer'.[18] The Soviet leader then demanded the establishment of a military–political commission, in which Russia would have an equal voice with the other two Powers. He also required the acceptance by the Badoglio regime of a Soviet diplomatic representative. This was at length acceded to by Britain and the United States, though only as late as April 1944. The Control Commission which took charge of the Italian surrender, however (the Italian armistice was signed on 8 September 1943), together with the Allied Military Government established in Rome, remained under exclusive Anglo-American management. The so-called Advisory Council for Italy, established on 30 November with headquarters in Algiers, in which the Soviet Assistant Commissar for Foreign Affairs, Vyshinsky, was allowed to act for Russia, played a wholly insignificant consultative role.

Excluded from Italy, Stalin determined that the same procedure in reverse should be applied to Rumania. That country's forces surrendered to the Red Army in May 1944 and on 23 August General Constantin Sanatescu, President of the Rumanian Council of Ministers, accepted Soviet armistice terms. Access to the Allied Control Council for Rumania, set up under the direction of the Soviet High Command, was denied to Britain and the United States. This was in accord with the famous agreement reached by Churchill and Stalin when the Prime Minister visited Moscow in October and spheres of influence for Britain and Russia in the Balkans were haphazardly decided: 90 per cent of Rumania to Russia, 10 per cent to Britain; 75 per cent of Bulgaria to Russia, 25 per cent to Britain;

90 per cent of Greece to Britain, 10 per cent to Russia; 50–50 for Yugoslavia and Hungary. Churchill, by his own account, seems to have been rather ashamed of this exercise when he saw it on paper and Stalin ticked it with a blue pencil, though it was Churchill who suggested the arrangement and even wrote down the formula, which he then wished to destroy.[19] Nevertheless, the agreement was in the main observed by Stalin, especially in Greece. When fighting broke out in that country in December 1944 between Left-wing ELAS/EAM forces and the British-backed government in Athens under Archbishop Demaskinos, Stalin never joined Bulgaria and Yugoslavia in aiding Greek Left-wing guerrillas. Churchill wrote to Eden on 11 December 1944, 'Stalin has kept off Greece in accordance with our agreement'.[20]

Despite angry altercations about such matters and quieter mutterings in the form of asides, the surrender of enemy forces went forward according to the agreed rule that they should as a general principle lay down their arms to the United Nations forces opposing them, which meant that the British and American high commands received Axis surrenders in western Europe and Russia's senior officers received those in eastern and central Europe and the Balkans. Inevitably, and however much the Americans might complain about the evils of power politics, this meant that western Europe, Italy, Greece and north Africa would come under the Anglo-American wing, and Bulgaria, Czechoslovakia, Finland, Hungary, Poland and Rumania under the Soviet wing, with Yugoslavia, liberated almost entirely by Tito's Partisans, temporarily and only through formal ideological association, in the Soviet camp. The manner in which the war ended was bound to govern the distribution of influence in Europe during the peace. However, this wrestling for positions during the surrender of Axis forces was avoided, somewhat surprisingly, in regard to the main enemy, Germany.

The management of the surrender of German forces in Europe in May 1945 was one of the few outstanding achievements of inter-Allied co-operation during the Second World War, carried through with scarcely any of the suspicious misunderstandings which marked the dealings of the two Western Powers with Russia on practically every other issue. Despite the strongest wish of almost every German soldier to hand himself over to the British or the Americans rather than the Russians, despite Churchill's aim to use the closing stages of the war to extract political concessions from Russia, Anglo-Saxon forces acted with impeccable loyalty towards their Soviet ally. They gave the most complete reports to Stalin of their talks with German emissaries in Switzerland in March, on the eve of Germany's collapse. They insisted in all their contacts with German forces that the surrenders on the different fronts should take place simultaneously. They agreed, in accordance with American demands, to withdraw their troops to the lines of demarcation in Germany, later to become the boundaries of their occupation zones, which had been drawn up by the European Advisory Commission in London. Churchill later stated in the House of Commons that this meant the retirement of Western forces in many places to 150 miles on a front of more than 400 miles.[21]

This was not done without strong protests from the British Prime Minister, who expected the Americans to join him in making extraordinary demands on Russia, even if it meant starting a war with her. By his own account, he thought Anglo-American forces should not withdraw to the agreed zones 'until we are satisfied about Poland and the temporary character of the Russian occupation of Germany and the conditions to be established in the Russianised or Russian-controlled countries of the Danube valley'.[22] On 18 April Churchill wrote to Roosevelt's successor, Truman, when he had only been six days in the White House, advising him not to halt the American advance in the central sector in Germany 'until the Russians agree to share food supplies in the occupied zones with the rest'. Truman had no heart for this bickering and refused. American forces halted on the Elbe, the then and later dividing line between East and West in Europe.

III

The great issues of the post-war treatment of Germany did not yet complicate relations between the Big Three. The division of the conquered country into three (later four, with the admission of liberated France to the inner circle) zones of occupation raised no considerable problem; agreement on this was reported by the three-Power European Advisory Commission on 14 November 1944.[23] In so far as it did, the problem was between Britain and America, rather than between them and Russia. The Americans, with their strong animosity towards France, were concerned that the occupation zone in south-west Germany assigned to them by the Advisory

Commission would mean that their lines of communication lay through France. They would have preferred to change places with the British in North Rhine Westphalia, with its access to the North Sea through Hamburg.

The Soviet Union's occupation zone east of the Elbe seemed logical enough, since that was where Soviet forces stood when the war ended. The fact that the Soviet zone included the capital of Germany since 1871, Berlin, was not generally regarded in London or Washington as a possible source of later conflict. The city was itself to be divided into four sectors for occupation purposes. Indeed, so little significance was attached to the fact that Berlin would be some 100 miles deep within the Soviet occupation zone that it was not considered necessary to set down anything on paper about arrangements for access to the western sectors of Berlin from the three western occupation zones in Germany. Ernest Bevin, the Foreign Secretary in the British Labour government formed at the end of the war, which had to grapple with the Berlin crisis in 1948, arising out of a Soviet attempt to shut off west Berlin from the western zones, told the House of Commons that:

There is a clear four-Power agreement for the occupation of Berlin, of the validity of which there can be no doubt . . . the regulations for travel to and from Berlin are not so clearly specified.

When the arrangements were made, he explained, 'a good deal was taken on trust between the Allies'.[24]

No doubt one reason why the position of Berlin within the occupation zone assigned to Russia gave rise to no great debate between the allies in their wartime exchanges was that they agreed at the three-Power Teheran conference in November–December 1943, and again at the Yalta conference of the three in February 1945, that Germany, besides being demilitarised, denazified and democratised at the end of the war, should also be dismembered. Ideas changed among the Big Three as to the form that dismemberment should take, the British clinging to the last to their demand that, whatever was done with the rest of Germany, Prussia should be amputated and robbed of its disastrous grip over the country. And coupled with dismemberment was the notion, endorsed for a short time by Roosevelt, and, to Eden's horror, by Churchill, too, that Germany should be stripped of its industry and reduced to the tending of sheep and cattle, with most of its manufacturing equipment shipped to Russia to repair ravages of war.

The Prime Minister went along with this bizarre plan at his Quebec meeting with Roosevelt in September, largely, it seems, because it originated with the American Secretary of the Treasury, Henry Morgenthau, and Churchill was mindful of Britain's probable need of American dollars after the war.[25] Stalin appeared to raise no objection either; it is not hard to understand his lack of sympathy for Germany and the Germans at the end of the war. At the same time, he had no wish to stiffen German resistance as the war drew to its close. The truth was that, even at the meeting of the three leaders at Yalta between 4 and 11 February 1945 and their Potsdam conference in July–August (by which time Truman had replaced Roosevelt, who died on 12 April, and Clement Attlee took over from Churchill in the middle of the Potsdam meeting), none of the three states had very clear ideas what they wanted to do with Germany. Much less had they reached a common mind about the defeated enemy.

They agreed about zones of occupation and the machinery of occupation, the Control Council for Germany and the Kommandatura for Berlin. They agreed on the elimination of Nazism; that Germany should be disarmed and militarism destroyed; and that the country should be democratised, whatever that meant. They agreed about the principles of German reparations, though only in such general terms as not to rule out angry exchanges about implementation once the grand alliance broke down; that, during the occupation, Germany should be treated as an economic whole, meaning, it seems, that surplus products from one region (if there could be any within the foreseeable future) should go to make up the deficits of another; and that Germany's industrial revival should not give the Germans a higher standing of living than their neighbours. And that was about all. The immense problem of how, and even whether, to put Germany together again, how a new government was to be formed, what sort of place Germany was to have in post-war Europe – all this was left to the newly formed Council of Foreign Ministers of the three, together with France. That debate could hardly be awaited with anything but foreboding, yet as long as the war-welded partnership of Britain, Russia and the United States held, German questions did not really disturb it.

The same could be said of Germany's major ally, Japan. Premier Stalin told Cordell Hull as early as 30 October 1943, the last day of the three-Power Foreign Ministers' meeting in Moscow, that Russia would enter the war against Japan after Germany's defeat. This was reaffirmed at the Soviet leader's meeting with Churchill and Roosevelt at Teheran in November–December 1943, when he said it would take Russia not more than three months after Germany's defeat to make war on Japan. When Stalin saw Churchill in Moscow in October 1944, he added that Russia would 'demand a price' for this.

What this price would be was formally spelled out at Yalta in February 1945, though Stalin had adumbrated it at the Teheran conference. First, the southern half of Sakhalin, appropriated by the Japanese in 1905, was to return to Russia, together with the string of Kurile islands north of Hokkaido. In Manchuria, which would remain under Chinese sovereignty, Russia's interest was recognised in the commercial port of Dairen, which was to be internationalised, and her lease of the naval base of Port Arthur was to be renewed, thus giving her a warm-water outlet to the Pacific, Vladivostok being frozen in winter. In addition, the Chinese Eastern Railway and the South Manchuria Railway were to be managed by Soviet-Chinese companies. To secure these concessions, Roosevelt undertook to obtain Chiang Kai-shek's agreement, and considering China's dependence upon the United States for all her hopes of liberation from Japan, the President could have foreseen no difficulties about this. What he did not anticipate, of course, was that, by the time Russia fulfilled her promise to make war on Japan and claimed her reward, that assistance would no longer be needed since America's atomic bombs, dropped on Hiroshima and Nagasaki on 6 and 9 August respectively, promptly ensured Japan's capitulation.

At Yalta, Churchill and Roosevelt were told by their military advisers of the discovery of the awesome new weapon, but it was said to be equivalent only to 500 tons TNT, compared with the 20,000 tons TNT of the bomb eventually dropped on Hiroshima. The Chiefs of Staff presented a final report to the two western leaders at Yalta which stated that it would still take 18 months to defeat Japan. It was on this understanding that Roosevelt paid the price for Russia's entry into the Pacific war. The only consolation remaining to his successor, Harry Truman, was the notification he received on 25 April that the first atomic bomb would be ready for use against Japan in four months, and the knowledge that America had in its hands the most formidable engine of destruction in history. Perhaps this explains

Truman's refusal to heed Churchill's call for a showdown with Russia as the war in Europe drew to its close. America had lost out at Yalta, but the new weapon might serve its turn if Churchill's fears proved well-founded. The American historian, Herbert Feis, writes of the first testing of the atomic bomb:

> The few who knew of this coming event thought it better to await the results of the test and let them speak for themselves: thus if a contest of will against the Russians involving possible transit into war should prove inevitable, it would be better to have it come after we and the world knew of this master weapon.[26]

IV

The views of all three major anti-Axis powers about the future of Germany were to undergo many changes in the years between 1945 and 1947, when the task of concluding a peace treaty with the former enemy state was temporarily laid aside. The partly connected problem of Russia's frontiers in Europe was relatively simple and stark, owing to her military control of the territory in question at the end of the war, though hardly less productive of bad blood between herself and the Western allies. The two basic elements in the problem were that, on the one hand, Russia was a revisionist power with unsatisfied territorial claims to settle, and, on the other, that for most of the war she was joined in partnership with two states, Britain and America, which could not ignore moral considerations in international questions, and which had made them the basis of their appeal for world-wide support against Hitler.

Russia had been a revisionist power since 1939 because the territorial settlement in eastern Europe at the end of the First World War was framed without her participation or consent, at a time when she was weakened by war with Germany and the internal struggle between Bolsheviks and Whites, and when Britain and France, then masters of the European system, supported the east European successor states against Russia and her contagious Marxist ideas. It would have been an event unique in history if Russia's communist rulers had not set themselves the goal of recovery of all, or a substantial part, of what they had lost in 1918–19. As it happened, Stalin's territorial claims during the Second World War, though considerable, were by no means inordinate: he did not seek the territorial *status quo ante*, but something appreciably less. Soviet claims against Finland (a part of Russia until 1918) we have referred to above:[27] as embodied in the peace treaty with Finland signed on 10 February 1947, they comprised Petsamo and territory in the Karelian isthmus for the protection of Leningrad, with compensation for Finland elsewhere. The Hangö peninsula, however, which the Russians leased under their armistice with Finland in March 1940, they now retroceded, receiving in return a 50-year lease of the Porkkhala-Udd naval base, which they handed back in 1955. The Baltic states, which Russia had annexed in 1940, were to remain within the USSR: they, too, had been Russian before 1918. The northern part of East Prussia, including the ancient capital, Koenigsberg, would pass to Russia. This was certainly not Russian *terra irredenta;* on the other hand, as the only German territory claimed by the Soviet Union, it could not be called excessive, especially when it is recalled that Prussia was the universal object of detestation for the United Nations during the war. The Soviet acquisitions from Rumania in 1940, embodied in the peace treaty with Rumania in February 1947, we have dealt with above.[28]

Then came the controversial Soviet claim to part of eastern Poland, controversial not so much because of its extent or ethnographical character but because of its intricate involvement with the larger question of Poland's independence. Again, the striking thing about Russia's territorial claim against Poland was its moderation when compared with the customary practice of victorious Powers. It amounted to the recognition of the so-called Curzon line, recommended as the Soviet-Polish ethnographical frontier by the Supreme Allied Council in Paris in 1919, and with some rectifications in Poland's favour, though with the old capital of Lvov assigned to the Soviet Union. In return, Russia proposed, and at Yalta it was agreed, that Poland should be compensated by a belt of German territory – up to the Oder and Neisse rivers – on her western side, though, in contradistinction to the Polish territories assigned to Russia, this was to be regarded merely as 'under Polish administration' pending a final peace treaty with Germany.

Stalin's border claim against Poland was argued chiefly on the ethnographical principles held sacred in 1919, although most of the Ukrainians and White Russians who used to live in the territories had either left or been driven out. The movement of Poland to the west, however, gave Moscow a distinct, though subtle, hold over any future government in Warsaw, whatever its political complexion. It meant that Russia would always be able to remind the Poles that, if they did not behave themselves, arrangements might be reached between Russia and Germany for the restitution of the Oder–Neisse lands, or part of them, to the Germans. At the same time, Poland's territorial shift to the west in 1945 could be regarded as strengthening the bond between Russia and Poland. So long as Russia opposed German unity, the Poles were bound to be pleased; when, in addition, Russia stood forth as Poland's protector against any later revisionist policies Germany might espouse, Polish gratification was doubled.

Finally, mention must be made of Russia's territorial expectations in regard to Czechoslovakia, that is, the cession of the eastern tip of that country, known as Sub-Carpathian Ruthenia, formerly a part of the old Austro-Hungarian empire. All told, Soviet territorial claims in 1945 extended over some 182,000 square miles, about the size of France or Spain, and embraced some 24 million people, about half the population of France. They were substantial claims, but not excessive by traditional international standards.

The remarkable thing was Stalin's anxiety to extract recognition of these claims, especially from Britain, at the earliest moment. When Anthony Eden went to Moscow in December 1941, Stalin pressed him insistently about Russia's territorial claims on 16 December, on the night of the 16th and 17th, and on 22 December, when German guns could be heard in the capital. It is a puzzle why he should have done so since to press territorial claims at such a stage of the war could not but irritate the British and Americans, to whom Russia looked desperately for help against the German attack. Stalin's explanation, which he gave to the Foreign Secretary, was that he did not want 'to have to fight at the Peace Conference to get our western frontiers'.[29] Yet he must have known that, if Russia lost the war and had to be liberated by Britain and America later on, the question of post-war territorial claims would hardly arise, certainly not in the form that Stalin wished. On the other hand, if she won the war, she would almost certainly be in a position to dictate her future borders whatever Britain and America might say.

However that may be, Britain, partly because of her own moral scruples, partly because of those of her American ally, could not endorse Soviet territorial aims so early in the war, though it might have been wiser to do so. Eden was in the odd position in his talks

with Stalin in Moscow in December 1941 in which he admitted that
Britain accepted *de facto* even the Soviet incorporation of the Baltic
states, but insisted that this could not be put in writing without
referring back to London, the Dominions and Washington. This was
largely because of the Joint Declaration, known as the Atlantic
Charter, which Churchill and Roosevelt signed on a battleship in
Placentia Bay, Newfoundland, on 14 August 1941. The first three
articles of the Charter ran:

1. Their countries seek no aggrandisement, territorial or other.
2. They desire to see no territorial changes that do not accord with
   the freely expressed wishes of the peoples concerned.
3. They respect the right of all peoples to choose the form of
   government under which they will live; and they wish to see
   sovereign rights and self-government restored to those who have
   been forcibly deprived of them.

Stalin had accepted the basic ideas behind the Charter in a
declaration on 6 November, when he said that:

We have not, and cannot have, such war aims as the seizure of
foreign territory, the subjugation of foreign peoples, whether it
concerns the peoples and territories of Europe, or the peoples and
territories of Asia, including Persia. Our first aim consists in
liberating our territories and our peoples from the German fascist
yoke.

The Charter was also included in the United Nations foundation
declaration of 1 January 1942, to which the Soviet Union was a party,
and was referred to in the Anglo-Soviet alliance signed in May 1942.
It should be remembered, however, that when the Charter was drawn
up, no Russian representative was present, nor were the Russians
consulted about it, even though the Charter was supposed to contain
the common philosophical foundations of the alliance, and although
Russia was at that time shouldering the main brunt of the war and the
United States, Britain's partner in framing the Charter, was still
neutral. The Russians were invited to adhere to the Charter at a time
when, owing to their dependence on the Western Powers for aid, they
could hardly do otherwise. Stalin was told by Eden when the two met
in Moscow in December 1941 that the Charter could certainly not be

ignored when Russia's territorial claims came up for consideration. The Soviet leader's comment was that 'it looked as if the Atlantic Charter were directed against the USSR'.[30]

Hence, Stalin did not receive British consent to his territorial claims either in his talks in December 1941 with Eden or in the following May, when the Anglo-Soviet treaty was signed. On Eden's return from Moscow, the Prime Minister, then in Washington and doubtless under the influence of American bias against wartime agreements on post-war territorial arrangements, wrote to the Foreign Secretary on 8 January 1942:

> There must be no mistake about the opinion of any British government of which I am the head, namely that it adheres to those principles of freedom and democracy set forth in the Atlantic Charter and that these principles must become especially active when any question of transferring territory is raised. I conceive therefore that our answer should be that all questions of territorial frontiers must be left to the decision of the Peace Conference.[31]

The force of the American veto was strong. Roosevelt clearly threatened the Prime Minister that he would dissociate himself from the Anglo-Soviet treaty if it included references to frontiers. He thought the prospect of a Second Front being opened up by Britain and America would reduce Soviet pressure for agreement about borders. Many on the British side took the opposing view that a frontier agreement in 1942 would make Stalin less importunate about the Second Front.[32]

There is a strong case for the view that failure to specify Russia's territorial ambitions in the Anglo-Soviet treaty of May 1942 was, for Britain, a serious mistake. In paying respects to principles, Britain and the United States lost an opportunity of having it stated, before the eyes of the world, that Russia had other purposes to serve in the war than merely the liberation of her own soil and the overthrow of Nazism. That demonstration might have been useful to the Anglo-American cause later on, and it might also have prevented that feeling of shock which seemed to overcome the two democracies at the end of the war, when the realities of the international situation were suddenly unveiled. More importantly, it might have been wiser to conclude an agreement about Stalin's territorial appetite at a time when Russia was locked in conflict with German forces and desperately needed Western help. Later, if Russia succeeded in repelling the invader (as all prayed she would), she would be strong enough to dictate her own terms and Britain and America would then have few means available for limiting them. As it happened, Russia's **claims, as Stalin made them known at the time of the Anglo-Soviet** alliance, scarcely differed from those he enforced at the end of the war, when Russia was victorious beyond all expectations and controlled all the territories to which her claims referred.

But there was a world of difference between Soviet frontier changes, which Russia's allies accepted, if grudgingly, and the freedom of her neighbours to decide their own affairs without dictation from the great powers. It was the latter which British people thought they had been fighting for. The most obstinate case was Poland. The problem was on the Anglo-Soviet agenda from the beginning of the Grand Alliance. It was one of the reasons, and more important than most of the others, for the break-up of the alliance and the onset of the Cold War after Germany's defeat.

The cause of this was the peculiar tenacity and inability to compromise of the two sides, the Russians and the Poles, with Britain pursuing the vain hope of mediating between them and preserving some vestige of Polish independence in the process. For Britain, it *was* Polish independence, and not Polish frontiers, which she had guaranteed and which was the immediate cause of her going to war. The story was of an irresistible force and an immovable object. The irresistible force was the Soviet government. They were determined to crush Poland, or the Poland of the inter-war years, even if it meant killing off its young military officers, the future source of Polish strength, as in the Katyn Woods massacre, which allegedly took place behind Soviet lines in Poland in 1940, or cruelly refusing to help the Poles in Warsaw when they rose in revolt against the Germans on 1 August 1944 and fought on for 62 days, while the Russians even denied the British the use of airfields under their control to drop aid to the beleaguered Poles until 9 December. Perhaps the Russians were not as indifferent to the Warsaw uprising as the world later made out. Air Chief Marshal Portal stated on 28 August that the Russians 'had suffered a setback, and all the evidence went to show that they were doing their utmost to reach Warsaw'.[33] But their antagonism to the revival of Polish nationalism was strong.

And there was a certain logic in that. Poland was the corridor through which German forces rolled into Russia in 1941; and no human contrivance could be relied upon to make sure they would never roll again. The Poles had demonstrated their inability to seal that corridor and in 1939 they had refused to allow the Russians to seal it for them. The Russians knew that the only way in which they could block the corridor after 1945 was to do it themselves, and that could only be done by taking over Poland, lock, stock and barrel, or by finding Poles who would combine with them to produce the same result. It would have been too much an affront to the much-publicised morality of the United Nations to do the former, and the sole alternative was the latter. There was a brief period of collaboration with the London-based Poles until, on 26 April 1943, Russia broke off relations with them when the London Poles requested the International Red Cross to investigate the murder of the 14,000 Polish officers in Katyn Woods near Smolensk. By this time, the Russians had, in January 1943, formed the Union of Polish Patriots in Moscow, a group entirely subordinate to Soviet purposes. The Union was remodelled in May 1944 through a merger with the National Council of the Homeland (KRN), formed from Polish radicals and communists who survived the Warsaw uprising, to become the Polish Committee of National Liberation (PCNL) established, first at Chelm on 21 July 1944 and then at Lublin, in south-eastern Poland. On 31 December, as the Red Army pressed further into Poland, the Soviet authorities recognised the Committee as the provisional Polish government.

Britain continued to recognise the exiled Polish government in London under General Wladyslaw Sikorski, then, after Sikorski's death in a flying accident in July 1943, Stanislaw Mikolajczyk, but at the Yalta conference in February 1945 the Russians succeeded in getting the Lublin regime accepted as the core of a new Polish Provisional Government of National Unity pledged to the holding of free and unfettered elections as soon as possible. The Provisional Government was to be formed from the Lublin regime with the inclusion of 'democratic leaders from Poland itself and from Poles abroad' and this reorganisation was to be supervised by a Commission, sitting in the first instance in Moscow and consisting of Molotov, Averell Harriman and Sir Archibald Clark Kerr.[34] The Commission turned out to be a farce, as the Russians intended. They argued that the Lublin group should actually select the new members; that these should be limited in numbers; and that the London Poles should either be excluded altogether or stringently restricted in the influence they should exert within the new regime. The Lublin regime was reorganised in no important respect. The Russians reaffirmed their recognition of it as the official Polish government, and, when Britain and the United States objected, refused to send Molotov to the San Francisco conference which opened on 26 May to finalise the new United Nations Charter, only relenting as a gesture to the memory of Franklin Roosevelt who had died on 12 April.

Stalin was resolved to make Poland a projection of the Soviet state, and, considering the frame of mind of the Poles, it is hard to see how he could have done otherwise. For if Russia was the irresistible force in the Polish problem, the Poles, certainly the London Poles, fully earned the name of the immovable object. Like Polish leaders in the inter-war period, they seemed to believe they could have it all their own way, regardless of the great powers on either side of them, and that, if they had to bow to the realities of their geographical situation, it was better to make friends with Germany than with Russia. With strange perversity, the Poles exhibited this preference even when Soviet forces were rolling back the Germans through their country in 1944. Eden told Roosevelt when he visited Washington in March 1943, 'how assertive the Polish government in exile was being: how utterly unreal in its notions of the place and power of Poland after the war; and how stubborn in its wish to keep the Eastern frontiers which it had between the two wars'.[35] At the Teheran conference of the Big Three in November–December 1943 agreement was reached on the Curzon line as the new Soviet-Polish frontier, with compensations for Poland at Germany's expense in the west. Churchill undertook, with the help of Eduard Benes, then head of the Czech provisional government in London, to prevail on the London Poles to accept these terms. On 6 January 1944, he wrote to Roosevelt that 'it will be their duty to the Powers of Europe, who will twice have rescued them'. Writing of the negative response of the London Poles to this British pressure, Herbert Feis describes the exiled government as:

concerned, not with its duty to Europe, but with its survival and place in Europe. It was still intent on regaining most if not all of the area which it had occupied between the wars and something more from Germany in the West. It felt entitled to emerge from the war as a larger as well as a freer power. And it was determined that it would neither change its political colour nor become bound to the Soviet Union.[36]

In reply to the appeals of Churchill and Eduard Benes of Czechoslovakia, the London Poles issued a statement on 5 January 1944 declaring that their aim was 'the sovereignty of Poland over its liberated territory, to be established as soon as possible'. Benes told Mikolajczyk that in issuing this statement the Poles 'had taken a wrong turn', and that they would be well advised 'to accept the chance Stalin was offering'. Churchill told the House of Commons on 22 February that he could not feel that the 'Russian demand for a reassurance about her Western frontier goes beyond the limit of what is reasonable and just'. By mid-October 1944, Churchill was telling Mikolajczyk that unless he accepted the proposed frontiers, he would be 'out of business for ever'. He added: 'you do not care about the future of Europe; you have only your own miserable interests in mind'.[37] Even Roosevelt, for all his American concern for Polish freedom, and possibly because of it, was on Stalin's side. In November 1944, he virtually washed his hands of the frontier question by telling Mikolajczyk that he would 'leave it to the Poles to settle'.[38]

V

The war was waged to its terrible end. The unnatural alliance between the Anglo-Saxon Powers and the Soviet state held together in the teeth of problems and discords related in this chapter. And there were others, over Austria, Bulgaria, Yugoslavia, the veto in the Security Council of the new United Nations, on which the three Powers first seemed in agreement at Yalta, then found they were as far apart as ever, a common experience. The alliance had its birth in iron necessity, with few roots in mutual sympathy or shared ideals, except as between Britain and America. Stalin, as almost every Western official or soldier who came into contact with him was forced to conclude, was interested only in one thing, the benefit of Russia as he saw it. His cruelty shocked Western leaders, as when he suggested at the Teheran conference in 1943 the shooting in cold blood of 50,000 or 100,000 German officers.

The fears of Churchill began to take shape as Stalin enforced his will on state after state in eastern Europe. March 1945 teemed with portents of things to come. On the 16th, Petru Groza, with Soviet backing, formed a National Democratic Front minority government in Rumania, in all things obedient to Moscow. In Bulgaria, the communist-dominated Fatherland Front, with the inevitable Soviet support, seized the reins of power. In Hungary, Marshal Voroshilov told the government what his directives for it were. In Czechoslovakia, Benes was bullied towards the end of March into taking more communists into his government.

Churchill recalled: 'at the end of the European war, this climax and apparently measureless success was to me a most unhappy time. I moved amid cheering crowds or sat at a table adorned with congratulations and blessings from every part of the Grand Alliance with an aching heart and a mind oppressed by forebodings'.[39] Yet it is hard to say that the alliance was as devoid of moral content as the melancholy war leader represents it. Certainly, Stalin decided the fate of eastern Europe at the end of the war with scant regard to the feelings of his allies or the peoples who fell within the control of the Red Army as it surged on, and with no respect for the lofty Declaration on Liberated Europe signed at Yalta, which reasserted the Atlantic Charter's principles and committed the three to consult each other on the formation of new governments in the liberated areas. But Russia had done most of the fighting. Russia destroyed the flower of the German army, at a cost of six million military deaths of her own people and possibly 20 million deaths in all, as compared with a third of a million military deaths each for Britain and America, hardly any civilian fatalities for America and 60,000 civil deaths for Britain. Was it to be expected that, after having repelled a vast and cruel invasion at enormous cost in blood and treasure, leaving herself a smoking ruin in the process, Russia would then retire and leave Germany and the east European states, many of which before the war were satellites and pawns of Germany, to decide for themselves what they should do in future and how they should live? A Soviet leader proposing such a policy in 1945 would have been massacred by his own people, and justly so. In 1945 America was telling the world she would retire from Europe within two years. Britain was bankrupt, so was the rest of western Europe. Who would defend Europe against Germany when she revived? Who but Russia? And who could deny her the means to do so?

What those who feared Russia in 1945 would have done well to remember was the France of 1919. The French then were unrestrained in their scheming to tie Germany in fetters. The British called the French 'pathological' about Germany. But, as it turned out, the French were right, and their advice about Germany, had it been followed, might have saved the peace. Unfortunately, after 1918 the French were not strong enough to enforce their views. The Russians in 1945 were.

But if Stalin was grasping in regard to Russia's national interest, Churchill could hardly have moved quicker than he did to thwart him. If Stalin was eternally suspicious towards the West, his suspicion could hardly have exceeded Churchill's suspicions of him. In May 1945, Truman was driven to send Joseph Davies, the former American ambassador to Moscow, to London to try to cool Churchill down about Russia, when the Prime Minister was calling for a tripartite meeting with the Russians for the sole purpose of having a show-down. Davies wrote back to the President: 'I wondered whether [Churchill] was now willing to declare to the world that he and Britain had made a mistake in not supporting Hitler, for as I understand him he was now expressing the doctrine that Hitler and Goebbels had been proclaiming and reiterating for the past four years'. 'I could not escape the impression', Davies told Admiral Leahy later, 'that [Churchill] was basically more concerned about preserving England's position in Europe than in preserving peace'. Davies was well known for his partiality towards Stalin's Russia, but Leahy commented on this statement that it was 'consistent with our staff estimate of Winston Churchill's attitude throughout the war'.[40] In so far as the Grand Alliance tragically dissolved after Hitler's death, Churchill can hardly be acquitted of some share of the blame.

5. Cold War and Détente

In the general election campaign in Britain which followed the break-up of the wartime coalition government in May 1945, Labour candidates used the slogan 'Left can speak to Left', meaning that a Labour victory in the election would give Britain a better chance of getting on with the Soviet Union after the war than a Conservative. Ernest Bevin, Labour's Foreign Secretary for the next six years, said at the Labour party's annual conference in 1945, 'Left understands Left and Right don't'. Christopher Mayhew recalls that his own election address included the words:

> I believe that Labour is better placed than the Conservatives, with their long record of unfriendliness towards Russia, to remove the mistrust now unfortunately existing between the two countries.

He adds, rather unnecessarily, that at the time of writing (1969), 'the belief that "Left understands Left" has virtually disappeared'.[1]

The belief was not implausible. As the war ended, people wanted to break away from the disastrous cold-shouldering of the Soviets by the mainly Conservative pre-war National Government. Labour politicians wished to capitalise on the immense stock of goodwill in the country towards the Russians, and the idea, nurtured in summer schools and in discussion groups in the Armed Forces, that Britain, facing social reconstruction, had things to learn from the Soviet model. The Left, however, was never homogeneous in Britain. Most Labour candidates in the 1945 election would have been about as willing to be classed with the Soviet brand of the Left as a duchess would have regarded herself as much a woman as any Birmingham housewife.

Besides, ideology has never much influenced British politicians in office, especially in questions of foreign policy. It is a remarkable fact that the Labour Government, returned in the 1945 election with a massive strength in the House of Commons of 393 seats as against 210 Conservatives, 11 Liberals and 2 Communists, heartily rejected, to a man, the National Government's hostility towards Russia; yet it almost at once adopted and steadfastly pursued a policy of opposition towards the Soviet state which equalled in rigour that of any Conservative administration before or since. Mr Attlee's and Mr Bevin's determination not to be outdone by the Opposition in hostility towards the Soviet Union, and to join with the United States in forging a containment belt around her, shocked many of their backbenchers and plunged the Labour party into argument. But this did not in any way affect the Government's policy. In the following general election, in February 1950, it was Mr Churchill, leader of the Opposition, who, in a speech in Edinburgh on the 15th, called for summit talks with the Russians and Mr Attlee who frowned on them.

Bevin's Labour critics accused him of having fallen under the influence of the old school of Foreign Office advisers, with their long experience of opposing the Russians. They gave the same explanation for his sour attitude towards the Zionist cause in Palestine when he refused President Truman's call for 100,000 Jewish refugees to be allowed to enter the Promised Land. But there were more important reasons for the Government's unhesitating decision to marshall Britain, and as much of western Europe as would go, into line against Russia, with the backing of American power.

First, the utterly unforgiving character of the Stalinist regime, and all its servants who had any contact with the bourgeois world, put all the arguments they needed into the mouths of Russia's most intransigent opponents in the West, and undermined the arguments of those sympathising with her and seeking to understand her predicament. Arthur Henderson's words of fifteen years before echoed again: 'Soviet . . . actions seem designed deliberately to play into the hands of opponents of continued Anglo-Russian relations'.[2] The old self-fulfilling prophecy was replayed: Russia fears a devastating Western assault when struggling to recover from the attack by Germany and when the West, or rather the United States, is not only not weakened, but vastly strengthened, by the Second World War. But explaining their fears is the last thing Soviet leaders wanted to do – all that they regarded as exposing their weakness, and so inviting attack. Hence their refusal to take part in the European Recovery Programme (ERP), based on Marshall Aid from 1948 to 1952. Their response was that of the frightened cat which tries to repel its tormentors by making itself look like a tiger, and the West reacted by showing its teeth and saying the best thing is to kill the animal before it becomes dangerous. Mr Bevin did not have time or inclination for probing into Russia's problems: he had too many of his own. Stalin's cold menaces made no impression. As he so often said, he had met that kind of thing before as a trade union leader and had no intention of letting his members down by giving in to it.

Secondly, Britain was in a hurry and the government with it. The hurry arose from the fact that when the war ended in 1945 the country was bankrupt. Attlee and Bevin sat with Truman and Stalin at Potsdam in August, but economically Britain was spent, and no country in that state can afford to have a foreign policy it can call its own. In order to win the war, or, rather, stay in the war, the government had to sell almost everything it had, including £1118 million worth of foreign assets – that is, almost all of them – from which dividends flowed before 1939 sufficient to pay for between one quarter and one third of imported food and raw materials. In addition, Britain had borrowed money all over the world to pay for the upkeep of troops and purchase of equipment during the war, and at the war's end she was called upon to repay these debts, amounting to some £2723 million, at a time when she was barely able to feed herself or buy the raw materials from abroad necessary for the revival of the economy. Stocks had run down during the war, plant needed replacement, bombing had damaged millions of homes and thousands of factories, foreign trade had been cut to shreds. An increase in exports of between 50 and 75 per cent was estimated to be necessary to finance the pre-war scale of imports; it would probably take between three and five years to achieve this.[3]

At the same time, the European continent was devastated through war and years of Nazi occupation, its peoples stunned and demoralised, with millions of displaced persons trudging from one country to another, not knowing where they were going or what they would do when they got there. Only one of Britain's friends, the United States, was fit and strong, stronger indeed, in both economic and military senses, than it had ever been in its history.

Britain's economic plight in the years following the Second World War affected all her foreign policy and foreign relations. In the bitter winters of 1946–47 and 1947–48, when Labour men and women thought they were building a new society, the country all but came to a standstill. The importance of this fact in the origins of the Cold

War, which almost at once sprang up between the Western Powers (the United States, Britain, France and other west European states), on one side, and the Soviet Union, on the other, can hardly be overstated. For Britain had not only to feed and supply her own 49 million people; she had commitments to many millions more, in many parts of the world. Some of these had grown with the rise of Britain's imperial power, others had come as a direct result of the war. Britain was a bankrupt, in a house with leaking roof and crumbling walls, trying to keep up a score of old palaces housing importunate relatives and retainers. Something had to give, and that soon.

Some imperial readjustments were effected with masterly skill. While Belgium, France, the Netherlands, Portugal, struggled to keep their imperial holdings in Asia and Africa, ignoring all the implications of the Allied cause in the Second World War and plunging themselves and their colonial subjects into bloodbaths in the process, Britain, almost surreptitiously, began to unburden herself of her overseas incubus, starting with India, the 'brightest jewel in the imperial crown', in 1947 and going steadily on with the decolonisation of a quarter of the world's population, inhabiting a quarter of the land surface of the globe. A host of new states emerged into freedom and their leaders, with multi-coloured robes and dark faces, came to Commonwealth Prime Ministers' conferences in London to the tune of Soviet denunciations of British imperialism. So far as it is known, Britain received no credit in the Soviet Union for history's most massive act of decolonisation, for the almost bloodless manner in which it was achieved. Her sole consolation was that hardly any of the African or Asian nations she had decolonised took the Soviet state or society as their model; instead, many of them, for a time at least, imitated the forms of the Westminster Parliament and the uniforms of British Service officers. Fears that Afro-Asian countries, once free from European rule, would go down the communist road have not been realised, except in so far as European states, including Britain, have helped to push them there. It was, however, at other points of the compass that the failure of Britain's resources to satisfy her vastly expanded commitments after the war aggravated relations with the Soviet Union and helped to shape that conflict of policies called the Cold War.

II

First, there was the Labour Government's decision in February 1947 that after 1 April they could no longer afford to give financial aid to the Greek Government in its struggle against internal communist forces, assisted from across the border in the north by Albania, Bulgaria and Yugoslavia. The Greek struggle coincided with mounting Soviet pressure against Turkey aimed at securing for the Soviet Union a share in defence of the waterway between the Black Sea and the Aegean. The notification of the British decision to Washington on 21 February precipitated the announcement of the Truman Doctrine by the American President at a joint session of the two houses of Congress on 12 March. It committed the United States to the support of 'free peoples who are resisting attempted subjugation by armed minorities and by outside pressures'.

The Truman Doctrine was a dramatic departure from the tradition of American isolation. Though immediately arising out of the predicament of Greece and Turkey, who were to receive $400 million to assist their defence, it was in reality unlimited in scope; any country anywhere might, on the face of it, qualify for American subsidies, provided it was threatened by communism. This at once sharpened the division between the two worlds – henceforward, governments seeking American assistance would know how to obtain it: they had merely to furnish evidence of the communist enemy at the gate. Moreover, the Truman Doctrine transformed an old-fashioned British practice of subsidising friendly countries whose policies were broadly similar to her own into a generalised ideological system which drew the line between good and evil in the world in the sharpest outline. The British, who had visualised the Russian naval threat in the Mediterranean through the eyes of Disraeli or Salisbury, now found themselves in the Cold War. This quickly took on the form, not merely of a confrontation of armed states, one group centred in Washington, the other in Moscow, but of a subterranean struggle against conspiratorial forces within the free world which never ceased.

Secondly, in that same year, 1947, as though to offset the combativeness of the Truman Doctrine, came Secretary of State Marshall's speech at Harvard on 5 June offering massive injections of sorely needed dollars to European countries, provided they drew up a co-operative recovery plan. 'The programme', Mr Marshall said, 'must be a joint one, agreed to by a number of, if not all, European nations.' The offer thus seemed to be open to the Soviet Union and the East European states she was now energetically converting to communism. The story of Mr Bevin's lightning response to the Harvard speech and his unreluctant acquiescence in Soviet Foreign Minister Molotov's refusal to take part in the Marshall plan on the ground that it violated national sovereignty, when the two met the French in Paris to discuss the plan from 27 June to 3 July, is well-known.[4] Mr Bevin wanted to press on with European recovery with American dollar help with all speed. As he told the Commons before setting out for the Paris meeting:

> The guiding principle that I shall follow in any talks on this matter will be speed. I spent six weeks in Moscow trying to get a settlement. I shall not be a party to holding up the economic recovery of Europe by the finesse of procedure or terms of reference or all the paraphernalia which go with it. There is too much involved.[5]

Britain had already received aid in December 1945 to the tune of £1000 million in loans from the United States and Canada, and that had gone down the drain in quick time; now there was a second chance, with greater safeguards against it being wasted, and that chance must not be missed. For Bevin, anything worse at that stage of Britain's affairs than the interminable squabbles with stone-faced men like Molotov as had deadlocked the four-Power Council of Foreign Ministers in their debates on Germany for the previous two years, could hardly be imagined.

The refusal of Russia to take part in the Marshall plan, welcomed with some relief by most Western politicians, and her denial of leave to participate in the plan to Czechoslovakia, Hungary and Poland, the governments of which did wish to take part, were of momentous importance. They meant that East and West would henceforward go their separate ways; that such international bodies as the Organisation for European Economic Co-operation (OEEC), which was formed from the 14 nations which, together with Britain and France, took part in the Marshall programme, would from now on bind these countries to the United States in an economic bloc sealed off from the Soviet bloc in Eastern Europe, which now began to travel its own road to economic recovery; and that the United States would be increasingly looked upon as the leader of a Western group of nations, which, if not positively hostile towards the Soviet Union and her friends in Eastern Europe, would be economically sundered from it. And these emerging rival blocs would before long be encased within hard military shells.

There is little evidence that these far-reaching implications of the American loan to Britain, the Marshall offer and the European Recovery Programme to which the Marshall offer led, were much pondered by Mr Attlee and his Cabinet colleagues, though many within the Labour movement were horrified at the way in which Britain was drifting into the American camp and further from the Soviet Union. The *Keep Left* group, founded in 1947 by R. H. S. Crossman and others and aimed at the formation of a 'third force' in Western Europe to which Britain would belong, and which would avoid commitment to either super-Power, was one example of dissent. The weekly journal the *New Statesman and Nation* regularly railed against Bevin's American involvement; on 13 July 1946 it commented on the Anglo-American loan:

Britain, with a Labour Government committed to a policy of evolutionary Socialism, is tied fast to a country of which the quintessence is aggressive, self-confident capitalism, impatient of all controls on the pursuit of money-making and determined to use its vast economic strength to impress its pattern on the business institutions of the world.

But politicians in office are necessarily dominated by immediate problems staring at them from their in-trays, and the most disturbing of these in the drab, austerity-laden post-war years, symbolised by the ascetic Chancellor of the Exchequer, Sir Stafford Cripps, with his glass of lemon juice at the despatch box, was Britain's total inability to pay for the food and raw materials vital to her industrial recovery. The only country with an abundance of food and raw materials to dispose of, even if it meant giving it away, was the United States. It would have been a strange way of rewarding British voters, who fancied in 1945 that they were opting for a better future, to condemn them to live indefinitely in siege conditions, ration book in hand, while the American horn of plenty was full to overflowing and the

Americans only too willing to share it.

The same pattern of sharp economic pressures clouding the longer-term political implications was evident at the end of the war with regard to Germany, in many ways the centre-piece of the Cold War. All the talk during the Second World War about the post-war treatment of Germany, within the Labour party and outside it, might never have been uttered for all the practical effect it had. Whether the Germans should be handled harshly or leniently; whether their country should be dismembered, split into separate states, occupied, and, if so, for how long; whether it should be pastoralised, socialised, internationalised, neutralised; whether its political revival should be internationally controlled and, if so, how: all such debate sank into silence in the post-war world beside the overwhelming need felt by the Attlee government to get the Germans off their backs as soon as possible and set them up as a self-governing community. Mr Bevin's perpetual refrain was:

> If the German people are going to rely on us or act as if we are going to feed them all the time, they must be suffering from a delusion. Germany must work and produce like other countries.[6]

In the European Advisory Commission, established in 1943, by means of which Britain, the Soviet Union and the United States agreed towards the end of the war on the post-war zones of occupation in Austria and Germany, Britain strove for and secured the north-western area of Germany (North Rhine Westphalia) as her zone of occupation. This was despite the American wish to occupy that zone in preference to the area in south-western Germany (Bavaria and Wurttemburg) eventually assigned to them.[7] But this British success was to prove disastrous. The British zone was predominantly industrial, with little agriculture. Before the war, most of its food came from east Germany, the 'bread basket' of the country, and from world markets. After the war, it took time for the devastated Ruhr to revive and its workers to get back to their jobs. Partly in anticipation of this situation, article 14 of the Potsdam agreement of July–August 1945 required the occupying powers to treat Germany during the initial control period 'as a single economic unit'. This meant, in the British view, that areas of food surplus, of which the British claimed that the Soviet zone of occupation beyond the river Elbe was by far the most important, should help provision areas of food shortage, notably the Ruhr. Accordingly, in the Allied

Control Council, established in 1945 for the co-ordination of occupation policies, Britain accused the Russians of violating three-Power agreements by refusing to allow food from their zone to enter the western zones in sufficient quantity, with the result that the burden of feeding 20 million Germans fell on the British when they were barely able to earn enough from world trade to feed themselves. As Mr Attlee told the House of Commons in June 1947:

> We desire that Germany should be treated as an economic whole. We have been placed in a terribly difficult position . . . in having an area which was always a deficit area from the point of view of food and, as I see it, in changing what were intended merely to be lines of occupation into rigid divisions of Germany, into zones with separate systems of administration. Our endeavour is that Germany should be treated as an economic whole.[8]

The economic blizzard blowing in the British government's face led to two developments which served as steps towards the great divide between East and West. The first was the decision to share the deficit in the British zone, estimated at £100 million a year, with the United States by the agreement reached in New York on 2 December 1946 for the economic fusion of the British and American zones.[9] By article 5 of the agreement the American authorities undertook to assume equal shares with Britain of the costs of imports into the two zones which were not covered by exports until 1949, when a self-sustaining economy for the area would hopefully be achieved. A year later the whole deficit was made a charge on American funds.[10] These arrangements marked the first move towards the formation of a separate independent state in western Germany; they were carried further by France's agreement in February 1948 to fuse her two small occupation zones with Anglo-American Bizonia. But the bizonal agreement also registered an important shift in the locus of decision-making in German affairs from London to Washington. Before the first bizonal agreement, Mr Bevin told the Commons on 22 October 1946 that 'our intention is that those [Ruhr] industries should be owned and controlled in future by the public'.[11] On 15 May 1947, after the first agreement had been signed, he said that 'the rights of allies must be safeguarded and German opinion had to be taken into account'.[12] So it was to be. He who pays the piper calls the tune.

The second consequence of Britain's economic plight for the

European situation in the early years of peace was that it much accelerated the movement to give the West Germans self-government, to set on its feet the Federal Republic of Germany (FRG) with its capital at Bonn, and to have done with the interminable, sullen struggle to agree with the Russians on how to put the four occupation zones together again and make peace with Germany as a re-united and sovereign state. The truth is that the movement towards a separate West German state was initiated by Britain, through Britain's desire to unburden herself of the costs and other responsibilities involved in the occupation of Germany. The French did not want a separate state in the West; they fought against it every step of the way until the inauguration of the Bonn republic in September 1949; they had to be cajoled by Britain with pledges of support against any future German aggression, like the Dunkirk treaty, signed in March 1947. The United States acquiesced; the idea of the Bonn republic in any case accorded with the well-established American desire to cut foreign commitments and let the rest of the world settle its own problems, though that desire was being disappointed as time went by. And it was most staunchly resisted by the Russians, who brought the world to the brink of war by their blockade of the western-occupied sectors of Berlin in 1948–49, partly as a protest against the formation of the Bonn republic. The blockade was lifted in May 1949 in return for the agreement of the three Western Powers on yet another round, predictably futile, of talks at Foreign Minister level on a four-Power peace treaty with a re-united Germany.

The Western version of how Germany came to be irremediably divided and how the FRG was formed was that the four-Power Council of Foreign Ministers, created by the Yalta conference in February 1945 to frame *inter alia* a peace treaty with Germany, tried and failed to do so; that the turning point was reached at the Council's session in London in November–December 1947, after which the three Western Powers decided, *faute de mieux*, to give effect to national self-determination in the western occupation zones, if it could not be done in Germany as a whole; and that the major share of blame for this sorry outcome lay with the Soviet Union, whose leaders did not want a freely united Germany or a central German government which genuinely reflected the national will and interests of the German people. What Moscow desired, in the Western view, was to sabotage all efforts to get the Germans back on their feet again, and that was part of their long-term campaign to destroy the Western democratic system and extend the frontiers of communism in its place.

As in the matter of the Marshall offer, however, the British aim, as Mr Bevin conceived it, was to make progress, and that meant restoring Germany, or as much of it as the three Western Powers controlled, to independence, with suitable safeguards against the Germans slipping back to their old aggressive ways. 'We cannot accept the Russian view', he said in January 1948, 'that Germany should be kept strictly in hand under an over-centralised government, nor can we let continued poverty and discord cause havoc in Germany and weaken all of Europe'.[13] If British policy meant a sharp break with Russia, so be it. The West would have to look after its own interests. And the Opposition agreed. 'I am sure that is the course the government ought to pursue', was Anthony Eden's comment.[14] That Bevin and his American colleagues, though not necessarily the French, itched to cut short the Foreign Ministers' talks on Germany is evident from the fact that, even before their final failure at the London sessions in November–December 1947, Britain and the United States had established in May in Frankfurt, in the American zone, a central economic administration for associating the Germans with the running of their own affairs, in accordance with Bevin's principle that they must increasingly look to themselves for their own recovery. As the Foreign Secretary explained to the House, the Economic Council created by this decision was formed from Germans nominated by the political parties represented in the elected Land Diets. It was an interim expedient pending the formation of a West German government should agreement with Russia on German unity prove impossible.[15]

In the event, the four Foreign Ministers, as recalled by the history books, did 'fail' to agree about making peace with Germany, and even about the sort of state that Germany should be, and responsibility for this has since been ascribed by the West to Russia and by Russia to the West. But what might have been the consequences of 'success' in re-uniting Germany and making peace with the unified state which resulted? Either, to be sure, a Germany committed by alliance to the West, which would have been intolerable to Russia, or a Germany commmitted by alliance to the Soviet bloc, which would have been intolerable to the West. Or – a more likely development, if Germany's history between the two wars is anything to go by – a Germany committed to neither side, but able to play off one side against the other, asking higher and higher prices for supporting either side, and hence becoming the master of Europe. Each of these possible outcomes is more horrendous to the West, or to Russia, or to both, than the divided Germany which eventually emerged. On the basis of that division, a doubtless unhappy, but nevertheless stable situation had somehow been created by the 1960s.

And, all things considered, the Western Powers have not done so badly. They have about as reliable an alliance with the lion's share of pre-war Germany, now forming the Federal Republic, as they could wish, while the Soviet Union, which made the greatest contribution to Germany's defeat in 1945, has had to be content with a third of the old Germany, and by no means the richest or most powerful third. The West could conclude that, for them, the Council of Foreign Ministers was not a failure, but a huge success.

III

Western policy in Germany since 1945 has been based to all outward appearance on the thesis that the overriding principle is that of national self-determination, and that the same applies to the smaller states between Germany and Russia, from Poland and the Baltic states in the north to Rumania and Bulgaria in the south. This has always meant, in Germany's case, that the two states which have grown up in Germany as a result of the failure of the four occupying Powers to agree on an all-German peace treaty should be dissolved, and that genuinely free elections to a constituent assembly should be held nation-wide over Germany; that the assembly should draw up a new constitution for the country, with its democratic character (in the Western sense) firmly entrenched and guaranteed; and that, after further free elections under this constitution, an all-German government should be formed from the new legislature, to be recognised by all the Powers and entirely free to decide its own foreign and domestic policy.

These proposals were placed by the Western Powers before the Russians at a four-Power Foreign Ministers' meeting in Berlin from 25 January to 18 February 1954, and in July of the following year at a four-Power summit meeting in Geneva. Sir Anthony Eden, the Conservative party's successor to Sir Winston Churchill, represented Britain, while President Eisenhower and Prime Minister Edgar Faure acted for the other two Western Powers. Messrs Bulganin and

Khrushchev, who took power as Prime Minister and communist party First Secretary respectively after the short-lived interregnum under Grigori Malenkov which followed Stalin's death in March 1953, spoke for the Soviet Union. The Geneva conference, though its famed 'spirit' is said to have improved the atmosphere of East–West relations, was inconclusive as far as its main subject, Germany, was concerned, as was also the four-Power Foreign Ministers' talks which resumed the debate in the same Swiss city in October.[16] But how could it have been otherwise?

The Geneva summit conference followed almost immediately upon the admission of the FRG into the North Atlantic pact, when the Paris agreements between the Western Powers signed on 20–23 October 1954 came into effect on 6 May of the following year. By declarations made simultaneously with these events, the three Western occupying Powers, Britain, France and the United States, stated that the government of the FRG was 'the only German Government freely and legitimately constituted and therefore entitled to speak to Germany as the representative of the German people in international affairs'; they also declared that the determination of Germany's frontiers must await a definitive peace settlement.[17] The NATO Council as a whole associated itself with these statements a few days later. The effect of the declarations was that the NATO Powers were now committed to regard Russia's newly created state in her zone of occupation in Germany, the German Democratic Republic (DDR), a communist dominated body, as a puppet, and no more, and the post-Yalta border between Poland and the DDR, that is, the Oder–Neisse line, as it came to be called, as purely provisional. On these two vital issues, the three Western Powers had predetermined their positions before meeting their Russian partner at Geneva, and, of course, without consulting him.

They were under no compulsion to do so. When the FRG's position was left in doubt after the French National Assembly's refusal in August 1954 to ratify the European Defence Community (EDC) treaty of 1952, by which the Federal Republic was to have been rearmed, there was some anxiety among Western governments whether the west Germans might, in desperation, seek to come to some sort of private arrangement with the Russians. When the new Federal Chancellor, Dr Konrad Adenauer, went to Moscow on 9–14 September 1955 (that is, after the Federal Republic had been firmly embedded in the North Atlantic system), newspaper headlines in

London, New York and Paris reverberated with the name 'Rapallo', the scene of Weimar Germany's notorious pact with Soviet Russia in April 1922. The Western Powers therefore seem to have felt that they must sweeten the FRG's entrance into NATO, and ensure that the Germans remained faithful to it, by identifying themselves with the FRG's position on German unity and German borders, in the process changing NATO from a decidedly status-quo organisation into a decidedly revisionist organisation. But there was no obvious need to do so. In 1955 the Federal Republic had no real option in foreign policy other than joining the Western camp. Isolation was intolerable to the majority of its people, as the consternation following the demise of EDC showed; joining the Soviet bloc would have been more so. In reality, it should not have been the NATO alliance which was courting the Germans in 1955, but the other way round.

Be that as it may, by the time of the 1955 Geneva summit meeting, the Western Powers had firmly bolted the Federal Republic into their alliance and had no intention of letting it go, except in the rather unlikely event of the Germans wishing to leave. Their expectation was that the Russians would eventually be persuaded to allow the 17 million Germans in their occupation zone to join the west Germans in NATO, with the further possibility that at some time in the future the Oder–Neisse territories might be added to this western-oriented united Germany. In addition, the country standing between this reconstituted, pro-Western Germany and the Soviet Union, Poland, would, if the three Western Powers had their way, have a freely elected government of its own, and it is as near certain as anything could be that such a Poland would be, if not implacably hostile to the Soviets, at least more friendly towards the Atlantic States than to its great eastern neighbour. The Western Powers considered, or spoke as if they considered, that these proposals would be acceptable to the Russians if combined with a security system by which the four Powers (the three Western states and the Soviet Union) would come to the assistance of any one of them if attacked by Germany – a country, that is, which, if things went as the Western Powers intended, would be a firm member of the Western alliance. As an additional security measure, the Western Powers assured the Soviet Union that if, under these arrangements, the re-united Germany decided to join the Western alliance, NATO forces would not be stationed in what was, at the time of the Geneva summit conference, the Soviet zone of occupation beyond the Elbe.

It was not explained how the agreement of the new all-German government to these arrangements could be taken for granted before it was actually formed, nor what sanctions would be available to enforce them, if the Russians were ever guileless enough to agree. In any case, the three Western Powers were adamant at the Geneva conference that there was no prospect of these security measures coming into effect until and unless the new Germany entered the Atlantic alliance.[18] In reality, this proviso was hardly necessary since, as the British Minister of State at the Foreign Office, Mr Selwyn Lloyd, let slip in the House of Commons, the assumption all along was that this was what the Germans would wish to do. 'These arrangements were drawn up', Mr Lloyd said, 'to meet what everybody admitted to be the probable contingency. It really was not worth wasting time on the others because it was confidently thought that this was the choice a free Germany would make'.[19]

It is hardly conceivable that such proposals could have been put forward by the Western Powers (and they were continually repeated in later years) in any expectation that they would be accepted, or even given serious consideration, by the Russians. To imagine that the Soviet Union, after having suffered an almost fatal attack from Germany in 1941, in which the Russians believed, not entirely without cause, that the Western Powers had connived, would retire from their zone of occupation and allow Germany to re-unite and join an alliance controlled, as any good Marxist was bound to think, from the citadel of the capitalist world, can only be regarded as an exercise in self-deception, if indeed that supposition was ever seriously entertained. But the probability is that it never was.

Admittedly, Soviet proposals on German unity, submitted at the Geneva conference and elsewhere by Messrs Bulganin and Khrushchev, were equally devoid of hope of acceptance by the West. They favoured a vague form of confederation between the two existing German states, the FRG and the DDR, which would involve the legitimising of the latter, and the disarming and neutralisation of this contraption (it could not be described as a state) under the guarantee of the four Powers.[20] It was evidently in the expectation that this formula would prove more acceptable to German opinion than involvement in the Cold War that the Russians agreed, after a decade of prevarication, to the state treaty with Austria, guaranteeing its neutrality and independence, in May 1955. What suited the Austrians, Moscow seemed to say, must surely suit the Germans. But the analogy was quite unrealistic and never stood any chance of acceptance, either by western Germany or the three Western Powers. Who wants to take over Austria or would ever have reason to subvert its neutrality? Substitute Germany for Austria and the hollowness of the analogy is clear.

The Russians had their own reasons, not dissimilar from those of the West, for joining in the game of pretence about German unity. Game indeed it was. For thirty years and more after German forces surrendered in May 1945, Russia and the Western Powers had publicly to profess interest in and the will to work for a united, 'democratic' and peaceful Germany, and to frame proposals, which they must have known stood not the slightest chance of acceptance, for achieving it. They 'had to' because that is what they had promised the world during and at the end of the war; because they thought that was what the world wanted; and, above all, because it was what they thought the Germans wanted, even though many Germans, in both parts of Germany, either did not want it or would not pay a high price to achieve it. But it is as plain now as it was then that no united Germany that is conceivably possible by agreement between the four Powers could be other than a permanent anxiety to some, if not all, of them. It is also plain that the divided Germany and Berlin which have grown out of the Cold War are about the least unsatisfactory solution to the dilemma that can be imagined.

The division of Germany is not merely, or even perhaps mainly, the effect of the East–West Cold War. It is a by-product of the whole German position within the European balance of power. But, to no small degree, this is obscured by the manner in which the Russians tend to explain their policies. In many major international questions in the twentieth century (we have no wish to say the same of matters arising in the internal administration of states), the Russians since 1917 have had a better case, as this book has sought to show, than superficial judgements imply, in many instances a stronger case than that of the Western states they have dealt with. But the language, and the diplomatic manner, employed by Soviet leaders in public, and perhaps in private also, tends to obscure this: it is often the language of brute force, of ideological battle, of threats and the tedious reiteration of sullen and stale catchwords, even when the reason of the case is on the Soviet side. The Berlin crisis of 1958–61, which interrupted the growing 'thaw' in East–West relations after Stalin's death in 1953, and which brought the two sides to the brink of nuclear war, is a good illustration of this.

Mr Khrushchev's conduct of the crisis, from his note to the three Western occupying Powers on the demilitarisation of west Berlin on 27 November 1958 to the building of the Berlin Wall on 13 August 1961, which effectively ended the crisis, was a hackneyed essay in faintly veiled aggression, coupled with appalling threats to the world if his threats were not heeded.[21] The effect was, on the one hand, to entrench the more 'hawkish' Western leaders of opinion in an inflexible refusal to yield an inch over Berlin, and, on the other, to thrust the 'doves', and all those who saw some sense in Soviet positions on Germany, into puzzled debate about Mr Khrushchev's real intentions. It later transpired that the Soviet leader was not primarily seeking to annex west Berlin in furtherance of the reputed Soviet aim of appropriating as much of other people's territory as they could, but was chiefly concerned with the loss of manpower to the West, with serious implications for the East German economy and the stability of the East German state. There is little evidence that this Soviet concern was known to the Western Powers throughout the Berlin crisis – judging from the expedients they suggested for solving the crisis, they hardly seemed aware of it – even though they themselves had contributed to it by building up the western sectors of Berlin as a 'glittering shop-window' of Western affluence and thus a temptation to the hard-pressed East Germans to 'vote for freedom with their feet'. During the tortuous four-Power Foreign Ministers' meetings in Geneva from 11 May to 10 June and from 13 July to 5 August 1959, when Western representatives strove for some alleviation of the tension which might have the effect of inducing the Russians to reaffirm Western rights in Berlin, there appeared to be no suggestion that the crisis might be due to Soviet anxiety about the economy of East Germany.

It could be argued that, had the Russians gone to greater lengths to explain their difficulties in East Germany, the effects might have been, not to make the Western Powers more sympathetic, but to increase their hostility, since they could retort that, if the Russians insisted on imposing on East Germany an economically disastrous communist regime, they had only themselves to blame for the consequences. But this brings us back to the basic dilemma underlying Soviet policy in Germany in and after 1945. On the one hand, it would surely have been madness for the Russians to lose control of their zone of occupation in Germany and allow a re-united Germany to come into existence, free to decide its own internal and external policies. If that happened, there could be no assurance that Russia would not once more have to suffer the experience of German invasion which she had already suffered twice, at enormous cost, since 1914. Or, at least, many years would have to elapse before the Russians felt secure enough to face that risk. On the other hand, given that the East Germans naturally wished to rejoin their fellow nationals in the west, just as the Germans between the two world wars wanted national freedom from the fetters of Versailles, what options lay before their Russian masters except to ensure that they would do no such thing, perhaps for ever, certainly for years to come?

IV

The German question, however, also needs to be considered within the context of the military consolidation of the West under the North Atlantic treaty signed in Washington by 12 nations on 4 April 1949, to which Greece and Turkey acceded in 1951 and the Federal Republic of Germany in 1955.[22] Britain, then a much more considerable power than she has since become, played a leading role in the formation of the Atlantic alliance. She may even be said to have been its author, along with Marshal Stalin. At a time when those Americans who saw the writing on the wall were still battling with isolationist forces in their country, British ministers were embarking on the military integration of western Europe, hoping thereby to win the support of the world's economic and military colossus, the United States. In March 1947, Ernest Bevin, in a town with a name of such emotive significance for Britain, Dunkirk, gave a pledge to France, which the French reciprocated, to be at her side in the event of renewed aggression by Germany. A year later, on 17 March 1948, Britain was the primary force in the creation of the treaty of economic, social and cultural co-operation and collective self-defence signed at Brussels with France and the three Benelux countries, Belgium, Luxemburg and the Netherlands.[23] This time, though the possibility of German aggression is alluded to in the preamble of the treaty, the source of the threat was envisaged as lying further to the east, without that fact being mentioned in so many words. As such, the Brussels treaty is to be understood as a signal to the United States of west European readiness to co-operate for defence, and an invitation to that country to throw its weight behind European efforts. This the Truman administration did, together with five other west European states and Canada, in the North Atlantic treaty.

The treaty, framed deliberately to meet the perceived danger of Soviet aggression and given strong institutional form by the creation of a Ministerial Council, a complex system of integrated naval and military commands and extensive provision for political, economic and cultural co-operation, was a triumph for British diplomacy, perhaps the greatest it had enjoyed since 1914. Accordingly, since 1949 Britain has stood out as the most faithful NATO member in Europe, exerting herself to the uttermost to preserve its unity and sacrificing opportunities for leadership in western Europe on its behalf. Despite grumblings on the Labour Left, the major political parties have never wavered in support for NATO, and no politician of any standing has ever adopted non-alignment as his cause. Britain has done more than any other country, the United States included, to rescue the alliance when threatened with disruption, as in the EDC crisis in 1954, when the American Secretary of State, John Foster Dulles, threatened an 'agonising reappraisal' of American foreign policy if the treaty were not ratified.

As far as the burden of defence within the NATO system is concerned, Britain has always contributed a larger share of her national income to defence than any other European NATO country, despite her chronic economic problems since the war. In the late 1970s, when NATO embarked on its Long Term Defence Programme (LTDP), involving an increase in defence spending of 3 per cent a year over a five-year period, the British government not only instantly agreed, but raised the figure to 4 per cent in the first year (1978–79). This was in the thick of the worst economic crisis since the war, which led to the formation of a Cabinet under Mrs Margaret Thatcher in May 1979 that drastically cut spending on some of the most vital social services yet left defence spending almost unaffected.[24]

Since the NATO system is, in everything but name, a self-defence arrangement directed against armed attack from the Soviet bloc, it might be supposed that Britain's exceptional loyalty to the alliance reflects exceptional fear of Soviet aggression. But this is not necessarily so. It is true that the Atlantic alliance was triggered off by the Soviet *Gleichschaltung* in eastern Europe between 1945 and 1948, culminating in the Soviet-engineered *coup* in Czechoslovakia in February 1948, and that, during the early years of the Cold War, Labour's Foreign Secretary, Bevin, seemed to have a pathological fear, both of Russia and communism, which many of his Cabinet colleagues and backbenchers shared. This was in spite of the fact that there never was in Britain that intense dread of communism which gripped the United States in the 1950s, nor was the communist party in Britain ever a force to be reckoned with, as it was in France and Italy.

Nevertheless, British support for the Atlantic alliance has in reality a more general and long-term basis than fear of Soviet aggression after 1945, and this may explain why fear of Soviet aggression became credible to well-informed men like Bevin when Russia was so weak at the end of the war as to be barely able to stand up. Whatever relations existed between Britain and Russia after 1945, the British desire to have a long-term alliance with the United States must have been basic to British policy, regardless of which party was in power in Westminster. For if there was one overriding fact at the root of the weakness in British foreign policy in the period between the wars, it was American isolation. The peace settlement which America helped to make in 1919, she did not stay to enforce. Britain, with France as her sole considerable assistant, was left to hold the balance against powerful dissatisfied states in Europe and the Far East at the same time, and it proved beyond her strength. The lesson in 1945 was that, never again, Russia or no Russia, must the United States be separated from Britain and her other friends in Europe. That was what Winston Churchill angled, pleaded, plotted for throughout the war: that was the idea he intrigued into the Atlantic Charter, signed in August 1941, the idea of the two English-speaking democracies under arms.

Britain was drawn into the Atlantic alliance after 1945, not so much because of Russia, and certainly not only because of Russia, but because of the logic of history. Britain, a small island, with a small standing army and a vast empire spreadeagled over the globe, anchored off an unruly continent which from time to time threw up great military empires, had always to link itself perforce with some great land power which could take the shock of aggression and act as the stone of attrition while Britain mustered its strength. Russia itself had acted as the stone of attrition in 1812, France and Russia together in the first years of the 1914–18 war, and Russia again in the war with Nazi Germany. After 1945, most people hoped that the stone of attrition in future would be the United Nations, with its concentration of force in the Security Council. But there was the veto, and the growing rift with Russia. If the world organisation failed, the Anglo-American base must be firm.

Yet it is almost inconceivable that the Soviet Union, in its devastated condition in the late 1940s, could have contemplated an armed attack in the North Atlantic area, with all the risks, even before the signature of the North Atlantic treaty, of finding itself at war with the United States, then in the full plenitude of its strength and armed with the atomic bomb. It *is* conceivable that Soviet leaders have entertained that possibility in the last decade or so, when Soviet military strength has been more on a par with, and in certain respects superior to, the West's, though even that takes some believing. All that we know of Russian history leads to the conclusion that Soviet leaders must wish above all else to bolt and bar the door against invasion (of which they have an inordinate fear), cost what it may, and that they will use their now vast military strength to exact all the political advantages they can, though the risks will always be carefully weighed. But it also suggests that direct aggression against well-defined external Powers is not in their tradition, especially when they have dubious allies, whose loyalty in wartime cannot be counted on, in their ranks and to the rear of their armies.

So much does all this work against the thesis that direct Soviet aggression was actually feared when the North Atlantic treaty was signed in April 1949 that it seems more likely that Mr Bevin and his Cabinet colleagues, surely the most enthusiastic of all the founders of NATO, inclined to exaggerate the dangers of a Soviet attack in order to secure their principal objective, a permanent American commitment to the balance of power.[25] Strangely enough, it is doubtful whether American leaders were convinced – or even felt that they needed to be – by such British exaggerations in order to be persuaded of the need for the alliance. The most passionate anti-communist of American statesmen during the Cold War, Mr Dulles, said in March 1949 that he did not 'know any responsible official, military or civilian, in this government or any government who believes that the Soviet government now plans conquest by open military aggression'.[26]

Britain was thus cast in the role of an initiator in the Cold War which sprang up between the Western Powers and the Soviet Union after Germany's defeat, or, to be more precise, in the intervening months between the three-Power conference at Yalta in February 1945 and the meeting at Potsdam in July–August of that year. The British government was actuated partly by alarm at the growth of Soviet power, partly by the realisation that, in the conditions following the defeat of the Axis, only the United States possessed the strength to form an effective balance against any aggressor facing Britain and her continental friends, partly by the idea that, of all the lessons to be learned from the Second World War, the folly of weakness in the face of an expanding power was the most important. In opposing Stalin in the late 1940s, Britain was doing what she thought she should have done in the 1930s. The irony was that, in the 1930s, it was Stalin who urged her to do those things.

Nevertheless, as soon as the Atlantic pact came into existence and a full-scale rearmament programme was initiated after the outbreak of the Korean war in June 1940, it was Britain who, above all her alliance partners, sought a rational negotiation of outstanding issues in the Cold War with the Soviet Union and her allies. She was rewarded by being charged by politicians in Bonn, Paris and Washington with pursuing the same 'appeasement' policies towards Stalin which she pursued towards Hitler before the war. The expression 'the English disease', since applied to so many British failings, was first coined as a description of Britain's search for accommodation with Moscow and Peking. The East–West *détente*, thought of, and denigrated, by most Americans as exclusively a super-Power affair, was, as a matter of history, invented and advocated by the British, only to be spurned in its early years by the United States, indeed by NATO in general.

Britain's old ally against Germany, France, was, until 1940, unrelenting in opposition to that state. Not so the United States, as Britain's ally against the other major revisionist power of the twentieth century, the USSR. Walter Lippmann once described his countrymen as 'too pacific in peace, too belligerent in war', and in nothing is this better illustrated than in their attitude to Soviet communism. America's physical detachment from the world's great centres of political conflict, as well as its continental size and strength no doubt help account for this. But there is also the emotional volatility of the American people, now credulous to the point of naivety, now combative to the point of mania. The American democracy, wrote George Kennan, 'is like a palaeolithic monster, slow to rouse, but which, once roused, lays about itself with such force as to wreck its habitation'. And that of others as well. A great deal of British foreign policy in the 1950s was spent in controlling the American giant, which British statesmen, more than those of any other country, had stirred to action. The Sorcerer's Apprentice found he had to tutor the demon he had unleashed. 'No annihilation without representation', cried Professor A. J. Toynbee.

V

British restraint of the United States – or, depending on the viewpoint, British appeasement of communism – began in the Far East, and shortly after the outbreak of the Korean war in June 1950, when Britain stood without hesitation at America's side in support of United Nations action in defence of invaded South Korea. We do not have to delve too deeply into old American protective feelings towards China, extending back into the nineteenth century, the American sense of outrage when Mao Tse-tung's victory in the civil war in 1949 took China into the hated enemy camp, or into American bitterness at alleged lack of allied support during the Korean war and the stalemated end of that war in July 1953, despite the loss of 54,000 American lives and 100,000 wounded, to understand the surge of emotion in the United States against Chinese intervention in the war. It culminated in the strong temptation, best expressed by the American commander-in-chief of UN forces in Korea, General Douglas MacArthur, to use the atomic bomb against the Chinese, to unify Korea under Western auspices, and to reinstate Chiang Kai-shek as ruler of the mainland. The horror which all this aroused in Britain, who had recognised the Chinese People's Republic as early as February 1950, was reflected in Prime Minister Attlee's dramatic dash to see President Truman on 4 December, in the strongest British reservations about American proposals to commit the UN to the unification of Korea and to name China as an aggressor at the world organisation, and in British support for the Indian Prime Minister, Mr Jawaharlal Nehru, in his efforts to intercede with Peking on behalf of a negotiated settlement.[27]

When the Korean war ended with an armistice signed at Panmunjom on 27 July 1953, the Anglo-American alliance, if not in ruins, was gravely strained. In the United States, there was not far short of a consensus of opinion that Britain, being herself something of a communist, or at least socialist, state, as the Attlee government's programme showed, did not shrink from harassing her major ally and source of financial aid, the United States, while it was fighting for the rule of law in Korea, from giving encouragement to the common enemy, China, behind America's back, and from consorting with a pack of neutralist states, led by India, which could not be described as other than dupes of the great communist Powers. These angry American conclusions were well illustrated by the elections in the United States in November 1952, in which the ultimate victor in the Presidential race, the Republican general, Dwight Eisenhower, promised, if elected, to cut through the Gordian knot of negotiations with the enigmatic Russians and the inscrutable Chinese by a campaign, vigorous and vague, to 'liberate' Russia and China, and all the states unlucky enough to fall under their sway, from their communist masters.

British Conservative governments under Churchill and Eden which followed the 13-year eclipse of the Labour party after its defeat in the general election in October 1951, could feel no sympathy with this windy and imprecise talk of 'liberation'. They clung to two fundamental principles: first, that it is a mistake to commit oneself in advance, and lead others into believing one is committed, to objectives such as 'liberation', which are probably impossible to fulfil except at quite intolerable cost; and secondly, that in dealing with revisionist countries, like China and Russia, the worst thing is to adopt policies likely to unite them, and the best is to drive wedges, or exploit existing wedges, between them.

The wisdom of the first of these principles was illustrated, at appalling costs in human terms, in 1956, when the Western Powers, having encouraged East European countries to rise against their Soviet masters by hints (though they were perhaps never more than that) of Western assistance if they did so, stood aside and confined themselves to expressions of moral outrage when the Hungarians took the West at its word, made a dash for freedom from the Warsaw pact and were mercilessly crushed by the Russians.

Britain always argued that the Atlantic treaty was designed strictly for collective defence against armed attack, not for the expulsion of communism from countries like Russia or China which had succumbed to it through revolution, or had had it imposed upon them, like Hungary or Poland, before the treaty came into existence. This position in fact emerged as the essence of United States policy in the Nixon–Kissinger years in the early 1970s. It is the inevitable position if it is assumed that, as the Hungarian tragedy showed, Western nations are not willing to regard the unseating of communism in areas in which it has become established as worth another war. But the British struggle to get this point accepted by the United States (which, after all, was bound to take the supreme decision on behalf of all the Western states if there proved to be no way of avoiding all-out conflict with the communist world) was by no means easy. It is no exaggeration to say that it was partly because British ministers considered it so important to get this matter of the *casus belli* (or rather, what should *not* be the *casus belli*) settled that they neglected the opportunities for leadership in the European integration movement at that time which they could have had for the asking.

The prudence of the second British principle in dealings with the communist Powers, that is, the importance of dividing them, or at least avoiding measures likely to have the effect of uniting them, was shown by Anglo-American disagreements about China in the 1950s. It is an extraordinary fact that the United States, which should have learned the folly of refusing on emotional grounds to deal with a stable foreign government from its experience with the Soviet regime in the inter-war period, went on to make the same mistake in China, from 1949, when the communists came to power, until 1972, when President Nixon made his first visit to Peking, preceded by his national security adviser, Dr Kissinger. America's ostracism of the Chinese communists was defended on the ground that they should not be allowed 'to shoot their way into the international community', in defiance of the elementary rule that the more dangerous to peace a state is, the more important it is to be in diplomatic contact with it. Moreover, by making China an enemy of the West; by building up Japan as a counter-weight to China, and at the same time forbidding Japan to have relations with China; by egging on the Nationalist regime in Taiwan to invade the mainland; by keeping up tension with China year after year over the offshore islands, Quemoy and Matsu; by lumping China and Russia together as aggressors in Vietnam; and by organising, in the teeth of the strongest British misgivings, the South East Asia collective defence treaty (SEATO) against China in September 1954: by actions such as these the American authorities did everything in their power to rivet the Sino–Soviet alliance together. The fact that it did nevertheless violently split apart is evidence of the opposition of Chinese and Soviet interests and policies, which the West should have exploited long before.

If the British never wanted to press the West's dispute with China to the point of endangering peace with the communist regime there, they also exerted themselves to the full to moderate the Cold War with Russia. Britain, the architect of the West's Cold War confrontation with Russia, was also the architect of the *détente*. The record is striking and unambiguous, with, remarkably, British Conservatives being even more active in the cause than Labour leaders. On 14 February 1950, Churchill, then leader of the Opposition, the pristine Cold War warrior of the West, called for summit talks with Russia in a general election campaign, at a time when the Cold War had hardly started:

> I cannot help coming back [he said] to this idea of another talk with Soviet Russia upon the highest level. The idea appeals to me of a supreme effort to bridge the gulf between the two worlds, so that each can live their life, if not in friendship, at least without the hatreds and manoeuvres of the Cold War.[28]

As soon as Stalin died in March 1953, Churchill, now Prime Minister, accepted much of Russia's international case in a speech in the House of Commons on 11 May:

> Russia has a right [he said] to feel assured that as far as human arrangements can run the terrible events of the Hitler invasion will never be repeated, and that Poland will remain a friendly Power and a buffer, though not, I trust, a puppet state.

He then went on:

> I must make it plain that, in spite of all the uncertainties and confusions in which world affairs are plunged, I believe that a conference on the highest level should take place between the leading Powers without long delay. This conference should not be overhung by ponderous or rigid agenda, or led into mazes and jungles of technical details, zealously contested by hordes of experts and officials drawn up in vast, cumbrous array. The conference should be confined to the smallest number of Powers and persons possible. It should meet with a measure of informality and a still greater measure of privacy and seclusion. It might well be that no hard-faced agreements would be reached, but there might be a general feeling among those gathered together that they might do something better than tear the human race, including themselves, into bits.[29]

This speech was made at the very time when the United States was using every means to persuade the French to ratify the EDC treaty, with its aim of strengthening Western Europe against Soviet aggression. On 4 July of the following year, 1954, a month before the debate in the French National Assembly which killed the EDC treaty, Churchill wrote to Mr Molotov proposing an Anglo-Soviet summit meeting to develop the suggestions raised in the Prime Minister's speech in May 1953.[30] These exchanges with Molotov petered out within a month, but in May of the following year Churchill was renewing his proposal.

In autumn 1956, when the Hungarian tragedy was unfolding, many British politicians, and many newspapers, too, so far from regarding the Soviet use of force against the Hungarians as reason for despair about Soviet policies and the prospects of peaceful co-existence with the Russians, considered the occasion one for renewing negotiations about arms control. One assumption in Britain about the Hungarian crisis, following as it did hard upon the heels of unrest in Poland earlier the same year, was that it might portend a Russian willingness to unburden themselves of some of their commitments in Eastern Europe, provided the Western Powers showed interest in some more acceptable system of general security in Europe than they had been prepared to envisage in the past. Or, if that proved too optimistic, that at least the Russians might be willing to contemplate some arrangement for thinning down armed forces on either side of the dividing line in Europe, which might have the further advantage of making possible the mutual inspection of forces and military installations on either side. This will-o'-the-wisp of disengagement became the *ignis fatuus* of both professional and amateur experts on British foreign policy in the middle and late 1950s. No sooner had one scheme of disengagement petered out than another emerged from the Foreign Office and the research departments of the political parties, while NATO defence chiefs and American senators struggled, not very successfully, to keep silent.

Disengagement, so the London government and their advisers believed, had the advantage of giving the West the means of continuously testing the durability of Soviet control in Eastern Europe. It gave the West the opportunity to pursue overtures about arms control from Russia's allies, or 'satellites', as the West was inclined to call them, in Eastern Europe, such as the Polish plan, put forward by Adam Rapacki, the Polish Foreign Minister, at the UN

General Assembly on 7 November 1957, for excluding nuclear weapons from Central Europe, and hence to encourage independent initiatives (if that is what the Rapacki plan was) from those allies. Mr Rapacki issued a revised version of his proposals on 4 November 1958, which took note of British criticisms, though this was rejected by the British Foreign Secretary, Mr Selwyn Lloyd, in the Commons on 4 December, presumably under pressure, especially from the United States and the Bonn republic, which had both been arguing that the Rapacki plan would impair NATO's defence capability and discriminate 'against the troops of a particular country'.[31]

Nevertheless, Conservative Ministers in the late 1950s continued to think that disengagement provided a practical theme of arms control after the United States, over British protest, had in the summer of 1955 given a dusty answer to the extraordinary acceptance by the Soviet delegation of the Anglo-French plan for general disarmament which those two countries had put forward on behalf of the West as a whole at the UN sub-committee on disarmament in London. This British quest for disengagement, or some version of it, persisted throughout the second Berlin crisis of 1958–61, when Mr Khrushchev, the Soviet Prime Minister and First Secretary of the Soviet communist party, attempted to bring to an end the Western occupation of West Berlin by having it converted into a 'free city' denuded of foreign troops.[32] In February 1959, the then British Prime Minister, Mr Harold Macmillan, broke away from the united NATO front at the very height of the Berlin crisis and unilaterally paid a visit to Moscow (or 'reconnaissance', as he preferred to call it) between 21 February and 3 March to discuss a wide range of questions, including cultural and trade relations, Berlin and Germany, disarmament, nuclear tests, and (with remarkable boldness) a non-aggression pact. Mr Macmillan sought to allay suspicions, not to say fears, among his allies by insisting that his purpose in Moscow was not to negotiate, but 'to try to seek a better understanding of our respective views on these grave issues and the reasons underlying them'.[33] Such British initiatives were criticised by West German politicians, now beginning to replace Britain as America's most reliable ally in Europe, on the ground that arms control schemes such as disengagement or nuclear-free zones would discriminate against Germany by reducing NATO forces on German soil. They were also frowned upon by NATO commanders.

Mr Khrushchev issued unambiguous warnings that, if anyone

assumed that, because he himself desired peaceful coexistence, he was ready to relax his grip on Eastern Europe, he would be making a serious mistake. In his article 'On Peaceful Coexistence' in the American Journal *Foreign Affairs* in October 1959, Mr Khrushchev wrote:

> Real facts of life in the last ten years have shown convincingly that the policy of 'rolling back' communism can only poison the international atmosphere, heighten the tension between states and work in favour of the cold war. Neither its inspirers nor those who conduct it can turn back the course of history and restore capitalism in the socialist countries.

But the British were not discouraged, certainly not Mr Macmillan. Throughout the Berlin crisis which began with Khrushchev's note of 27 November 1958, no-one worked harder than he, though to no immediate avail, to arrive at some understanding with the Russians which, while reaffirming the three Western Powers' legal rights in Berlin, which they had won by their victory in the Second World War, would reassure the Russians that a free West Berlin was in no sense a threat to them or their allies. In the course of the crisis, the Prime Minister, almost singlehandedly, dragged a reluctant President Eisenhower and General de Gaulle to a summit meeting with Mr Khrushchev in Paris on 16–19 May 1960, only to see the Soviet leader storm back home before the conference began on the pretext that the Americans had sent a U2 spy plane on a mission over the Soviet Union which the Russians had shot down on 1 May. The American President refused to apologise or to punish those responsible, as the Russians demanded, but promised that the flights would be discontinued.[34] It was perhaps the greatest disappointment in Mr Macmillan's life. Of the last day in Paris, 19 May, he later wrote, 'there was little now to be done, except try to conceal as best I could my disappointment, amounting almost to despair – so much attempted, so little achieved'.[35]

The British, too, worked, perhaps harder than any other Western ministers, to get the conference launched in Geneva in August 1958 to illegalise the testing of nuclear weapons, with the Americans and Russians as their partners in the negotiation. Once the conference began, Britain, to a greater extent than either of the super-Powers, strove to keep it alive in the face of repeated threats of breakdown, until the test ban agreement, which did not, however, apply to underground tests, was finally signed in Moscow by the three nuclear states on 5 August 1963. Britain played much the same kind of active and inventive role, under different Prime Ministers and Foreign Secretaries, in the negotiation and completion of the nuclear non-proliferation treaty in 1968 and in the three years which culminated in the signature of the Final Act of the Conference on Security and Co-operation in Europe by 35 nations at Helsinki in August 1975.

The story has its countless incidents and variations. Some British ministers have taken a harder and more unforgiving line towards the Soviet Union than others, and have been rather more benign towards the Chinese communists as a result. A notable example, which stands forth pre-eminently in the performance of high-level British politicians since 1945, is the Conservative Prime Minister, Mrs Margaret Thatcher, who won a 42-seat majority at a general election in May 1979 and hence could look forward to a secure four- or five-year term of office. Almost from the outset, Mrs Thatcher took up a 'hard-line' stance towards Russia, winning from the press and propaganda agencies of the Soviet Union the designation 'Iron Lady'. Under the Thatcher government, at time of writing, the Soviet Union has received from Britain the most severe strictures; Britain has been ahead of all the European NATO countries in agreeing to accept on its soil improved American weapons, in accordance with a NATO decision in November 1979, and in approving the three per cent increase in defence spending per annum over the next ten years which NATO has voted; Britain, with more alacrity than any of its other European allies, sprang to President Carter's support in his opposition to the Soviet Union's armed intervention in Afghanistan in December 1979; and Britain refrained from such unilateral approaches to the Soviet Union after its move into Afghanistan as President Giscard d'Estaing's visit to Warsaw to see Mr Brezhnev in June and the visit by Chancellor Schmidt of the FRG to Moscow in July 1980. But this is unusual in Britain's post-Second World War history, reflecting perhaps the strong, or headstrong, temperament of Mrs Thatcher, which has been noted in other issues, foreign and domestic.

At the same time, the Soviet move into Afghanistan in 1979 also represented something of a departure from Russia's traditional practice, to which British politicians are accustomed. When, after 1945, the Soviets resorted to the use of force outside their own frontiers, they generally did so within their recognised 'sphere of influence', that is, for the most part, Eastern Europe. Now, in her incursion into Afghanistan, Russia was using force on a major scale, involving something like 90,000 troops, in an entirely independent and non-aligned country. For many British people, this looked like a disturbing parallel with the situation in March 1939, when, for the first time, Hitler, by his invasion of Bohemia, attacked a country which had no conceivable ethnic connection with Germany.

Apart from the Thatcher period, however, British policy towards the Soviet Union since 1945 has followed a consistent course of armed vigilance against aggression, coupled with a search for *détente* and all manner of agreements to ease international tension, as and when opportunities for making these presented themselves. There is a striking resemblance between this policy and the so-called 'double line' pursued by the National Government towards the Fascist and Nazi dictators in the 1930s, with, however, the all-important difference that then the dominant principle was conciliation towards the revisionist states, followed, when conciliation failed, by hastily organised armed resistance, whereas, since 1945, priority has generally been given to armed resistance, with the offer of conciliation when armed resistance has demonstrated to the revisionists the drawbacks of trying to snatch advantages by force.[36] The policy has surely been correct in its grasp of essentials: namely, the assumption behind it that the expansion of Soviet power in Eastern Europe at the end of the Second World War was to a large extent inescapable, whatever its moral quality, and that the rest of the world could not be expected to commit suicide in a vain attempt to reverse it. At the same time, the policy took for granted that the more Soviet leaders were given to understand that attempts to crush by force the independence of peoples living beyond those limits of Soviet expansion would be met by equal or greater counter-force, the less would they be tempted to challenge Western interests, and hence peace. Today, of course, in so far as she pursues the same line of poliicy, Britain must do so from a position of diminished strength in the international community, and in partnership with other members of the European Community.

But it cannot be stated too strongly that it is well for Britain, and all those thrown into contact with the Soviet state, to refrain from beginning their analysis of the Soviet phenomenon by attributing to Russia and her leaders that unique share of wickedness which most people have been inclined to ascribe to them. As we have argued in this and the foregoing chapters, there is not much in the record of Russian foreign policy since the revolution which is significantly more depraved than the policies of other powerful states in history, or which does not make a certain sort of sense in the light of that country's experience of international affairs. Before we resort to words like 'aggression', 'expansionism', or 'imperialism' to describe Russia's international behaviour, we should remind ourselves of the necessities of state which her rulers must ponder in making their decisions. It may be that, in the end, we will conclude that Russia's foreign policy is as wicked as we tend to think her internal policies are. But we cannot be sure of this without making an effort to discover why the Soviet state acts as it does.

Assuredly, Soviet spokesmen afford the world little help in that task of understanding. By their secrecy, by their repellent manner of explaining policies which are often in themselves justifiable by the standards and usages of this age, they have done their best to destroy the chance of other people catching a glimpse of the inner meaning of their policies and thoughts. But that does not relieve other people of the heavy duty, in their own interests and those of their descendants, of trying to come to terms with the baffling Soviet phenomenon as best they may.

Part II

The Cultural and Economic Aspects

6. Russophobia and Russophilia

FOR two hundred years Russia has never failed to arouse strong feelings in Britain, whether of admiration and affection – Russophilia – or fear and mistrust – Russophobia – though the latter has generally been more powerful. The physical remoteness of Russia, the vast differences between its history and Britain's, which were referred to in the first chapter of this book, and the widespread ignorance about Russia in Britain, go some way to explain why these feelings have been so strong and why they have affected British thought about Russia and its policies. Moreover, favourable and unfavourable reactions towards Russia, in both Tsarist and communist times, have alternated rapidly: the pendulum has swung from one extreme to another, and this because Russophilia and Russophobia have been more matters of emotion than reason, and because, more often than not, both have stemmed from sources unconnected with the real nature of the Russian phenomenon.

During the eighteenth century Britain and Russia had too little to do with each other for coherent attitudes to form in either country towards the other. In the colonial field, Britain was acquiring Canada, disengaging from the American colonies and expelling France from India. In Europe, its main concern was the destruction of French domination. Russia under Catherine II began to control the northern shores of the Black Sea and extended into central Europe by joining in the three great partitions of Poland (1772–95). In 1791 came the first serious eruption of Anglo-Russian hostility with Pitt's application to the House of Commons, which failed, for funds to restore to the Ottoman empire the fortress of Ochakov, which guarded the estuary of the Dnieper and Bug rivers, and which Tsarist forces had captured at great expense.[1] For the first time, the British press discovered Russia, and its despotic government and expansionist policies. The *Morning Chronicle* decided that the Tsars had designs on Europe and Asia: 'would our rotten boroughs continue to be compensated for in the manner proposed by Mr Pitt', it wrote in May 1793, 'if government by one person were introduced here by foreign means?'[2] By 1817 the *Morning Chronicle* was warning that:

> A very general persuasion has long been entertained by the Russians that they are destined to be rulers of the world and this idea has been more than once stated by publications in the Russian language.[3]

Britain and Russia, as comrades in arms, celebrated Napoleon's defeat at the Vienna Congress in 1815, but that event, like the defeat of Germany in 1945, left British politicians to ponder the rising threat from the east.

Sir Robert Wilson, in *A Sketch of the Military and Political Power of Russia in the Year 1817*, published in that same year, gave the cue for British mistrust of Russia which dominated British thinking about foreign affairs for the rest of the century. With the exaggeration that has always affected British views on Russia, he contended that:

> Russia, profiting by the events which have afflicted Europe, has not only raised her ascendancy on natural sources, sufficient to maintain a preponderating power, but, farther, she has been presented by her rivals with the sceptre of universal dominion.[4]

An ideological element was injected into this nascent Anglo-Russian antagonism by the *guerre des idées* which followed Waterloo, the eastern courts, Austria, Prussia, Russia, championing the rights of monarchs against constitutionalism, Britain and France objecting to the use of the Congress system for the restoration of the *ancien régime*. In contrast with the pattern in the twentieth century, British Tories were less affected by these anti-Russian feelings, thinking of the Tsars as the bulwark of conservatism in Europe. The Whigs, gaining strength from the Reform Act of 1832 and the school of Romantic writers of the period, saw in Moscow the chief threat to freedom.

The Greek war of independence (1821–32) brought Britain and Russia together in a strange alliance, for the first and only time, in defence of national self-determination in the Ottoman empire in the

Balkans. But otherwise Russia's pressure against the Porte–in 1828–29, in 1833, when the Tsars wrested the highly favourable treaty of Unkiar Skelessi from the Sultan, and in 1853, when British opinion was swept to the pitch of hysteria by the Russian invasion of the Turkish provinces of Moldavia and Wallachia, the later Rumania, and, again, in Persia in 1826–28 and 1836–38 – solidified British suspicions. 'Within the United Kingdom', writes J. H. Gleason in his authoritative *The Genesis of Russophobia in Great Britain*, 'there developed early in the nineteenth century an antipathy towards Russia which soon became the most pronounced and enduring element in the national outlook on the world abroad'.[5]

The Polish uprising in 1830 and its brutal suppression by forces of the Tsar, and likewise the Russian incursion into Hungary in 1849 to help Austria with the liquidation of the revolution in that country, gave shape and form to the anti-Russian stereotype in Britain. The leading British Russophobe in the mid-nineteenth century, David Urquhart, had little difficulty in stimulating by his writings the mood which underlay British attitudes during the Crimean War (1854–55), described by Disraeli as 'just but unnecessary'. Despite the fact that it was the Sultan who rejected the famous Vienna Note of the Great Powers for settling the Russo-Turkish quarrel, and the Russians who accepted it, British jingoism swept to the defence of innocent Turkey against cruel Russia. The jingle of London streets, 'Oh! Lovely Albert!', dedicated to the Prince Consort, ran:

> I will tell thee, Al, we never shall,
> Although you played the deuce then,
> Allow the Turks to be run down
> By the dirty, greasy Russians.

In the Commons, Palmerston, the master of the hour, warned that Russia, 'bestriding the Continent from north to south', would, if allowed to defeat Turkey, 'become dangerous to the liberties of Europe' and its power 'would be fatal to the independence of other states'.[6] Bulwer Lytton called on the reluctant Prime Minister, Aberdeen, to:

Check the ambition of Russia and preserve Europe from the outlet of barbarian tribes that require but the haven of the Bosphorus to menace the liberty and civilisation of races yet unborn – that the liberties of our children may be secured from some future Attila and civilisation guarded from the irruptions of Scythian hordes.[7]

'The Eastern Question', writes Kingsley Martin in his book on Palmerston's manipulation of British public opinion during the Crimean War, 'had indeed become a sporting encounter between Russia and Turkey – with the betting heavily on the latter'.[8] It was to be the same a quarter of a century later, when Russia and Turkey were again in conflict in the Balkans and Disraeli was prodded by a feverishly anti-Russian public opinion in Britain to force the Tsar to moderate his drive to replace the Porte with Russian power. 'We don't want to fight, but by jingo if we do' turned out to be one of the last acts of Victorian defiance against the Bear, and it was followed, as the century neared its close, by doubts and fears about Britain's entire position in the world. With the Anglo-Russian Convention of 1907 the two countries agreed to settle their differences about Persia, the source of so much Russophobia in Britain. In 1914, the Russia which had seemed such a threat for a hundred years, was now turning its Scythian hordes against Britain's new enemy, Germany, and Russian soldiers, allegedly sighted in Scotland on their way to the Western front – and with snow on their boots, too – were comrades in arms again. Turkey, the championship of which against the Tsars had been one of the strongest factors in Russophobia, was now a main source of Russophilia, and, by an agreement in 1915, Constantinople and the Straits, the greatest prize Russia had striven for throughout the nineteenth century, were resignedly made over to the Romanovs. The First World War was one of the moments in Anglo-Russian relations when 'imperial rivalry was transcended by a common menace of major proportions'.[9]

Yet, even though abhorrence, fear, mistrust, clouded the British image of Russia during the last century to a far greater extent than admiration or affection, much of this was at the surface level of mass opinion. It was highly sensitive to newspaper scaremongering, the press having become by mid-century a dominant force in politics. In other, and perhaps more profound respects, the standing of Russia in less volatile sectors of British opinion was different. In the first place, few British ministers really succumbed to popular anti-Russian clamour: Aberdeen in the 1850s mistrusted it, and even in the great crisis of 1877–78 the Prime Minister, Disraeli, was widely accused of 'dragging his feet'. The inner circle of policy-makers were little affected by the vulgar stereotype of Turkey as the defenceless maiden ravished by brutal Russia. In 1844, the Tsar, Nicholas II, came to London with Foreign Minister Nesselrode and discussed with British ministers the problem seriously confronting both countries, that of dealing with the moribund Turkey. It was not simply a question of sending the Light Brigade against the second Attila.

Above all, as travellers from western Europe penetrated Russia and wrote books about it and its people, one aspect of the country began to captivate British people, and the fascination has remained powerful to the present day: that is, the famed simplicity and faith of the ordinary Russian people and the sense of sadness which western writers have perceived in their sufferings. One British writer who expressed this root of British Russophilia in the ten or twenty years before 1914 was Maurice Baring. In *The Mainsprings of Russia*, published in 1914 and widely read in Britain owing to the wartime alliance, Baring wrote of the 'curious possibilities of sympathy, curious analogies and still more curious differences which complement each other' between the Russians and the British. He was struck by the 'charm' of Russia:

> The charm is there . . . once you have felt it you will never be free from it. The aching, melancholy song, which Gogol says wanders from sea to sea through the length and breadth of the land, will for ever echo in your heart and haunt the recesses of your memory.

And it is, at bottom, the ordinary people who provide the charm. 'What I love and admire in the Russian people is nothing barbaric, picturesque or exotic – but something eternal, universal and quiet – namely, their love of man, and their faith in God'. In another passage Baring writes, in typical vein, of 'a kind of biblical and dignified simplicity of utterance and paucity of idiom which is the precious privilege of the poor in Russia'.[10] Thirty years later, when Britain and Russia were once again fighting a war against Germany, Winston Churchill appealed to the same image: 'I see the Russian soldier guarding the land'.

II

The revolution of 1917 and Russia's subsequent abandonment of the war against the Central Powers exerted a profound influence upon

Russophobia in Britain. In the first place, it changed its incidence among the political parties. The Conservatives, who, as Tories, had been on the whole the pro-Russian party for most of the nineteenth century, became the most violent opponents of the new breed of men in Moscow. After their departure from Lloyd George's coalition government in October 1922, they pushed the Bolsheviks further into isolation, culminating in the breach of diplomatic relations in May 1927. The Labour party, which became the chief rival to the Conservatives after the split in the Liberals caused by Lloyd George's breach with Asquith, emerged as the friend of the new socialist state, though there was the widest variation on this between the official Labour leaders who formed the two Labour Cabinets in the 1920s and whose strongest wish was to distance themselves as far as possible from the Bolsheviks, and the Left wing of the party, whose admiration for the Soviet regime was less inhibited.[11]

The nature of Russophobia and Russophilia was changed, too, by the 1917 upheaval. Before 1914 fear of Russia had mainly centred upon the colonial and naval threats: it singled out expansionism as a theme of Russian history, originating with Peter the Great and directed towards warm-water ports and the high seas of the world, where the British navy ruled supreme. The nodal points were Constantinople and the Straits, Persia, Afghanistan, Manchuria and the Yellow Sea. The threat dwindled with the rise of German industrial and naval power and after Russia's defeat by Britain's ally, Japan, in 1905. Following 1917 and the civil war in Russia, Britain had little to fear at sea and colonial rivalry was almost non-existent. There was a brief period of rapprochement between Lenin and Kemal Ataturk, which momentarily stirred the embers of the old Eastern Question, but fears were set at rest by Lord Curzon's great achievement in driving a wedge between the Bolsheviks and the Turks at the Lausanne conference, which made peace with Turkey in 1923.[12] The Bolsheviks were no more than an irritant in China: when the British struggled to defend their commercial and other rights·in China against Kuomintang nationalists in the 1920s, they suspected Russian communist fingers in the pie, but it was all too evident that Chinese nationalism was the real source of the trouble. In any case, the Kuomintang broke with Russia in 1927 and towards the end of the 1920s Chinese nationalist leaders were beginning to realise that they must come to terms with western capitalism if they were going to obtain the economic assistance essential to national reconstruction.

India was a different case owing to its exceptional position in the British empire and the rumblings of a real revolt in that country after the First World War. The Foreign Office under Curzon and Austen Chamberlain were positive that the trouble-makers in Moscow were behind all this and lost no opportunity to tell the Russians and the rest of the world how angry they were about it.[13] They were vociferously backed by Conservative MPs in the Commons and up and down the country, who had little difficulty in finding people willing and able to furnish documentary support for the campaign. The Bolsheviks, the cry went up, were out 'to set India aflame', as for instance by supplying 'smokeless power' to a mysterious Dr Hafiz of Kabul for blowing down the ramparts of the British Raj.[14] At the same time, through their treaty with Persia in 1919 and their intrigues in Afghanistan the Bolsheviks meant to complete their seditious tasks. Little of this could have been taken with much seriousness by the real managers of British policy in the 1920s, certainly not by Chamberlain. But, amid all the troubles which beset Britain after the war, from unemployment to the harassments of the Irish question, the feeling that sinister men in Moscow were, if not responsible for the pressures, at least active in stirring the pot, must at least have afforded some satisfaction. The Eastern Question, however, and the central role it had long played in arousing hostility in Britain against Russia, had, for the moment, disappeared from the scene.

Russophobia had in fact quite a different basis among British Conservatives, and those who sympathised with them, after the First World War. It arose, first, from a sense of the entire strangeness and unknowability of the new rulers of Russia. They might have some of the features of previous holders of power, but their outlandish language, their strange doctrines, their fanaticism and violence, were all new and frightening. Russophobes who had welcomed the fall of the monarchy in 1917 as signalling the long-awaited advent of democracy in Russia were cruelly disappointed and their bitterness towards the Bolsheviks was all the greater. They saw the Leninists rejecting democracy and parliamentary government as they knew it; gagging the press, or what was left of it; summarily shooting all who disagreed; and proclaiming that their cruel and vicious system would soon be the standard and norm for every country in the world.

But perhaps the worst aspect of the Bolsheviks, in the eyes of British Conservatives and indeed all politically moderate people, was the frank, undisguised appeal they made to dissatisfied sectors of working-class opinion throughout the bourgeois world. The immediate aftermath of the war for that world was a drastic rise in unemployment, after a temporary and short-lived boom, and the onset of social conditions, in Britain as in other capitalist countries, which provided an ironic comment on the wartime promises of a new and better life which would follow once the fighting was finished. Conservatives had no doubt that these troubles were merely the short-term price which had to be paid for the country's effort during the war, but if the Bolsheviks continued their practice of working up political unrest in other countries, that price might not be so short-term. The anxieties aroused by the so-called 'Zinoviev letter' of 1924 and the General Strike of 1926 were typical of the times.[15]

One great portent for the politically orthodox was the implications of the Russian decision to quit the war in 1917. However deeply felt were the grievances of British workers against the capitalist system in the 1920s, the shock imparted by the 1914–18 war might prove of even more long-term importance. The war was the first total war; all the country's resources were mobilised for the conflict, distinctions between combatants and the rest of the population were blurred, the loss of life was unprecedented. Questions had been asked during the war, and were bound to be asked with even greater insistence as it became a memory, about the aims which war on such a scale was supposed to serve; it was evident that, in any future war of similar dimensions, ordinary people would probably not be satisfied with any war aims other than their own interests. Events in Russia in 1917 had shown that the masses, who are expected to pay the price of war, could end it if it did not serve their purposes. This could not but have far-reaching effects on all world politics. When Conservatives considered the future of the social system after 1917, they saw that it was coming to depend on its ability to offer more to the ordinary, unpropertied person than the Tsarist system had offered when the Russian soldier had decided to quit the war and go back home. Since Conservatives tended to regard Russia's new leaders as having brought about this situation, their dislike of the new regime was naturally unbounded. A century before, Tsarism had looked to the British Right like a pillar of order in Europe. Now its successor was a recipe for chaos.

Conservatives who denigrated the new order in Russia were matched by Left-wingers who saw in it the triumph of their own class, the working class. The fact that the process of building socialism involved putting democracy, free speech and a free press into cold storage for a generation or more was not too serious a consideration: the Russians themselves had never had much experience of such luxuries anyway, and for the unemployed miner in South Wales or the slum-dweller in Leeds or Glasgow in the 1920s, these liberties were small compensation for the ill-luck of having been born at the wrong end of the social register. Of course, very few who sympathised with the Left in Britain knew enough about Russia to wish, in their innermost feelings, really to change places with the Soviet worker. But there was a sense nevertheless, as bitterness about the war and its aftermath spread, that the Russians had, as Lenin said, 'grasped the next link in the chain of history', while the West was stuck fast in its tracks.

Admiration of Russia in the 1920s also involved the defence of Russia against its enemies, and since it was surrounded by enemies – the whole world was its enemy – the country tended to symbolise the defencelessness of the working class itself. In doing so, it no doubt evoked some of that feeling of 'fair play' said to be so common in the British psychology, which had worked on the side of the Turks *against* the Russians in the high noon of Victorian England: not only siding with the underdog, but searching for an underdog to side with. And, in defending Russia, the worker and his spokesman were fighting for that 'better' Britain in which his present miseries, and his feelings of humiliation, would be ended. Douglas Hyde was typical of the many hundreds of thousands of working-class men and women who, knowing practically nothing about Russia and its history, and never having visited the country, nevertheless came to regard it as their promised land:

In order to get my communist Britain [Hyde wrote] I must at all costs work to assist the continued survival of the socialist sixth of the world. Who attacks Russia attacks my hope of a communist Britain. In helping Russia 'with all the means at my disposal and at any price', therefore the British communist is working for a better Britain, the French communist for a better France . . . .. He is, in his own eyes and that of his Party, the super-patriot.[16]

The last word is significant. By an odd twist of events, the Russophile of the inter-war period, reviled by Russophobes as willing to wreck his own country for a 'pot of Moscow gold', and actually willing, in some notorious cases, to betray his own country in the 1940s and 1950s to the KGB, was also able to find, in his attitudes towards Russia, a release for his pent-up feelings of patriotism. Russia for him was the kind of homeland his own country could become if and when the worker received his rights. Marx had declared that the worker 'has no fatherland', and that might be true under capitalism. But the worker would be less than human if he did not yearn for a fatherland which he could call his own, to love and make sacrifices for.

Douglas Hyde's book, relating his conversion to and subsequent disenchantment with communism, is also revealing on account of its title, *I Believed*. Hyde began his adult life as a Methodist lay-preacher and, after quitting his job on the *Daily Worker*, entered the Catholic Church. It suggests that, in an age in which monstrous world events and the sheer pace of scientific discoveries have placed immense strain on the ordinary person's belief in God, the authoritarian ideology, such as communism, and the all-powerful institutional apparatus, such as the Soviet political regime, can exercise a certain psychological compulsion. The Soviet system, it seems, has many of the attractions of the great world religions, with the exception of the promise of a personal life after death, which in any case not all religions offer. Perhaps it was with wisdom that Marx taught that the classless society, once realised, would never die.

Russophilia in Britain in the twenties mobilised such feelings. But, in people of a different mental cast, it appealed to the desire for order, for system, for an escape from the chaos and meaninglessness rife in the after-war years. The old order of the world before 1914 was supposed to be regulated by a 'hidden hand' – the mechanism of markets and prices in economics, the gold standard and the balance of power in international relations – just as the invisible Almighty presided over the universe, like Michelangelo's Jehovah in the Sistine Chapel. But the upheavals accompanying the First World War had proved too vast for these unseen mechanisms to control, and the result was seen in the slumps, the mass unemployment, the hyper-inflation and shrinking trade of the age. Thinking men and women everywhere wanted order brought back again, and this time it would have to be in the form of conscious human intervention: there must be planning for peace and welfare, as during the awful years 1914 to 1918 there had been planning for death and destruction. Thinkers who idolised planning – people like H. G. Wells and Sidney and Beatrice Webb – went to Russia in droves to see a new civilisation being planned: they saw the future, as they put it, and it worked. Julian Huxley described Russia's five-year plans as expressing 'a new spirit, the spirit of science introduced into politics and industry'.[17] No matter that their knowledge of Russia was as scanty as their visits to it were short: no matter that, as their critics alleged, they saw in Russia what they went there to see. The fact is that, for the planners, Russia was not so much an experience which they tried to understand, but the fancied embodiment of a pre-existing aspiration. It was because they wanted a planned society, and Soviet Russia was, as from 1928, the first of the planned societies, that they fell in love with it, though the love was not always to last.

The intellectuals, as we will see more fully in the next chapter, crowded the ranks of British Russophiles in the 1920s, as well as the class-conscious militants. But there were also men of affairs, technicians, engineers, construction workers, business men and traders. British capitalists and their technologists did not all scorn the Red Empire: some of them thought of it as one of the few places where things were moving, new factories being built, bridges thrown across rivers, the earth scoured for its wealth. The old industrial revolution could be carried forward by a handful of enterprising men, the Henry Fords and Andrew Carnegies, but, as Marx said, for the scale of production which science had made possible in the twentieth century, organisation had to be of nation-wide size, and that was how things were moving in this new Russia. The business world in Britain, or at least the less blinkered members of it, began to join the pilgrimage to Utopia.

One such was Allan Monkhouse, who worked in Russia on the construction of electric power stations until 1933, when he was expelled after his conviction in the famous Metro-Vickers trial.[18] Contemptuous as Monkhouse naturally was of the Soviet legal methods from which he suffered, his admiration for the constructive achievements of the communists was unstinted:

Whatever may be the ultimate outcome of events in the USSR [he wrote in 1933], we must give the communist party authorities and the Soviet government the credit for having tackled a great problem with energy and thoroughness.

'It is my considered opinion', Monkhouse concluded, 'that the majority of the men responsible in the Kremlin are acting sincerely and in accordance with their convictions and are neither seeking personal power or self-aggrandisement'.[19]

If such laudatory statements sound strange in a well-to-do British engineer of impeccable Right-wing political views, they are no stranger than the similar admiration voiced by a Conservative Prime Minister, Harold Macmillan, during a visit to the Soviet Union in February 1959, when he said in proposing a toast:

> This is a truly constructive life work which you have undertaken. The future before the Soviet people is one of expanding horizons. Across the steppe glows the furnace of industry beckoning to a promised land. This is no mirage which you see before you. It is sober reality. The rate and quality of your progress is indeed extraordinary and – so far as I know – unparalleled in history.[20]

Mr Macmillan could have nothing but loathing for the Soviet style of politics: but no doubt, as with many other pilgrims to Russia, he was warmed by the factory furnaces which once blazed in industrial England and now seemed unaccountably forlorn. Two years before Macmillan's toast, the British press had acclaimed a Soviet triumph, the launching of the first space-satellite: 'they have beaten America to it. Nobody would try to play this achievement down'.[21] Two years later, when the first Soviet astronaut travelled in space, *The Times* gave its accolade: 'all credit then to the Russians. They have stirred the imagination as, in the fifteenth century, did the voyages of discovery by sea'.[22] Strange that Britain should admire the Russians for reminding it of its youth.

III

The pattern of Russophilia and Russophobia in Britain in the 1920s, then, was variegated: it did not quite conform to the political spectrum. With the 1930s, the lines were etched more deeply. First, the Great Slump consolidated the Right wing in defence of the status quo, as the formation of the National Government in August 1931 showed. If the world economic crisis really did suggest that the capitalist system, and parliamentary democracy which was linked with it, were in peril, there could be no doubt where the allegiance of British patriots must lie. There might be, here and there among Conservative ranks, some admiration for Continental fascists, and

their unimpressive local variety under Sir Oswald Mosley, and hence
some sympathy for their anti-Soviet campaign. But, on the whole,
British Conservative leaders, even in the 1930s, did not believe that
things had reached such a pass. Some, men like Churchill and Eden,
even thought that Russia's hand must be grasped as an ally against
the even greater evil, Hitler's Germany.

The general view on the Right was that, somehow, Britain would
ride out the storm: with careful housekeeping the economy would be
kept afloat, and, even if the old 'depressed' areas were incurable, new
industries in the south of England would take root and restore
prosperity, while, in the international field, Hitler and Mussolini
might in time come to see the folly of sabre-rattling and settle down to
the revival of international trade. Russia remained an irritant, but it
was weak and remote and perhaps, given luck, the rest of the world
could get along without it. The Right saw very little to like about
Russia and certainly nothing which the West could take as a model
for dealing with its own problems. This was Russophobia, but of a
passive, ritualistic sort.

For the Left, the slump was a great portent. It showed that, after
all, the nations had no future to look forward to except in socialism,
whatever the precise form that was to take – and, in order to know
how to get there, they could do no better than study the Soviet model.
The most glaring proof of this was the tragedy of unemployment:
three million in Britain in 1932, six million in Germany, survivors of
the holocaust of 1914–18, the litter of the scrap heaps of the times,
men without hope or a future, waiting to be swept into the next war
or the uniformed legions of the dictators. Russia, the planned society,
had no unemployed: the possibility that the unemployed in Russia
could be filling the labour camps, and not the streets, received little
consideration.

With all this was connected, by a satisfying kind of iron logic which
appealed as much to the not so well educated worker on the dole as it
did to the university don, the darkening international situation.
Perhaps the private armies of the fascists, and later the national
armies they formed when they seized power, were the Right wing's
answer to capitalist unemployment. Perhaps the war, towards which
the fascist states were plainly heading, was intended to play the
capitalists' game: by providing the arms makers with fat profits; by
disciplining the working class all over the world and moving their
thoughts from revolution to self-destruction; and by attacking and

destroying the Soviet Union.

This Left-wing analysis could not have more effectively identified the interests of the Soviet Union with those of the unpropertied masses. The Soviet Union had raised itself from nothing in 1917 to a powerful state in which the needs and interests of workers by hand and brain came first. It had done so in the teeth of opposition and threats from capitalist states which had conspicuously failed to utilise their resources for the common good. The Soviet Union had no interest in war: all its energies since 1917 had been devoted to socialist construction. On the contrary, it was now calling for a front among all freedom-loving people against the real threat to peace and democracy, the fascist states, which left no doubt in anyone's mind that they meant to go to war and were making ready their people for it by every means. If the ordinary person did not, in these cicumstances, see in Stalin's Russia his most effective form of defence, he must be blinded by prejudice.

There were not lacking skilled and learned writers to provide the intellectual foundations for this argument. Russophilia, in those days of Nazi Germany's ascent to dominance in Europe, was not only emotionally satisfying to those who shared it: it had a solid, almost unassailable, intellectual content and theoreticians, British and foreign, of the highest distinction to deploy it. The list of prominent British Russophiles of the 1930s reads like a *Who's Who* of the brightest and the best: natural scientists, artists, historians, students of politics, economics, law – the company was as diverse as it was talented. It was almost impossible to be well educated in Britain of the 1930s without being, at the very least, an admirer of Russia.

One of the most prolific and persuasive tutors of the Russophiles was Harold Laski, so well known that in the thirties and forties his name was, in the British mind, almost synonymous with that of the London School of Economics, where he was a professor of political science. Laski combined a flair for sweeping generalisations with a lack of any really specialised knowledge about Russia; this led him to declare in 1934 that 'there has been far more realisation of personality under the Soviet regime than in any comparable period of history'. In Russia, he reported, he had found 'a buoyant and optimistic faith I have never before encountered'.[23] But Laski, like the millions whom he influenced, did not really need to know Russia in order to have strong feelings about it. It was sufficient that the name 'Russia' stood for the opposite of the 'capitalist system', the demise of which he considered to be imminent. Lecturing in 1943, he said:

> The war of 1914 and the present war make it obvious that capitalism has reached the end of its period of expansion. Its economic consequences are therefore in direct contradiction with the ends which political democracy seeks to achieve. And, while this is so, the Soviet Union provides a capacity for expansion which makes its principles a challenge to capitalist societies: the greater, moreover, the security of its international position, the more profound that challenge is likely to be.[24]

The difficulty, of course, about basing admiration for another country on convictions about the approaching demise of the system prevailing in one's own is that, once that system changes, or the conviction withers, the admiration is likely to wither, too.

This genuflection before Russia and the Soviet system suffered a shock with the Nazi-Soviet pact of August 1939 and Stalin's subsequent annexation of the Baltic states and eastern Poland. The attempt by British communists to write off Britain's struggle with Nazi Germany as an 'imperialist' war made little sense to the island race and the expected chorus of rage swelled when the Russians attacked Finland in November 1939. But perhaps the lingering Russophilia in Britain of the 1930s was still too affected by sheer bewilderment to turn into its opposite. If so, it never had the chance to do so in view of the overwhelming adulation of Russia which swept over Britain and the rest of the world following Hitler's attack on that country on 22 June 1941.

With Russia's entry into the war on the same side as Britain, Russophobia for all practical purposes ceased to exist. Criticism of the USSR became tantamount to treason. All the partisans of the Soviet state, including the communists and fellow-travellers, who had had the painful task of defending Stalin during his period of friendship with Hitler, were now taken into the bosom of the community and welcomed everywhere as experts on the new ally. Lord Beaverbrook, who resigned from the government in February 1942 in order to campaign for the Second Front in Europe as a means of assisting Russia, described communism under Stalin as having 'won the applause and admiration of all the Western nations'.[25] The government became concerned lest admiration for Russia encourage support for the communist party: its membership, about 12,000 in 1941, shot up to 65,000 in 1942. The Prime Minister, Churchill, asked the Ministry of Information 'to consider what action was required to counter the present tendency of the British public to forget the dangers of communism in their enthusiasm over the resistance of Russia'.[26]

It was not merely that the Russians were applauded to the skies as heroes, and, along with that, went not a little relief that, so long as they held out, Hitler's wrath was diverted from Britain. But, as the war went on and the German invaders took their punishment, the idea inevitably crept back that the Soviet social and economic system must be far in advance of the West's, as the Russophiles had always contended. Soviet education, social and medical services, the place of Soviet women in society, the rights of national and other minorities, the distribution of wealth and income, Soviet housing, trade unions, the press, were all re-examined and lectured upon and their strong points noted. Even the well-known purges of the 1930s, which had done so much to reduce Russophilia in Britain, were found to have been right after all, since, without them, Russia – if it was not heresy to breathe such an idea – might have gone the way of France or Norway in 1940. But perhaps the most important thing about this wartime Russophilia was that it combined a patriotism as authentic as the Union Jack with the welfare-state thinking of the Beveridge Report. Just as the Russians fought for their country the more heroically because it *was* their country and vindicated their rights, so the British, standing up to air raids and trouncing Rommel in North Africa, were, this time, really fighting for a land fit for heroes, and were doing so *because* of their partnership with Russia, which already was such a land. The Anglo-Soviet treaty of 1942 was in fact the guarantee that the promises of wartime would not be dishonoured.

It was possibly because of this intermingling of Russophilia with British patriotism that young, well-to-do and highly educated men and women at the old universities felt no compunction about betraying state secrets to the KGB when they entered government service in such large numbers during and just before the war. It was not so much that men like Anthony Blunt, Guy Burgess, Donald Maclean and Kim Philby sold their country when their masters in Moscow told them to because they were drunk on communism. The truth perhaps was that they found in service to Moscow a more genuine kind of patriotism than that to which they were used. The old country which they had loved had been taken over by traitors, in the Marxist world-view, by capitalist exploiters and their henchmen. If it was to be liberated, as Stalin liberated Russia and Tito Yugoslavia from fascist conquerors, the old patriotism must be temporarily renounced. It is only on some such assumption that we can explain how the hundreds of thousands of young men and women who had been, if not exactly communists, adulators of the Soviet system in the 1930s, fought like tigers in defence of their country when war came. They did so no doubt partly because it was allied with the Soviet Union.

In the 1980s it is impossible not to regret that the pendulum swung so far in Russia's favour as it did between 1941 and 1945. In itself, Russia's heroic defence against Germany is not evidence of the greater acceptability of the Soviet system, or even perhaps of its greater efficiency. The Russians certainly fought well, but this is not uncommon in their history: they fought heroically for three bitter years during the First World War. Moreover, other factors than Soviet efficiency contributed to Germany's defeat, such as the vast size of the Russian land, its vicious winters and the almost inexhaustible manpower of Russia, thrown into the furnace with little regard for the losses. If fighting capacity is to be reckoned as an index of a nation's political or social advancement, we have to explain how Germany under Hitler was numbered one of the world's greatest military forces.

If Russia's wartime achievements had not been so readily interpreted in Britain as evidence of a social system of superhuman excellence, the revelation, after the war, that there *was* a dark side to the Russian moon might not have come as such a shock. If the god failed in the years after the war, perhaps the British, who for a few years turned a human people into a god, had only themselves to blame. Evidence of the lengths to which admirers of the Soviet Union went to place that country on a pinnacle of excellence owing to its exploits during the war is seen, for example, in the writings of the historian, E. H. Carr. In *The Soviet Impact on the Western World*, published in 1946 and consisting of six lectures given at Oxford, Carr twists contemporary history in all directions in order to show that the Soviet way is the way of the future. Soviet democracy is the only true democracy because, though the 'broad lines of Soviet policy may be dictated from the centre', the Soviet Union 'has never ignored the human element or underestimated the extent to which the execution of any policy depends on the enthusiasm or initiative of the individual citizen'. Strikes are 'meaningless' in a socialist state because there is no capitalist class to strike against. Carr continues with remarkable credulity: 'there does not appear to be any record of a strike in the Soviet Union for many years past . . . . In this respect the world is travelling far more rapidly than most people yet realise along the Soviet path'. Russia has a reputation for taking over small countries, but, says Carr, that is the way of progress: 'the smaller nations can no longer remain . . . neutral and remote from the decisive currents of international affairs. Sooner or later they will be drawn into the orbit of one or other of the Great Powers'. 'The choice before Britain . . .' the deadly exegesis unwinds. Russia is totalitarian, and Russia succeeded in the war: therefore, 'all but the blind and the incurable' must realise that 'the forces of individualism have somehow lost their potency and their relevance in the contemporary world'.[27] With champions like this to defend her, the stock of Russia in Britain was bound to fall as soon as the Axis Powers were defeated.

Disenchantment was not long in coming. Russia's imposition of regimes of its own choosing in one country after another in eastern Europe, culminating in the fall of Czechoslovakia in February 1948, almost ten years after Munich; Stalin's orders to western communist parties to fight against economic recovery under the Marshall Plan; his brutal pressure against west Berlin during the year of the airlift; the Soviet-countenanced attack on South Korea in June 1950, making Stalin look like Mussolini, the conqueror of Ethiopia, in the year of the League's demise, 1935; above all, the savage Soviet assault on Hungary in 1956 and on Czechoslovakia, for the second time, in 1968: one horror after another dissipated the image the British had of the Russians as the Second World War ended. After the fall of Czechoslovakia in 1948 the Labour party became reconciled to an alliance with the world's greatest capitalist power, the United States, though its more Left-wing members continued to speak up for the Soviet Union whenever there was a shred of a case for doing so.[28]

The alarming thing was, as the Cold War eroded piece by piece the Russophilia of the war years, that fear of Russian expansionism into Asia and Africa began to revive, with its reminiscence of the nineteenth century. Russia's war of nerves against Turkey immediately the war ended; its delay in withdrawing troops from

Iran, coupled with the suggestion of a Kremlin plan to form a
separate state in Azerbaijan; and, most recently, the Soviet incursion
into Afghanistan in December 1979, with worrying implications for
security in the Gulf and the West's supply of oil from the Middle
East: from such incidents even British people sympathetic to Russia
were left to draw conclusions not dissimilar from those drawn by their
great-grandfathers about the Bear's movements towards India. *The
Daily Telegraph* spoke of Russia's 'global designs'.[29] *The Times*
described the Afghanistan incursion as being 'in the long tradition of
expansion southwards towards warm water', though it added that
Russia's action seemed more like 'an act of defensive aggression'
than naked expansion.[30] The *Guardian* was less worried, seeing
Afghanistan as 'a mixture of one-off military adventurism and
political blunder'.[31] But the general reaction was one of concern.

There were ways, too, in which the less sophisticated and less well-
informed began to think again about Russia as the Great Patriotic
War receded into history. A disturbing incident occurred in 1946,
when British servicemen who had married local women in Russia
during the war found to their astonishment that their wives were not
allowed to come back to Britain with them when the war was over.
The number of women concerned was small, not more than thirty,
and their fate could hardly compare with great questions like the
problem of Germany or international control of the atomic bomb.
Yet it is arguable that the affair of the Russian wives did more than
many great diplomatic wrangles to turn British sympathies away
from the Soviet state after the war. Nor is this remarkable. The
pointless cruelty shown by the Soviet authorities in refusing
permission to a few harmless women to leave the country, as though
the security or prestige of that vast super-Power could be damaged by
their going, was, after all, indicative of how the rulers of that state
regard the human beings who are in their charge. The wife of
Douglas Hyde, a veteran supporter of the communist cause, once
gave vent to anger at the brutal stubbornness the Russians knew so
well how to dole out in those years: after listening to the news one
evening, she cried: 'I'm sick of old Molotov saying No, No, No, the
whole of the time. And I'm utterly fed up with Russia's behaviour
since the end of the war!'[32]

Sometimes one wishes that the makers of Soviet external policy
were able to understand how, by sheer lack of imagination, they
damage their own cause by infuriating the very people in the outside

world who are doing their best to help them. Perhaps to a determinist, like a Marxist, the goodwill of other people is unimportant: only the iron laws of history matter. And yet the Russians obviously do go to a great deal of trouble, in other ways, to win other people's respect and credence.

IV

The wheel has come full circle. The fear and mistrust of Russia which characterised British opinion in the nineteenth century, and which could at times reach fever pitch, has returned, it seems, to dominate the field. Its focus seems much the same as in the last century: the Russian tradition of governmental despotism, the secret police, the suppression of dissent, the centralised control of opinion, all accompanied externally by the old territorial expansion, the drive to the high seas, the subversion and domination of smaller states which stand in the way. Remnants of the Russophilia of the thirties and forties linger in the form of continuing respect for Russia's scientific and technological skills, its educational achievements in those fields, its ability to mobilise a marvellously gifted and patriotic people for its national ends. But as 'the worker's paradise', or as one of the world's most advanced social systems, the Soviet Union no longer warrants a mention in Britain. In some respects, this may be due to the very success of the Soviet argument, as its spokesmen in this country have mediated it. In the last 40 years or so, British society has become more compassionate and considerate: the losers in life's race are not so apt to be ignored by the rest as they once were. The stimulus provided by the Soviet model to those who worked with this end in view served its purpose.

Yet, despite the coldness towards Russia which the strains of East–West relations since 1945 engendered, it is probably true to say that the mass of British people still retain much respect for the Soviet state and are not wholly convinced by the harsh words directed by their own leaders and mass media against it. Words used by people questioned in Mass Observation surveys after the signature of the Nazi-Soviet pact in 1939 have their echo today: 'you never know with Russia: she's a dark horse. I still believe she'll come in on our side'. Tom Harrison, the Mass Observation expert, wrote in 1941 that ordinary people 'have preserved a respect, if not regard, for Russia and have shown considerable scepticism as regards the news and views about Russia which have generally been available'.[33]

Perhaps, along with the deeper mistrust of Soviet leaders which has come with the years, that still represents the attitude of large numbers of people in Britain. 'People hope that America will change', Mass Observation reported in 1948, 'but are not greatly expecting it. They expect Russia to change, but are slowly becoming accustomed not to hope for it'.[34] They have become even more accustomed in the intervening years. It is probably still true to say, however, that if the Soviet government were to take the lead with definite proposals for the improvement of East–West relations, the genuineness of which was not so obviously in doubt as super-Power proposals so often are, there would be a readiness in Britain to listen, and an impatience with those who dismissed such an offer as propaganda. The Soviet Union, in short, still seems to have a reservoir of goodwill in Britain, working on its behalf and waiting to be tapped. Unfortunately, history since the war seems to have shown that Russia's leaders either care little about that goodwill or have practically no skill in appealing to it.

7. Russia and the Intellectuals

THE interest aroused by the Russian Revolution in British intellectuals (that is, those who spend their lives in creating and developing ideas and in artistic expression) is not surprising. It was the same with the French Revolution of 1789: writers like Shelley, Swinburne, Wordsworth acclaimed the fall of the Bastille as opening a new door on the future of mankind. To Bertrand Russell, one of the first Western thinkers to grasp the significance of the events of 1917, the Russian convulsion had an even greater meaning. The revolution, he wrote in 1920:

> is one of the great heroic events in the world's history. It is natural to compare it with the French Revolution, but it is in fact of even more importance. It does more to change daily life and the structure of society; it also does more to change man's beliefs . . . Bolshevism combines the characteristics of the French Revolution with those of the rise of Islam; and the result is something radically new, which can only be understood by a patient and passionate effort of the imagination.[1]

That Russell, the advocate of reason in politics, should speak of the need for passion in understanding what had happened in Russia shows how deeply the revolution stirred the hearts as well as the minds of British thinkers.

In the first years after their seizure of power, the sheer defiance and incorruptibility of the Bolsheviks caught the admiration of people like H. G. Wells, who went to see for himself in September 1920 and received an impression of a 'vast, irreparable breakdown', yet one from which only the Bolsheviks stood any chance of rescuing the country:

The Bolsheviks [Wells wrote] albeit numbering less than five per cent of the population, have been able to seize and retain power in Russia because they were and are the only body of people in this vast spectacle of Russian ruin with a common faith and a common spirit. I disbelieve in their faith, I ridicule Marx, their prophet, but I understand and respect their spirit. They are – with all their faults, and they have abundant faults – the only possible backbone now to a renascent Russia.[2]

Wells returned home with the conclusion which, if it had been adopted by Western governments, would have made later relations with Russia less fraught with disaster: 'there is only one being in Russia with whom the Western world can deal and that is the Bolshevik Government itself'.[3]

Wells emphasised the capacity of the Leninists to afford hope for the future, and that was a powerful reason for the admiration of many intellectuals. For British, as for many continental European and American writers, Russia in the 1920s came to represent that ancient and persistent vision, Utopia, the revolt from the present and yearning for a lost happiness. 'The revolutionary's Utopia', wrote Arthur Koestler, who was a member of the German communist party in the 1930s, 'which in appearance represents a complete break with the past, is always modelled on some image of the lost paradise of a legendary Golden Age'.[4] The lost paradise symbolised the sense of despair with the present, the feeling of nullity and disintegration which came with the end of the First World War. 'The war', wrote Bertrand Russell in his book on Bolshevism, 'has left throughout Europe a mood of disillusionment and despair which calls aloud for a new religion, as the only force capable of giving man the energy to live vigorously'. 'Bolshevism', he went on, 'has supplied the new religion'. Because, according to Russell, 'the present holders of power are evil men and the present manner of life is doomed', what was needed was hope, and 'the chief thing that the Bolsheviks have done is to create a hope or at any rate to make strong and widespread a hope which was formerly confined to the few'.[5]

Bertrand Russell was astute enough to realise – which many later Western admirers of the Soviet system failed to appreciate – that much of the attraction of the Russian Revolution to outsiders was that it satisfied one of the emotional needs of the time; but that need often had little to do with the actual problems the Bolsheviks were facing in their own country and the inhuman methods they were driven to adopt to overcome them. 'The effect of Bolshevism as a revolutionary life', he wrote, 'is greater outside Russia than within the Soviet Republic':

> Grim realities have done much to kill hope among those who are subject to the dictatorship of Moscow. Yet even within Russia, the communist party, in whose hands all political power is concentrated, still lives by hope, though the pressure of events has made the hope severe and stern and somewhat remote.[6]

Having seen communist methods at close hand and judged them 'rough and dangerous' and Bolshevik policy 'too heroic to count the cost of the opposition it arouses', Russell concluded that he could not support any movement which aimed at world revolution. Nevertheless, the dilemma remained for all who pondered the meaning of the Russian Revolution: how to move from the intolerable present back to the lost paradise without falling under a despotism at least as intolerable in the process.

But the heroic quality of the communist effort to make a new world continued to have its attractions for the trickle of British visitors who paid the then still unfashionable visit to Russia in the 1920s. Most of them were all too well aware of the tragic self-destructiveness shown by the capitalist world during the war and the return to 'poverty in the midst of plenty' after it. One such was Arthur Ransome, the British writer, who published a favourable report in his *Six Weeks in Russia in 1919*. He bore witness to an immense social transformation. He visited the theatre, for example, and saw it no longer filled with bejewelled elegance, but with lean and shabby workers and soldiers. A Russian performance of Saint-Saens's *Samson and Delilah* was symbolic:

> Samson's stirring up of the Israelites reminded me of many scenes in Petrograd in 1917, and when, at last, he brings the temple down in ruins on his triumphant enemy, I was reminded of the words attributed to Trotsky: 'if we are in the end forced to go, we shall slam the door behind us in a way that the echo will be felt throughout the world'.[7]

'Bringing the temple down in ruins' was not an entirely unwelcome idea for sensitive spirits who had lived through the agony and misery of the Great War. The revolution in Russia could be read as a sign that the human race could rise from all that and live again.

An agency which brought British writers and educators more into contact with the Soviet regime was the Society for Cultural Relations with the USSR, founded in 1924. Its first president was the sociologist, L. T. Hobhouse, followed by the poet and critic, Lascelles Abercrombie. Their names, and those of the first two vice-presidents, J. M. Keynes and H. G. Wells, are indicative of the place in the highest reaches of British intellectual society which the Soviet Union was beginning to win for itself. With the establishment of diplomatic relations between Britain and the Soviet state in 1924, opportunities for British people to go and see for themselves multiplied. Inevitably, it was the already sympathetic who tended to take these opportunities; in fact, making the pilgrimage to Moscow soon became *de rigeur* for the British intellectual or social reformer. Equally inevitably, their necessarily short visits generally served the purpose of confirming their existing views.

Malcolm Muggeridge, for all his socialist leanings, was too sensible to be captivated by this intellectualist tourism. Writing in 1940 – when the Soviet Union was under a cloud with British public opinion – he makes fun of the antics of the inter-war flow of visitors to the 'Worker's Paradise':

> Their delight in all they saw and the expression they gave to this delight, constituted unquestionably one of the wonders of the age. These earnest advocates of the humane killing of cattle who looked up at the massive headquarters of the OGPU with tears of gratitude in their eyes, earnest advocates of proportional representation who eagerly assented when the necessity for the Dictatorship of the Proletariat was explained to them, earnest clergymen who walked reverently through anti-God museums and reverently turned over the pages of atheistic literature, earnest pacifists who watched delightedly tanks rattle across the Red Square and bombing planes darken the sky, earnest town-planning specialists who stood outside overcrowded, ramshackle tenements and muttered: 'if only we had something like this in England'.[8]

The appetite of the intellectuals for things communist, or, better still, Soviet communist, grew to a lust in the 1930s. The 1930s has been called the Pink Decade, but the colour should more properly have been somewhat darker.

The three great developments which propelled thinkers, artists and writers from their inner worlds into the vortex of social forces were the economic slump with its massive unemployment, the advent of fascism seen at its brutal worst in the Italian attack on Abyssinia in 1935 and on the Spanish republic in 1936, and, as the decade wore on, the approach of war, prophesied as far more terrible than the one which seemed only just ended. The intellectual could hardly escape some form of social or political commitment, though many did, and, since the Soviet Union had evidently solved the unemployment problem, was bitterly opposed to fascism, and consistently called for a united front to resist fascist aggression and the drift back to war, it was almost equally impossible for the intellectual not to move to Moscow's side. If he had been born in the working class, this was obvious enough. But if, like most professional intellectual workers in Britain at the time, his economic position was more secure, the mere fact that it was became an even stronger source of his sympathy for the Left. Koestler, relating in the 1950s the path of his own conversion to communism, emphasised the role of guilt, perhaps even more important to a generation reared on Freudian theory. 'Every contact with people poorer than myself was unbearable', he relates, 'the boy at school who had no gloves and red chilblains on his fingers, the former travelling salesman of my father's reduced to cadging occasional meals – all of them were additions to the load of guilt on my back'.[9]

Hence, according to the poet, Stephen Spender, 'from 1931 onwards, in common with many other people, I felt hounded by external events. There was ever-increasing unemployment in America, Great Britain and on the Continent. The old world seemed incapable of solving its problems and out of the disorder Fascist regimes were rising'. Seemingly without realising it, Spender touches upon the essential ephemerality of the intellectual's obsession with social questions at that time, and hence with Marxism and the Soviet Union, by differentiating it from the characteristically inward world of the artist and thinker, now condemned by the Soviet authorities: 'perhaps, after all, the qualities which distinguished us from the writers of the previous decade lay not in ourselves, but in the events to which we reacted. These were unemployment, economic crisis, nascent fascism, approaching war'.[10] What, however, when these problems disappeared, or were superseded by those arising from the practices of the Soviet Union itself?

The list of admirers of the Soviet system glitters with the names of leading publicists in Britain during the Pink Decade: political writers and reformers, like Sidney and Beatrice Webb, G. D. H. and Margaret Cole, Harold Laski and John Strachey; men of letters such as Bernard Shaw, Spender and C. Day Lewis; and scientists of the standing of J. D. Bernal and J. B. S. Haldane. But there were exceptions: J. B. Priestley, for all his concern with social problems, never really joined the Russian bandwaggon, nor did Aldous Huxley, Arnold Bennett or T. S. Eliot. Many writers, notably Wyndham Lewis, inclined towards the other end of the political spectrum.[11] It should be remembered, too, that the intellectual in Britain, unlike his counterpart in France or Italy, for instance, has never enjoyed a place of highest esteem in the community; even parties and other political groups on the Left were never dominated by intellectuals to anywhere near the same extent as their opposite numbers in continental Europe. Nevertheless, that the Soviet cause should have captured such a substantial slice of the British intellectual élite was remarkable, especially when one recalls the hostility of most of the country's political leaders towards Soviet Russia at that time. Later, members of that élite could not understand exactly what the attraction had been: Koestler, who became a British subject during the Second World War, represents the lot of a communist in the 1930s as being one which no intelligent person could tolerate in the symposium *The God that Failed* (1950). Yet he remained a party member for seven years (1931–1938).

The Left-wing intellectual tended to glorify the working man, or rather his own image of the working man. At Oxbridge in the thirties well-to-do undergraduates pretended to have uncles who were miners, and wore corduroy trousers tied below the knee with string, like navvies. But they had little contact with the working class, and the workers, on their side, could not afford to visit Russia and did not flock to join the communist party. Their most active organisations, the trade unions, were highly suspicions of communism and discouraged their members from joining the party. The 'Black Circular' issued by the TUC in 1934 prohibited trades councils from accepting communist delegates and urged that communists should be excluded from any trade union office.

However much British intellectuals, as Spender points out, were actuated in those times by external events rather than internal experiences, their separation from the ordinary workers in the country around them could not have been more complete. No doubt it was because they shared such an utterly unreal image of the worker that the Soviet Union, conceived as the worker's state, assumed the place in their thinking that it did. Spender describes in his autobiography the 'literary social life' he lived in the 1930s, consisting of 'week-end parties, luncheons, dinners, teas'. The working man occupied no prominent place in this 'manner of living in which whole days were wasted'. In London, he explains, 'it often takes an hour to get to a luncheon, which perhaps lasts till 3.30. It then takes an hour to return home and at 6.30 you may have to leave again for a dinner engagement'.[12] When at last the poet did encounter working-class people during the Second World War, he was disgusted by them: they were 'as petty, grabbing, malicious, self-seeking, irresponsible, prejudiced, as members of any other class'. 'I am sure', he writes, rather confusingly, 'it is wrong to assume that proletarian virtues will inevitably remain with the poor when they are no longer oppressed'.[13]

How remote some of the big names of the times were, not only from the real situation in the Soviet Union, but from the lives and thinking of the ordinary people around them, is well shown in the experience of Sidney and Beatrice Webb, who fell under the spell of Sovietism in their seventies, after a lifetime of social investigation and public service. On 7 May 1932, the Webbs, 'with a draft of their foregone conclusions safely stowed in their luggage', set out for a three-week visit to the Soviet state, their combined ages being 147.[14] Their infatuation with the Soviet system knew no bounds; all sense of reality seemed cast aside. On one occasion, the then leader of the Labour party, Arthur Henderson, mildly protested, at which Beatrice reacted 'by wildly dancing to the strains of the *Internationale* in defiance'.[15] It was like a love affair in which reason is equally abandoned. Beatrice wrote of it that 'old people often fall in love in extraordinary and ridiculous ways – with their chauffeurs, for example: we feel it more dignified to have fallen in love with Soviet Communism'.[16] It was just like the Webbs to take it as a matter of course that falling in love with the chauffeur was undignified and ridiculous.

The book which issued from their labours in 1935 – the year when the great purges began in Russia following the murder of Kirov on 1 December 1934 – was called *Soviet Communism. A New Civilisation?*

The question mark was omitted from the Russian translation and from the second English edition, which appeared two years later. The book is massive, two volumes of 1174 pages, written in the colourless Royal Commission prose of the Webbs. It is also 'extraordinary and ridiculous': extraordinary, for these high priests of social research, because based on no considerable prior knowledge of this vast and baffling country, and on no other sources than those provided by the official Soviet authorities, which are reproduced uncritically; ridiculous because accepting at their face value all that Soviet agencies reported about their own system. Some indication of the value of this vast tome is provided by the Webbs' flat statement that 'it is a distinctive feature of the social arrangements of the Soviet Union that, to a degree unparalleled elsewhere, they provide for every person, irrespective of wealth or position, sex or race, the poorest and the weakest, as well as those who are "better off", in all cases equality of opportunity for the children and adolescents, and, increasingly, also a common and ever-rising standard of living for the whole population'.[17] The same theme is projected throughout the book and, as in official Soviet publicity, no evidence to the contrary is entertained.

Strangely enough, Mrs Webb had not always been so credulous. After listening to a lecture by Krassin in 1920, for instance, she had confided to her diary that

> One is tempted to wonder whether this creed does not consist almost entirely in an insistent demand for the subordination of each individual to the 'working plan' of the scientifically trained mind of the expert.[18]

On the other hand, it was perhaps precisely that aspect of the Soviet creed that later appealed to the Webbs, when their dedication to the planned society was complete.

It is true that, with the trials and purges in Russia in the mid-30s, Beatrice's doubts grew. Asked to write an article on the Soviet Union for the *Anglo-Soviet Journal* just before war broke out in 1939, she used the expression 'the disease of orthodoxy' to characterise Soviet society and refused to delete it when the editors objected. The offending phrase was incorporated in a new edition of *Soviet Communism* in 1941. There is evidence, too, of Mrs Webb's second thoughts about the

Soviet system in the remark she reputedly made about her nephew Malcolm Muggeridge's disillusion with the USSR: 'why did he imagine he would like Soviet Russia? He ought to have smelt a rat and carefully avoided discovering its stinking body'.[19] For all that, *Soviet Communism* remains impressive testimony to the emotional power aroused by the Soviet system in some of the most highly intelligent British people when faith in their own society crumbled. One is reminded of the distinction drawn by the American writer, Gabriel Almond, in his book *The Appeals of Communism* between two kinds of communists or fellow-travellers in the West: the militant who is a communist owing to genuine belief in the truth of the Marxist doctrine, on which he may be something of an expert, and the alienated person, who migrates to communism owing to disenchantment with the standards and practices of his own society.[20] The Webbs, like so many other intellectual workers in the West who experienced the seductions of Moscow, seemed to fall into the latter rather than the former group.

Stephen Spender's *Forward from Liberalism*, published in 1937, when the Spanish civil war, the struggle to keep alive the hope of a better future, was at its height, argued that there was no conflict between individualism and the Soviet-type system, simply because the freedom of the individual was already being crushed, or threatened with being crushed, in the capitalist state. 'To go forward', Spender wrote:

> The masses must be given, not merely political, but also economic freedom, so that they may produce their own free individuality and their own culture. The future of individualism lies in the classless society. For this reason, the social revolution is as urgent a problem for the individualist as it is for the worker: he must break down big artificial barriers and join the worker in building a new civilisation.[21]

Accordingly, *Forward from Liberalism* reads, or much of it does, like a paean of praise for the new order of Russia, with only occasional twinges of doubt about Stalinite repression. 'Since I wrote these pages', Spender adds to his book by way of postscript, 'the execution of Zinoviev and his fellow Trotskyists has taken place'. This trial, Spender glumly continues, 'emphasises the fact that unless the democratic constitution is quickly introduced, there must be many more such trials'. There follows a sentence tinged with a certain despair: 'if criticism in Russia is not to become a pernicious disease, it must be legalised'.[22]

But would it ever be? That was the question. Some evaded it by contending that the repression of opposition in the Soviet state was hardly worse than the brutality of capitalist society, and that it had at least the merit of being directed towards social justice and the ending of human misery. They employed the image of violence in the redress of wrong, the analogy with the surgeon's knife. In a birthday tribute to Christopher Isherwood, W. H. Auden encouraged him to:

> Reveal the squalid shadow of academy and garden,
> Make action urgent and its nature clear.[23]

C. Day Lewis echoed the same message in his strictures on the uncaring rich:

> At bay in villas from blood relations
> Counters of spoons and content with cushions
> They pray for peace, they hand down disaster . . .
> It is now or never, the hour of the knife,
> The break with the past, the major operation.[24]

By a strange turn of events, the Left cause, originating in revolt against the drift to war which was so endemic in the 1930s, also gave a certain satisfaction to the interest in violence, which, according to the prophet of the times, Freud, lurks in all of us. At the same time, violence was made acceptable to the pacifically inclined intellectual by being yoked to the struggle for social betterment.

The question of how to step from the drift to disaster inherent in the capitalist scheme of things to the new society of the common man – whether through violent revolution or parliamentary change – perplexed the pre-war generation of thinkers and their answers varied. Many wondered whether there was time for the process of peaceful change to work itself out – time, that is, before the war catastrophe overwhelmed the world, as few as that time doubted that it would. John Strachey, a leading force on the Left, though he never actually joined the communist party, believed that the socialist system was not only inevitable, though it would have to be fought for, but would be a far higher form of democracy than anything the West had so far known. Moreover, Western countries, Strachey contended in *The Theory and Practice of Socialism*, published in 1936, should be able to carry Marxist socialism to more advanced levels than the Soviet Union itself:

> When the British and American peoples establish institutions as democratic as those of the Soviet Union, their peoples should be able to develop an all-pervasive system of genuine self-government even more rapidly than have the Russians.[25]

Of one thing, however, Strachey was confident, and that was that Russia needed no expansion. Her socialist economy, he explained, 'with its ability to sell internally every single good it can produce, frees her from any need whatever for imperialist expansion'. For Strachey, however, as for so many other British Marxists of the thirties, that optimism gave way before Russia's palpable expansionism of the early war years. Ironically, when the Labour government was formed in 1945, Strachey, after first serving as Minister of Food, became Minister for War at the time of Britain's greatest rearmament drive in its peace-time history, inspired by fear of Soviet expansion.

Harold Laski, whom we have mentioned in the previous chapter as embodying some of the traits of the British Russophile, was Marxist in accepting class conflict as a basic force in history, though his attitude towards violent revolution was always ambiguous. He was much impressed by the fragility of parliamentary democracy in the capitalist state. When, according to the Marxist prognosis, capitalists feel the pressure of shrinking foreign markets and investment opportunities abroad, and at the same time the demands of their own workers for expanded welfare, they do not scruple to shut down the democratic system, either by calling in the strong man, as had happened in the fascist states on the continent, or by united opposition to any further social progress, as happened with the formation of the National government in Britain in 1931. 'No ruling class ever abdicates voluntarily' was Laski's *leit motif*. In the ensuing conflict between capitalist states making their last stand in the form of fascism and the surviving democracies like Britain and France, the Soviet Union was democracy's natural ally.

Laski's first reaction to Soviet Communism was mixed. In his *Communism*, published in 1927, he called the Bolshevik seizure of power the 'greatest event in history since the Reformation', but could not acquit the Soviet regime of terrorism, though he admitted that 'no party could have wrought order from this chaos' without methods which savoured of terrorism.[26] Laski visited the Soviet Union in 1934, returning as an admirer of Soviet law; his pamphlet on Soviet justice, Law and Justice in Soviet Russia, published in 1935, pleaded that British judicial practice had much to learn from Russia, though the preface frankly admitted that there was no reference to the OGPU, 'because I know nothing at first hand'.[27] In 1936, with the rise of fascism in Europe, Laski abandoned his opposition to Labour party co-operation with the communists and called for a popular front with them.

In 1939, like Strachey and many thousands more, Laski withdrew his support from Russia as a consequence of the Nazi-Soviet pact, but but the influence of the Soviet state continued to be strong with him. In 1943, he urged the Labour party to nationalise the 'commanding heights of the economy', a phrase which Lenin had introduced into the vocabulary of socialism. After the Second World War, he made himself one of the most trenchant critics of Bevin's policy of linking Britain with the United States in collective defence against Russia. In an article published in October 1947 he charged the Western system with responsibility for the Cold War owing to its inability to find markets at home to employ its full productive capacity because of the capitalist structure of social relations.[28]

Laski and Strachey, together with the publisher Victor Gollancz, were the driving forces behind the publishing venture which became the essential symbol of British support for the Soviet Union and the struggle against the capitalist evils of the day, the Left Book Club. The LBC was founded by Gollancz in May 1936 with the object of producing a series of books, which members received monthly and for which they paid a small fee, dealing with the 'three closely related questions of fascism, the threat of war and poverty, aiming at effective resistance to the first, the prevention of the second and socialism as the cure of the third'.[29] The books were selected by Gollancz, Laski and Strachey. In 1939 membership reached a peak of 57,000; in addition, no less than 1500 discussion groups had been organised up and down the country. The club extended its activities into drama with the formation of the LBC Theatre Guild and had its own periodical, Left News. There was even a Christian Book Club formed, edited by the 'Red' Dean of Canterbury, the Rev. Hewlett

Johnson, though for some reason it never flourished.

In all, the LBC produced 44 books, most of which were directed towards stimulating support for the Popular Front. It effectively died in the Second World War, another victim of the Nazi–Soviet pact and the communist effort to denigrate the war against Hitler. The club was only one of the intellectual forces of the times working for an alliance with Russia as the only effective opposition against Nazism, but its success was phenomenal. It was Russia's most influential line of communication with intellectual circles in Britain. 'At this time', wrote the organiser of the LBC's discussion groups in his account of the club, 'the tide of intelligent opinion was running our way . . . we were the voice of the times, as far as the fear of, and the anger at, fascism was concerned, as far as the passionate desire for peace and a more humane future for society was concerned'.[30] Nor did the LBC draw its support only from the committed Left; the welcome given to the idea of co-operation with Stalin against Hitler was broadly based: Lord Cecil, Duncan Sandys, Wilson Harris of the *Spectator*, Dingle Foot, Sir Arthur Salter, the Liberals – Sir Archibald Sinclair, Gilbert Murray, Sir Walter Layton – such names were included in the 'considerable body of opinion which held that both our safety and that of Russia was dependent upon the participation of Russia in a firm declaration of military action against further aggression'.[31] The agreement signed by the Soviet and German Foreign Ministers in August 1939 proved the grave of it all.

There were two other intellectual sources of sympathy for the Soviet cause in Britain in that day, and the fact that there was some incompatibility between them shows how widespread that sympathy was. One was science and the other religion, even though science, like everything else in the Soviet Union, was firmly subordinated to the interests of the state, as interpreted by the ruling communist party, and even though the Soviet state, while not precisely persecuting religion, was officially atheistic and sought by every means to downgrade religion. Again, it is evidence of the compulsive attraction exerted by the Soviet cause on highly intelligent British scientists and religious leaders that these evident disqualifications of the Soviet Union for winning their support did not in fact much discourage them.

The mere fact that the Bolsheviks wrenched Russia away from the obscurantism of the Orthodox Church under the Tsars was a recommendation to Western scientists.[32] Moreover, Marxism claimed to be a science and undertook to substitute for the rule-of-thumb style of traditional politics the precision and methods of the laboratory. British admirers like Wells and Julian Huxley were impressed, too, by the importance attached to science in the new Russia, to the teaching of science in schools and universities, and the provision for scientific research. The Russians had to drag themselves out of mediaeval darkness into the light of the twentieth century and the resources of modern science were indispensable for doing that. Besides, Stalin was the first of modern statesmen to introduce the system of planning into every facet of his country's life, and this had an irresistible fascination for the scientist; in the world of the future, the whole human race looked like being as responsive to the scientist's will as the specimens under his microscope. The outstanding geneticist, J. B. S. Haldane, sometime editor of the *Daily Worker*, became one of the most prominent apologists for the Soviet Union in Britain; he was closely followed by J. D. Bernal. The perversion of science for military and imperialist ends by the fascist dictators on the continent naturally strengthened the commitment of such men and women to Russia's support. For a scientist, the commitment united two of his most powerful interests: the desire for a social cause to identify with against the evils of the times, and the wish to employ his scientific knowledge in the service of that cause.

Joseph Needham, the biochemist, was much preoccupied with the dilemma, as he saw it, facing scientists in the 1930s, and had no doubt how it should be resolved.

> There are two ways open to the scientific worker at the present time. All the backward pull of respectability and tradition urges him to throw in his lot with the existing capitalist order, with its corollaries of nationalism, imperialism, militarism and ultimately fascism. On the other hand, he can adopt the ideas of social justice and of the classless state; he can recognise that his own best interests lie in the triumph of the working-class, the only class pledged to abolish classes. In a word, he can think of the Kingdom literally and can work for its realisation. A Kingdom not of this world but to be in this world.[33]

It is interesting to see in this passage how readily Needham slips into biblical language when describing the idealised future of the classless society, showing how the politically conscious intellectual migrates into the realm of faith. Yet the faith is all the more compelling because strengthened with scientific certitude. Thus, in his Herbert Spencer Lecture, delivered at Oxford in 1937, Professor Needham bestowed the authority of science on the predestined victory of the worker society:

> As I write, there rages in one of the most beautiful of European countries a tragic and terrible struggle between the People and their Adversary. The sound of its gunfire penetrates any college court . . . some faith may be needed to assert with boldness that, even if Spanish democracy be overwhelmed, even if the great democracy of the Soviet Union itself were to be overwhelmed, no matter what shattering blows the cause of consciousness may receive, the end is sure. The higher stages of integration and organisation towards which we look have all the authority of evolution behind them.[34]

Thus, *scientia* – as in the Marxist ideology – *vincit omnia*, even commonsense, even compassion.

Perhaps it is not surprising that Soviet agents should have chosen the University of Cambridge in the inter-war years for the recruitment of their British assistants, and, in some cases, spies. Cambridge had a greater reputation for the natural sciences than any other place of learning in Britain: it was the home of the Cavendish Laboratory, where the bases of atomic physics were being laid. Yet, as a matter of history, the scientific profession in Britain did not serve Soviet masters; almost all the defectors to the Soviet Union from British nuclear research establishments after the Second World War were refugees from other countries, like Fuchs and Pontecorvo. Moreover, Cambridge men who embraced communism in the thirties and later, when in government service, passed on secrets to Russia, such as Blunt, Burgess, Maclean and Philby, were arts students on the whole.[35]

The support of British scientists for the Soviet system was badly shaken by mounting evidence of the system's 'disease of orthodoxy'. The facility with which communists throughout the world discarded their long fight against fascism when ordered to do so by Stalin in 1939 was a bitter pill to swallow. So was the notorious Lysenko controversy in 1947, showing that, in Soviet eyes, truth, in the scientific, as in other fields, tends to be that which promotes the political cause. The Soviet geneticist Lysenko gained world prominence by denying the established theories of Weismann and Mendel and substituting a theory of environmental forces in heredity more in accord with Marxist views. The Soviet authorities upheld Lysenko's ideas as the only admissible ones and persecuted scientists who disagreed. The British Communist party urged its scientist members to endorse Lysenko's theories, at which several of them, including Haldane, left the party.[36]

The Slansky trials in communist-controlled Czechoslovakia in 1952 had a further disturbing effect on the British scientific community, many members of which included distinguished Jews, and Jews figured prominently among the defendants at the trials. A year later the arrest of certain Jewish doctors in Moscow on a charge of attempting to murder Stalin intensified fears of mounting anti-semitism in Russia. In 1956, the *Daily Worker* (now the *Morning Star*) actually admitted that these fears were soundly based. 1956, too, was the year of Khrushchev's secret speech at the twentieth Soviet communist party congress, in which he detailed the crimes of Stalin, and the year of Russia's suppression of the Hungarian uprising.

The second of the intellectual tendencies in Britain to which Soviet communism appealed was that of religion. We remarked in the previous chapter that the decline of religious faith in the twentieth century may have had some influence in the rise of the secular faith, Marxism.[37] Certainly, some British writers have seen in the Soviet brand of communism either a creed with all the emotional satisfactions of religion or a truer kind of religion than their own. Freda Utley, the economic historian, testifies to the former: 'perhaps in my case, as in that of many young people today, the instinctive desire for a religion was the compelling force leading, step by step, into the Communist trap'. Trap it was for her. Visiting Russia in the early 1930s in the full flush of her conversion, she saw the horrors grow around her: the same inequality, perhaps more so, as in the West, the deadening uniformity, the fight for existence absorbing the energies of the masses 'while the struggle for position and affluence seemed the main preoccupation of those fortunate enough to belong to the communist party'. Then came the arrest of her husband on a trumped-up charge – she never saw him again – and her decision to leave Russia for ever.[38]

Nevertheless, the Soviet system attracted reflective Christians in Britain who considered that a society in which thousands starved while others dined in luxury was not following Christ's teaching. Christianity might be more evident in the communist ideal of sharing and producing for the common good. Such a Christian was Conrad Noel, the vicar of Thaxted from 1912 to 1942, who upheld the communist way of life as exemplifying Christ's teaching. Among his disciples were the composer Gustav Holst and Joseph Needham. Needham agreed with Spengler that Christian theology is the 'grandmother of Bolshevism'.[39] It was from Christianity, so Needham argued, that the Marxist hatred of oppression had sprung:

> It cannot be a coincidence that Marxist morality grew up in the bosom of Christianity after eighteen Christian centuries, as if the phoenix of the Kingdom should arise from the Church's failure.[40]

'Communism provides the moral theology appropriate for our time', and, as against the objection that communism denies belief in God, Needham argued that communist ethics 'engendered a sense of the holy', and, in any case, he contended, the immanence of the Christian godhead was more to be found in communism than in any other form of society. But what should be said about the communist's denial of immortality and the power of prayer? Needham gave no answer.

Needham believed that Soviet communism heralded the Kingdom of God. He was closely echoed by the most famous of all Christian supporters of the Soviet Union, Dr Hewlett Johnson, who owed his preferment as Dean of Canterbury in 1931 to Prime Minister Ramsay MacDonald. 'When all was said and done', he wrote in his autobiography, 'the Soviet people were actuated, in the major operations of life, by a moral purpose. They were working for a common good that seemed to me essentially Christian in its morality, however much they deny the fact'. [41] Elsewhere he had written: 'Jesus challenged class, as class. Communism builds the classless society'.[42] It was in this spirit that the 'Red' Dean wrote perhaps the most famous eulogy by a British writer on the Soviet Union, *The Socialist Sixth of the World*, which reached 22 editions. Shortly after its publication, Canterbury Cathedral was presented with the piquant spectacle of Archbishop Cosmo Lang saying prayers for Finland on 31 December 1939, with Hewlett Johnson officiating. In 1951 the Dean was awarded the Stalin Peace Prize.

After the Soviet Union became Britain's ally as a result of the

German invasion in June 1941, several Church leaders saw in that event a signal that Britain should decisively move towards a more equalitarian and compassionate society. Cosmo Lang's successor at Canterbury, William Temple, who held the See from 1942 until 1944, was a highly influential spokesman on behalf of this argument. But there were British Christians who had always mistrusted the Soviet system and continued to do so. A prominent example was the Christian communist and literary critic, John Middleton Murry, the editor of the *Adelphi*. Murry was confident that Britain should constitute a communist society, but was equally sure that it should not follow what to him was an oppressive Soviet example.[43]

Not surprisingly, eminent British Roman Catholics who took an interest in the Soviet experiment did not often approve it. Like Freda Utley, some were repelled by the disproportionate share of income and amenities enjoyed by the ruling minority and by the low living standards of the masses. One of these was John Heenan, a priest who became a cardinal and the Archbishop of Westminster. Heenan travelled in Russia in the 1930s in the role of a psychiatrist, visiting schools, hospitals and the homes of ordinary people. Here he encountered some of the fear permeating the land. He visited a Jewish family in which the father and husband had lost his job as result of an anti-semitic drive and was terrified of meeting Westerners for fear of being accused of spying for them. He refused to accept money from them, though he and his family needed it:

> He thought it bad enough to have entertained foreigners without accepting foreign currency. So we departed.

'I felt I had learned more about Soviet Communism than if I had read the whole Lenin Library'.[44]

At the other social extreme, Heenan met another Russian family, the husband being in this case a party member. Eager to see their living quarters, he accompanied them home, but when he called on the family the next day and entered their apartment unannounced, he discovered it to be luxuriously appointed, nothing like that of the Jewish family:

> I was back in the street within two minutes. As a social call, my visit had not been a success. But I had achieved my purpose. I had seen the home of a prosperous party member.[45]

Heenan also professed to be shocked by the Soviet persecution of religion, which, from personal conversation and pamphlet literature, he found to be much in evidence.

At the same time, there were aspects of the Soviet system which Heenan admired. Like Laski, he was impressed with the judicial system, which he saw as a happy medium between the old-fashioned pomp of the British courts and the frequent discourtesy of the American variety. He observed a trial in which he was struck by the judge's humanitarian concern and compassion, and compared the mild sentence given with a British sentence handed down in similar circumstances. Like Bernard Shaw, he was impressed, too, by the Labour Commune for young criminals, the Bolshova, which taught them trades and sometimes prepared them for the university.

Thus, British intellectuals, including the critics, like Heenan and Muggeridge, and those in the end bitterly disillusioned, like Koestler and Freda Utley, tended to see different aspects of the vast and complicated Soviet situation. A comprehensive, objective view was almost impossible. The human mind is apt to select evidence which suits its existing dispositions; thus visitors often went to Russia to confirm their previous ideas. Beatrice Webb's niece, Kitty, asserted that the Webbs had made up their minds that they admired the Soviet model before they set foot on Soviet soil.[46] In her own reminiscences, Barbara Wootton observed of the people in her group of visitors to Russia that it was easy to predict what their views would be when they returned.[47] This was as true of the admirers of the Soviet system as it was of its critics.

One piece of evidence that foreign intellectuals who admired the Soviet regime did so more because of their sense of alienation from their own society than of the intrinsic merits of that regime is that they were not much influenced by the literature or other artistic products of Russia. Soviet writers admired by Western critics were apt to be rejected by the official guardians of taste in the Soviet Union, and in any case their work was not usually taken as a model in the West. Boris Pasternak's *Dr Zhivago* could not be published in the Soviet Union and only appeared in western Europe as a result of the manuscript falling into the hands of the Italian publisher Feltrinelli. It became an outstanding success in the West and Pasternak was awarded the Nobel Prize in 1958, which the Soviet authorities forced him to reject. Alexander Solzhenitsyn's two books *The First Circle* and *Cancer Ward* similarly met with official Soviet disfavour; perhaps for that reason, he, too, was awarded the Nobel Prize. His first work, however, *One Day in the Life of Ivan Denisovich*, was published in Russia during the 'thaw' in 1962 and even received the public blessing of Prime Minister Khrushchev. But such writers were acclaimed in Britain and the West generally more because they were critics of a Soviet regime which Western intellectuals had grown to reject than as literary pioneers to be taken as models. Otherwise, the great bulk of Soviet writers, playwrights, novelists and poets were totally without influence on the professional work of their opposite numbers in Britain.

This was not only because of the language barrier, but because, by the 1930s, Soviet writers able to earn a living from their work had virtually become spokesmen for the regime, 'engineers of the human soul', participants in the state plan, like everyone else. The basic principle of their art was 'socialist realism' and they were permitted no expression of thought or feeling which did not serve the ideological cause. Describing the reasons for his own apostasy (he was a member of the party for only a few months in the winter of 1936–7), Stephen Spender explains that 'socialist realism is the death of all original art':

> To destroy the freedom of art is really a kind of madness, like destroying the freedom of the individual to have ears to hear sounds to which his mind is sensitive, and to replace them with microphones which are tuned in to hear only what the State directives wish him to hear, which are the sounds relayed by the State amplifiers . . . the destruction of this freedom is justified by the slogan that freedom is the recognition of necessity. The political freedom of necessity is the necessity of the State version of the needs of generalised collectivised man. The freedom of art speaks for the individuality of each human being.[48]

Art in the Soviet Union is required to have an express social purpose, otherwise the artist is denied a livelihood. For this reason, it has had scarcely any influence in Britain.

It is possible that, in the world of music, some minor Soviet influences on British work may be detected. The Soviet composer, Dmitri Shostakovich, was obliged to eschew developments in Western music known as serialism, or the Schoenberg school, whereby patterns of notes are substituted for the traditional keys, the effect being often dissonant, hard to appreciate and therefore not acceptable to official Soviet critics who expect music to be a 'socially relevant' form of art. Nevertheless, Shostakovich may have had some influence on the British composer, Benjamin Britten, with whom he was often in contact. It was possibly because of Shostakovich's influence that Britten tended to adhere to traditional forms capable of being popularly appreciated. Other British composers have expressed admiration for Shostakovich. Ronald Stevenson, for example, was so impressed with his work that he composed a passacaglia based on the letters of Shostakovich's name, which was presented to the Russian at the Edinburgh Festival in 1962.

But it is in the realm of cinematography – possibly because of the necessity for films to have a large audience owing to the cost of production, and hence to avoid catering for eccentric minorities – that Soviet artistic influence in Britain has been most in evidence. Two outstanding Russian film directors, Eisenstein and Pudovkin, had a dramatic impact on film-making in the West. In particular, Eisenstein's use of 'montage', the collision of images designed to stimulate the audience to new responses, made an impressive effect on foreign film-producers, British included. The British Film Society invited Eisenstein to Britain to give a series of lectures in 1929. Partly as a result of his teaching and films, especially 'Battleship Potemkin', British cinematography developed new techniques and turned its attention to everyday life for new subjects. Eisenstein's realistic portrayal of daily life in Russia inspired the foundation of the British Documentary Film Movement. The Scottish film producer, John Grierson, was one of those much influenced by these developments, as can be seen in his film 'Drifters', a study of the North Sea herring catch. But cinematography stands out as an exception, for the reasons given, to the general rule that the influence of Soviet art in Britain has been minimal.

II

Intellectuals, Richard Crossman has written, succumbed to communism, or admiration of it, because of their 'quite unusual sensitivity' – they had a 'heightened perception of the spirit of the age, and felt more acutely than others both its frustrations and its hopes'.[49] For that very reason, intellectuals were among the first to feel the disenchantment with Russia in Britain which began with the Great Terror of the mid-1930s, reached a climax with the Nazi-Soviet pact in August 1939, faded in the great surge of feeling towards Russia which came with the Great Patriotic War, and then returned with the Soviet repression of nationalism in Eastern Europe after the war. Since then, the intellectual has turned a cold eye on the Worker's Fatherland, without, however, becoming greatly enamoured of its world adversary, the United States.

It is only fair to say, however, that this disenchantment reflects, not only a decline in respect for Soviet communism, but a revision in the minds of intellectuals, and perhaps of all of us, as to what politics is about and what can be done with it. Because so much was expected of political action in the thirties, Soviet communism, the quintessence of political action, was adulated by many; now the zeal for political action has evaporated, and with it, adulation of the Soviet model. The point was well stated by Stephen Spender in his autobiography *World Within World*, when he wrote that the thirties 'saw the last of the idea that the individual accepting his responsibilities could alter the history of the time'. From now on, Spender continues, 'the individual could only conform to or protest against events which were outside his control':

> The tragedy of the 1930s was the blindness of the many: the tragedy of the 1940s was the ineffectiveness of the few. Today, there is more realisation of problems than there is faith in solutions.[50]

The British writer who has best expressed this disillusionment with political action, and with the Soviet dream which has gone with it, is George Orwell, originally known as Eric Blair. Orwell has probably done more than any other British writer to ridicule and condemn Soviet communism, and, in doing so, to destroy the hope of half a century ago that, through politics, the world could be transformed and the organised paradise of Wells and the Webbs realised. Orwell, then a socialist, served in the Spanish civil war with the POUM militia, the Spanish Trotskyists. Having witnessed the persecution of POUM by the communists, Orwell was better placed than most British Left-wingers to believe the stories then circulating about the horrors of Stalinism. He became convinced of the necessity to explode the Soviet 'myth' if socialism in the West was to be saved. For him, the USSR was not only not socialist; it was becoming less socialist than it had been in 1917:

> . . . in my opinion, nothing has contributed so much to the corruption of the original idea of socialism as the belief that Russia is a socialist country and that every act of its rulers must be excused, if not imitated.[51]

After some difficulty – the book was rejected by Victor Gollancz, though the author was evidently not much worried by the fact – Orwell eventually found a publisher for his savage satirical attack on Russia, *Animal Farm*, in Secker and Warburg, and it appeared in 1945, two years after it was written.[52] Its popularity, which was instantaneous, mounted in Britain as that of its subject, Russia, declined. Three years later, when the Cold War had settled down as the seemingly permanent state of Russia's relations with the West, when Stalin was threatening to push his erstwhile allies out of Berlin, and when Czechoslovakia, the victim of 1938, now fell to another form of dictatorship, Orwell's nightmarish portrayal of the thought-controlled totalitarian state, *1984*, saw the light of day. The book was the culmination of the intellectuals' retreat from their love affair with Russian communism:

Plaisir d'amour ne dure qu'un instant,
Chagrin d'amour dure toute la vie.

The intellectuals, or many of them, had worshipped Russia and the communist system, not so much for what they were, but because they represented the antithesis of the capitalist West which the intellectuals abhorred.[53] In doing so, they overlooked, and did not bother to inform themselves about, the uglier face of the Soviet phenomenon. When disenchantment came, and the pendulum swung to the opposite extreme, few paused to ask whether it was not Russia that had failed, but those who used her as a receptacle for their own emotions. Russia had had her own history and that made her different from the well-ordered, antiseptic haven Fabians dreamed about. Instead, however, of inquiring why and how Russia was different, most people found it enough to voice their dislike. If this was unsurprising in the case of most people, it *is* surprising that it was found sufficient for people 'of quite unusual sensitivity'.

8. The Impact on the Left

THE Soviet Union has done two things for the Labour Movement in Britain: it has provided an inspiration and a model, though the force of both has steadily declined since 1917, and it has served as a warning of the destructive effect socialism could have on the democratic environment in which the Movement grew to its present strength. In this chapter we will consider these effects on the three major branches of the Labour Movement: the Labour party, the trade unions and the communist party. Many fringe organisations have proliferated on the Left in Britain since the war, partly as a result of disillusionment with the Soviet model, but space does not allow these to be discussed in any detail.

I

The Labour party began life as the Labour Representation Committee founded by a conference held in London in February 1900 and attended by delegates from 65 trade unions and three socialist societies, the Independent Labour Party (ILP), with a membership of 13,000, the Social Democratic Federation (SDF), with 9000 members, and the Fabian Society, with its small, though distinguished, membership of 861. The Committee's secretary was Ramsay MacDonald and its object was (its name was changed to Labour party in 1906) to promote the return of Labour (not called socialist) members to Parliament and to co-operate with any party to promote legislation 'in the direct interest of Labour'. The new party won 29 seats with Liberal support at the general election in 1906 and by the end of the war formed the second largest party in the Commons. Two of its members, G. N. Barnes and Arthur Henderson, sat in the War Cabinet formed by Lloyd George in December 1916, though Henderson resigned in August 1917 owing to a dispute with his colleagues about his attendance at a meeting in Stockholm summoned by Dutch socialists to discuss a negotiated end to the war.

In 1918 a Labour conference drew up a new constitution which provided for individual membership – previously the party had been a federation of trade unions and socialist groups; nevertheless, most members remained affiliated. The constitution also declared in its famous Clause IV that its aim was the common ownership of the means of production. The first Labour government was formed with Ramsay Macdonald as Prime Minister in January 1924 and depended upon Liberal support; the Liberals never recovered from the split between Lloyd George and Asquith during the war.

The revolution in Russia in 1917 was greeted in Labour circles with varying shades of enthusiasm.[1] One Left-wing Labour MP recalled later that 'it was like the coming of a new Messiah. It was the great event of the century: it seemed like a prelude to world wide revolution'.[2] Others were nervous about the implied abandonment of constitutional processes, such as there were in Russia at that time. Henderson, who went to Russia in May on behalf of the War Cabinet, feared the revolutionary Left, destined to sweep into power in November. In June a Labour party conference in Leeds showed a mixture of hopes and fears about the course of events in Russia. Once the Bolsheviks had come to power, however, there was no support – quite the reverse – for Allied intervention in Russia, certainly not after the Central Powers had laid down their arms. The party was also unanimously opposed to any support being given to Poland in its war with Russia in 1920. It was not so much that Labour men identified with the Bolsheviks; they simply wanted no more fighting.[3]

The real issues raised for the Labour party were two, neither of which has been fully resolved to this day. One was the question of how much socialism the party should commit itself to, and whether, in pursuing its objectives, it should rely wholly upon persuasion and constitutional processes, or whether it should, if necessary, follow the Bolsheviks' example and use any means, including force, to achieve their ends. The other question was one of tactics, though it was closely connected with the substantive issue. It was: if British people were frightened by the violence unleashed by the revolution and its evident threat to their institutions and property, would not any form of association with the Russian communists be a kiss of death to the young party? Some Labour men's patriotism had already been questioned during the war, when the party split into pro-war and anti-war sections, and leaders of the latter, notably Ramsay MacDonald and J. R. Clynes, were in the forefront of the party after the war. MacDonald, who had been drummed out of the Lossiemouth golf club because of his opposition to the war, became Labour's first Prime Minister. The last thing he and his colleagues could afford, even in the retreat from patriotism which followed the war, was any suggestion that they lacked national loyalty, or would serve Lenin's purposes if entrusted with office.

In its early years the party won support from people disillusioned with the social system, yet who did not know whether they were communists; at the same time, its leaders were bound to deprecate communism because that was the only way in which they could acquire national respectability. But the political programme adopted by the party in 1918 was decidedly 'Left of centre', a moderate type of social reformism. The declaration was entitled 'Labour and the New Social Order' and was drafted by the Fabian gradualist, Sidney Webb. It called for a minimum wage and a maximum working week, the democratic control of industry, a revolution in national finance involving heavy taxation to subsidise social services, and the nationalisation of land, railways, mines, electric power and insurance. The programme was to be achieved entirely by constitutional means: the electorate would have to be persuaded to vote for it, or as much of it as it could stomach, and presumably any Labour government elected to office on the programme would do nothing extra-legally to prevent a successor government being elected to restore the *status quo ante*, if that was what the voters wanted.

This British brand of socialism – 'more Methodist than Marxist' – was as far removed as could be from the hundred per cent transfer of economic resources to the state under the supervision of one ruling party, with no opposition parties allowed, which comprised the Soviet formula. MacDonald, for all his description of the Russian revolution as 'one of the greatest events in the history of the world', could not have been more plain in insisting that the Labour party's idea of socialism was gradualist from first to last:

Above all [he wrote in 1920] it discards lightning changes as the way to realise itself . . . it believes in democracy, not only as a moral creed which alone is consistent with its views of humanity, but because it is the only practical creed. It knows that, revolutions or no revolutions, public consent is the basis of all social order and that the good builder makes his foundation sound before he puts up his storeys.[4]

MacDonald never had any illusions about the meaning of Bolshevism or the intentions of its practitioners:

> When they say dictatorship, they mean dictatorship, when they say revolution, they mean bloodshed and violence.[5]

Labour gradualism, Labour constitutionalism, did not require party members or Labour MPs to abandon their protectiveness towards the Soviet system, or their almost instinctive feeling that simply because the new Russia was socialist, or called itself socialist, it *must* be right in the basic things, whatever its critics might say. Hence, as we have seen in a previous chapter, the party worked for *de iure* recognition of the Soviets in 1924, for more trade with Russia, for loans and export credit guarantees.[6] They opposed Conservative governments' campaigns against Russia, culminating in the diplomatic breach in 1927, and urged MacDonald to renew diplomatic relations when he formed his second administration in 1929. When three prominent members of the Parliamentary Labour party, Aneurin Bevan, John Strachey and George Strauss, went to Russia in September 1931, they reported back to their colleagues on the contribution trade with that country could make to removing the tragic unemployment of the times:

> However much observers' views may differ as to actual conditions in that country, all must be agreed that the economic life of old Russia has been churned up to the depths. She will never return to her primitive methods of production either in industry or in agriculture. Her large-scale and intensive methods have come to stay. This means that 150 million people have become for the first time buyers and sellers in the world market and their purchasing power is likely to increase in geometrical rather than arithmetical progression.[7]

Whenever anyone had a good word to say about Russia, it was usually a Labour man or woman who said it.

But Labour's leaders had to be careful. MacDonald's experience over the Campbell case and the Zinoviev letter in 1924, and the countless scares about Post Office savings being confiscated under a 'Bolshie' Labour government, showed how careful.[8] Trying as all this made life for the party, it did mean that moderates within the pary had a weapon against the militants in the form of evidence of the political suicide which association with the communists would imply. At the same time, it was evident that the communists did not much object to gradualists committing suicide: it might even be a positive advantage since it might demonstrate that there is no future for gradualist socialism within capitalist society.

But just how much association with communists, or with any revolutionaries, should the Labour party allow itself? After the formation of the British communist party in 1921, the Labour party was repeatedly faced with the question of whether it should accept affiliation with the communists, which it always refused, and, if it did not, what it should do to prevent infiltration into the party of 'crypto-communists', 'fellow-travellers' and others whose commitment to gradualism was not conspicuous. The fact that, for historical reasons, a self-defensive xenophobia has always characterised the Labour party, made the problem of relations with communists difficult. The fact, too, that the communist, with his persistence and feeling of dedication, had good ability to penetrate other organisations, did not help. Harold Laski, in a pamphlet published by the Labour party in April 1946 and appropriately entitled *The Secret Battalion*, provided an acute analysis, both of the nature of the communist infiltration problem and Labour psychology in dealing with it.[9] Fear of the party being 'taken over', fear of its being 'betrayed', combined with a sense of guilt about harbouring suspicions about fellow socialists, were elements in the situation. Mr Khrushchev, who visited Britain with Soviet Prime Minister Bulganin in 1956 and faced sharp criticism from Labour MPs about the treatment of social democrats in the Soviet bloc, commented on this experience that he 'would rather vote Conservative than Labour'.[10] The treatment he received seemed to underline the general rule that social reformers, such as socialists and communists, tend to abuse one another more than their opponents. Lenin said it was a sign of affection, but there are other explanations.

The Labour party's problems of dealing with revolutionary communism increased with the years. In the 1920s, when the Soviet Union was following its so-called 'class against class' policy, under which social democrats were lumped together with bourgeois parties as the workers' enemy, all the more dangerous because thinly disguised as friends, the problems were easier: the dividing lines were clear. Difficulties arose with the Soviet Union's adoption of Popular Front tactics in the 1930s – the call for a bloc of all opponents of fascism, socialists, communists, liberals and the rest, who should sink their differences and face the common foe. It was a call hard to resist because it made such eminently good sense. One who failed to resist it was Sir Stafford Cripps, later a member of Churchill's War Cabinet and Chancellor of the Exchequer in Attlee's post-war government from 1947 until 1950. In 1932 Cripps formed the Socialist League designed to bring under one umbrella the whole of the socialist Left in opposition to fascism. In 1936, he called for the creation of a Popular Front with the communists and two years later broadened this out into a general Popular Front against fascism, for which he was expelled from the Labour party.

Cripps considered that the risk of communists winning out in the Popular Front was a small price to pay for unity in the struggle against fascism. He saw little importance in Lenin's dictum that, against the common enemy, communists must support social democrats, 'as the hangman's noose supports the condemned man'. But few top-ranking Labour leaders agreed to go along with him, despite the party's weakened state and its need for all the support it could get after the débâcle of 1931, when the National government was formed with its leader, MacDonald, as Prime Minister and some of his old party aides as colleagues in the Cabinet.

A complicating factor in the party's attitude towards the communists and the Popular Front was the undoubted appeal, in the disarray of capitalism in the early 1930s, of Soviet planning, the first five-year plan being under way when MacDonald's second Labour government was formed in 1929. Planning became vital in the socialist vocabulary. In the Labour Party's general election manifesto for October 1931, 'Labour's call for action', were the words, 'we must plan our civilisation or perish'. Attlee went as far as to say in 1933 that:

> There must be a Five-Year Plan drive put into the work. This can only be done by associating the party in the actual work at every stage. Thus I conceive the district commissioner as something more than a public servant. He is the local organiser and interpreter of the will of the Government. He is not impartial. He is a Socialist and therefore in touch with the Socialists in the region who are his colleagues.

Attlee continued, rather audaciously: 'it may be said that this is rather like the Russian plan of commissioners and communist party members. I am not afraid of the comparison. We have to take the strong points of the Russian system and apply them to this country'.[11] By the mid-1930s, Labour's programme of nationalisation was complementing the planning philosophy.

The Second World War brought up the question of collaboration with the communists, now exposed beyond doubt as Stalin's minions, in a new and more acute form. But this did not happen at once. The Labour party was as shocked by the Nazi-Soviet pact of August 1939 as everyone else, except the communists. The party denounced Stalin's annexation of eastern Poland and his aggression against Finland in November 1939 as vehemently as the Conservatives: it published a fierce attack on the war against Finland as an act of 'Hitlerism'.[12] But then, with the Nazi attack on Russia in June 1941, the communists not only returned to favour in Britain, they were positively acclaimed as friends and spokesmen of heroic Russia. They had turned out right after all. As rallies, exhibitions, concerts, public poetry-readings were organised by the communists as part of the 'All Aid to Russia' or 'Second Front Now' campaign, the Labour party, like everyone else, felt almost squeezed out. No doubt their resulting resentment, whether or not consciously felt, had some role to play in intensifying Labour disenchantment with Russia once the trend in the opposite direction set in.

As if this were not enough, the Labour party's basic philosophy, which for a time seemed vindicated by the events of the 1920s, when continental militarism seemed in retreat and two Labour governments could be formed without the Right being provoked into overturning the constitution, suffered a severe shock with the slump of the 1930s. The premise of Labour politics, that working-class standards of living could be gradually raised until an equalitarian society was achieved, was brought into question. Would the propertied classes allow their wealth to go on being taxed to make life good for the many when that wealth was already being decimated by the slump? Would they not make a last stand rather than permit the confiscatory process to go further, and had they not already given a foretaste of that in 1931, when they demanded of the MacDonald government that it cut working-class living standards or get out? According to Harold Laski, when there was a 'contradiction' between democracy and class relations in capitalist society, it was democracy which went to the wall. Barbara Wootton, certainly no Marxist, records in her memoirs that she had never believed this prognosis, but that the great slump convinced her that it was so.[13] The fall of the Weimar Republic to the Nazis in Germany in 1933, and of the Spanish Republic to Franco later on, were evidence of the same thing. The fact that these developments were condemned by the Soviets and regarded with indifference by most of the rest of the world showed how emerging doubts in the Labour party about the constitutional road to socialism mingled with dilemmas about the party's attitude towards Moscow.

It says a great deal for the stability of the party that, after all, the belief in gradualism was not much shaken by these deeper questionings which the slump provoked. One reason no doubt was the resilience of the British economy, symbolised by the recovery in the 1930s. The old depressed areas remained depressed, but in the south of England new industries prospered; they were assisted by the protected market afforded by Commonwealth and Empire after the Ottawa agreements of 1932, and by the relatively greater fall in prices of raw materials and food during the slump. By the outbreak of war in 1939 Labour knew that it wanted no return to the dole, the means test and all the rest, but neither did it want fundamental change in the economic system and the British way of life. With a better planned economy, with Beveridge-type social insurance, more money spent on housing, education, hospitals, with full employment maintained by the government using Keynesian techniques, and with state ownership of the basic industries, coal, steel and transport, there was good hope of a future brighter than the past.

The party's Left wing remained strong, but it served rather to put the party's real leaders, almost always moderate men, more on their mettle than fundamentally to alter the party's political direction. For a time after the war, Aneurin Bevan led a 'ginger' group which split him from his senior colleagues and caused his resignation from Attlee's post-war government as Minister of Labour; he criticised what he called British subservience to the United States, wanted less money spent on defence and more on foreign aid, and would have liked rather larger doses of nationalisation. But, as Labour approached power again, after its long sojourn in the wilderness in the 1950s, Bevan returned to the fold; he identified himself, for instance, with Attlee's successor as party leader, Hugh Gaitskell, in his fight to keep the British independent nuclear deterrent at the party's annual conference in Scarborough in 1960.

Gaitskell himself, who was robbed of the chance to become Prime Minister by his early death in 1963, fought to commit the Labour party to what it actually believed in, which was social equality, rather than socialism. This meant, in his view, deleting from the party constitution the famous Clause IV with its pledge of the public ownership of the means of production. Gaitskell lost the battle and the ironical result was the party's adoption at the Scarborough conference of Lenin's phrase about nationalising the 'commanding heights' of the economy. But nobody really believed that a Labour victory at the polls would mean the making of Britain into a socialist state on the Soviet model. When Labour returned to power under Harold Wilson and later James Callaghan from October 1964 until May 1979, with the intermission of a Conservative government (1970 until 1974) under Edward Heath, the character of Britain as a mixed economy remained unchanged. Possibly the frustrations of militant socialists arising from such an outcome determined them to swing the party to the Left once it left office in May 1979.

The theoreticians of the party played a part in keeping it to the middle road, and their abhorrence at the Soviet police state was a factor in their thinking. Evan Durbin (he lost his life by drowning in 1939) wrote his *The Politics of Democratic Socialism*, published in 1940, partly in protest against inhuman treatment of people by the Soviet state. Democracy was essential to his socialism:

> Democracy [he wrote] is not related to socialism as gilt to gingerbread, as coffee to cream – a decorative addition or a great improvement – but as air to breathing, as earth to fire . . . the *fons et origo* of all our social hopes.[14]

Fifteen years later, another Durbin, Anthony Crosland, and another victim of an early death, was writing in affirmation of the same democracy:

> What really matters [he wrote] is the degree to which management is autocratic or democratic, the extent of joint consultation and participation . . . in all these respects, the Soviet worker is more proletarianised than the British worker. He has no free Trade Unions to protect him, no right to strike, no freedom to change his job, no elaborate system of arbitration, and no political party to

represent his interest in a democratic parliament. Deprived of individual rights and subject to autocratic management, he might well envy the British worker.[15]

Another factor in Labour moderation was the change in the social composition of the party, and of the electorate, too, which came with the affluence, however temporary it proved to be, of the 1960s. The old 'cloth-cap' image of the party faded, and Labour had to appeal to newer sectors of suburban and professional voters. 68 per cent of new Labour MPs returned in the 1966 general election were university graduates, and only 14 per cent manual workers, as compared with 41 per cent and 37 per cent respectively in 1951. The old rallying cries in the party sounded less stirring, and Gaitskell's wish to strike out Clause IV reflected this.

The leaders of the party who ran the government after the election in 1945 – Attlee, Bevin, Morrison, Dalton, Cripps – set the tone of undramatic pragmatism in the post-war period. They were essentially practical men, humane and moderate, the enemies of violence and violent change. Almost all of them had served in senior government posts during the war, in which their sense of the limits of the possible grew. When Churchill in the 1945 election called them revolutionaries who would run the country with whips, he lost the election by this flight of fancy. One reason why the electorate preferred Attlee to Churchill was that it had had enough of heroics during the war. It wanted a quiet life, though an economically secure one.

Admiration for the Soviet war effort in the Labour party was unbounded; so was the hope, tinged with doubt, that Russia would co-operate with Britain and America in making a peaceful world after the war. There was also, especially among professional workers, a desire to learn from Soviet practice, in medicine, education, welfare services, technology, but no wish to bring Soviet communism to Britain. Labour's statement of its post-war policy, *The Old World and the New Society*, evidently drafted by Laski, who was later to become chairman of the party, was entirely in the party's tradition of moderate reform.[16]

The party went along with this, and since there were in Britain sizeable arrears to be made up in the social service field, as for instance through the setting up of a free national health service, the party remained reasonably united on domestic policy. The same was not true, however, for foreign affairs. After so much adulation of the Soviet system during the war, Labour was confronted with Attlee's and Bevin's unflinching decisions, first, to place Britain in the forefront of the American plan for European economic recovery, Marshall Aid, and, second, to stand with the United States in armed resistance to Soviet encroachments throughout the world, and especially in the North Atlantic area. The uproar from the Left was deafening. When the government joined with the Truman administration in June 1950 in opposing the communist regime in North Korea, supposedly backed by Russia and the People's Republic of China, in its attack on western-oriented South Korea, backbench Labour MPs thought, with Omar Bradley, that this was 'the wrong war in the wrong place at the wrong time'. Left-wing Labourites who criticised United Nations action in Korea in 1950–3 asked whether America would have been so keen on taking up arms on South Korea's side if South Korea had been a communist state. They might have asked if they themselves would have opposed the war if South Korea had been a communist state.

Labour MPs who disliked the Attlee government's alignment with the United States in opposition to Russia had an opportunity to organise themselves against it when the *Keep Left* movement was formed within the party by Richard Crossman, Ian Mikardo and Harold Wilson. The pamphlet which they wrote in 1947 with that title advocated more socialist legislation and a posture of neutralism, or non-alignment, as against the collective defence pacts then in process of formation on both sides of the ideological divide. But *Keep Left* fizzled out in 1948, partly because the West European governments with which its authors wished to team up fell under Right-wing control, partly because incontrovertible evidence of Soviet expansionism began to come in thick and fast. The fall of Czechoslovakia to communism in February, the threats the western sectors of Berlin were exposed to in the East–West war of nerves, the unflagging news reaching London of Russia's determination to drive out of government in eastern Europe everyone refusing to submit to its will – all this showed that no-one was more skilled than the Russians in binding together the British Labour party as a solid force against them, even though the bulk of its members would rather be on the Soviet side of the ideological fence if they could.

From time to time in the thirty-odd years since the formation of the Atlantic pact, the Soviet government has appealed to Left-wing support in the Labour party, inside and outside Parliament, by proposing new disarmament measures, nuclear-free zones, the thinning down of forces in central Europe, the neutralisation of intermediate areas between the two armed camps, or by the general denunciation of American misdoing. But the support such appeals have won has never seriously deflected Labour governments from approval of the Atlantic pact, or even of American policy. Labour MPs may visit the Soviet Union and make complimentary remarks about the Soviet system. Mr Kitson Clark went there in 1977 to attend the fiftieth anniversary of the revolution. He praised the absence of unemployment and inflation in the Soviet system and said that:

> Perhaps we do not recall often enough that whatever differences separate us from time to time from our Soviet comrades, it remains a fact that you have managed to achieve much that we are still far from achieving.[17]

But such aberrations have not so far affected the pro-American leanings of Labour, as of Conservative, governments in foreign policy.

At the height of the Vietnam war in the 1960s, Prime Minister Harold Wilson was able to endorse American policy when almost all of America's other allies opposed it. Britain has continued to spend a higher proportion of her national income on defence than any other NATO country, except the United States, and has maintained her independent nuclear deterrent, in the teeth of Left-wing Labour criticism, at increasing cost. Perhaps because of their realisation that Left-wing criticism has had little effect on British defence or alliance policies, the Russians have never refrained from following up their gestures of goodwill to the British Left with acts calculated to destroy any sympathy they gained by doing so, Their protests against Britain's 'ganging up' with capitalist America in 1946 and 1947 was followed by the Czech *coup* and the blockade of Berlin in 1948. Mr Khrushchev's talk about the horrors of nuclear war and his calls for *détente* were drowned by the clatter of Soviet tanks rolling into Hungary in 1956. Mr Brezhnev's long campaign for the Helsinki agreements in 1975 was coupled with new drives against dissidents in the Soviet Union and Russia's incursion into Afghanistan in

December 1979. It is a thankless task to be an apologist for Russia in Britain.

With the advent of a tougher line in American policy towards the Soviet Union after Jimmy Carter's victory in the presidential race in 1976 and Ronald Reagan's in 1980, the Labour party seemed to swing further to the Left. One effect of this was the breakaway of some of its moderate leaders, and their formation of a new group, the Social Democratic party, in March 1981. It is doubtful, however, whether either of these developments have much to do with admiration for the Soviet Union in Britain, or the reverse. In so far as Left militants in the Labour party oppose nuclear weapons and British membership of the Atlantic alliance, for example, it seems more due to genuine fear of a drift back to war, owing to a worsening of East–West relations, than to any partiality for the Soviet cause in world controversies. Conceivably, the preference of the new Social Democrats for the 'middle road' in politics, and the seeming public approval for this in opinion polls, may reflect a general aversion for political extremism which recent dismay over Soviet behaviour has encouraged. There is still some political advantage to be gained by the Soviets by appealing to emotional socialism in the Labour party, but it is perhaps less today than at any other time since 1917.

Thus, the Labour party, while always anxious to distance itself from communism, has served as a factor of some strength for the Soviet Union in Britain. The party, or rather its more doctrinaire members, has generally been more willing to see justice and reason in the Soviet argument than either of the other major parties. To some extent, this might at times have had the effect of weakening the vigilance of the country against Soviet pressures within the international system, though this can never have been more than minimal. At the same time, it is in accord with the British wish, which few would probably deprecate, to have points of view publicly stated even if not shared by the majority, or rather, especially when not shared by the majority. But, paradoxically, perhaps the greatest advantage of the ideological link, slender as it is, between the British Labour party and the Soviet Union has been to keep that party even more committed to the path of constitutionality and peaceful change than it otherwise would have been. The fact that there never has been – partly as a result of the Bolshevik revolution – tolerance in Britain for the politics of violence has meant that the Labour party, in order to become a major party, has had to dedicate itself to gradualist socialism. Whether it will continue to do so is another question.

II

British trade unionists have generally manifested an ambiguous attitude towards socialism, and the Soviet Union as the longest surviving example of a socialist state. In so far as socialism is vaguely identified with 'worker power', the trade unions favour it. At the same time, their ideal is free collective bargaining and the absence of wage controls, which are more characteristic of the private enterprise economy. They also oppose the subordination of trade unions to the state, which is the basis of Soviet economic planning. Nevertheless, trade union leaders in Britain have generally been slow to condemn Soviet policy. It is uncommon for union leaders publicly to condemn such Soviet actions as the incursion into Afghanistan in 1979, or to come out openly in support of workers' activities in the Soviet bloc of which the communist authorities disapprove, such as Solidarity, the independent trade union movement which emerged in Poland in 1980, or the attempts to form free trade unions in Russia.

British trade union leaders who have avowed their socialist convictions and given their unions a militant twist have often belonged to the communist party at one time or another. Hugh Scanlon, former president of the Amalgamated Union of Engineering Workers (AUEW), for example, who resigned from the communist party in the mid-1950s, admitted that Marx's vision of a socialist society might not be soon realised in Britain, but claimed that:

> My approach to trade unionism has always been that it can never be an end in itself, it must be a means to an end. That end is the establishment of socialism. If we merely see the trade union movement as a means only of getting better conditions, only of getting a few more crumbs from the table rather than being at the table itself, then I think we are completely underestimating the role of the trade union movement. Undoubtedly, the final role of the trade unions must be to change society itself, not merely to get the best out of existing society.[18]

Similarly, Lawrence Daly, then the General Secretary of the miner's union, who left the communist party in 1956, wrote in 1969 that:

For me the lesson is that the movement should formulate ideas about the society it would like ultimately to see, and be less satisfied with minimal short-term objectives: more demands and less compromise . . . . Preoccupation with short-term problems and with 'what is possible in the existing situation' breeds the attitude that it is not possible to change things very much.[19]

It is a matter of dispute to what extent industrial unrest in Britain since the war has been stirred up by communist troublemakers and their fellow-travelling assistants. In 1966, Prime Minister Harold Wilson coined an oft-repeated phrase when he said of a seamen's strike that it was led by a 'tightly-knit group of politically motivated men', and named eight communists, whom he accused of working to overthrow the government's prices and incomes policy. Communists themselves, with some show of pride, have admitted it. Bert Ramelson, speaking from experience gained as the communist party's industrial organiser, declared in the 1960s that 'there had not been a single mass industrial movement of any size in this country in the last decade where you don't find communists at the centre'.[20]

Perhaps the biggest contribution of the Soviet Union to the development of trade unions in Britain has been to convince them that the raw deal they used to get under capitalism, and may still get, is not essential, and that it can be improved by collective action, whether or not that collective action involves the transition to a fully fledged socialist state. Harold Laski wrote that 'nothing has done so much as the impact of Soviet Russia to demonstrate among trade unions everywhere the conviction that mass unemployment is not a necessary element in economic organisation'.[21] However inconsistent Soviet practice with the British tradition of free trade unions, it has shown British working people that they need not accept their status and conditions in capitalist society, and that through struggle they could improve their lot.

Most trade union leaders welcomed the Bolshevik advent to power in 1917 with a mixture of excitement at the implications for socialism and horror at the violence and chaos which ensued. One section of the movement was beside itself with enthusiasm: this was the militant National Shop Stewards and Workers' Committee, a thorough-going Marxist organisation which merged with the communist party after its formation in 1921. It opposed the general agreement among union leaders to put restrictive trade union practices into cold storage for the duration of the war.

Allied intervention in Russia in 1918 temporarily united the unions in giving aid to the Bolsheviks. The unions, now a powerful force in British life owing to their contribution to the war effort and the financial and moral support they were giving to the new Labour party, joined with the party to form 'Hands Off Russia' committees aimed at ending Allied intervention. At the annual Labour party conference in 1919, Herbert Morrison declared that intervention was:

> not war against Bolshevism or against Lenin, but against the international organisation of socialism. It was war against the organisation of the trade union movement itself, and as such it should be resisted with the full political and industrial power of the whole trade union movement.[22]

When British troops were finally withdrawn from Russia in November 1919, a further basis for trade union assistance to the new regime in Moscow was provided by the outbreak of war between Russia and Poland in 1920. London dockers refused to load a ship with arms for Poland. At a conference a week later, their leader, Ernest Bevin, persuaded them to ban the loading of any ship with weapons to be used against Russia. In July a critical situation arose when the Bolsheviks pushed Polish forces into Poland itself. Prime Minister Lloyd George hinted at British action in defence of Poland, though he later assured Parliament that such action was unlikely.[23] The reaction of the Labour party and the Parliamentary committee of the TUC was to set up a national Council of Action empowered by a delegate conference in August to stop the war 'by any and every form of withdrawal of labour'. Bevin told the meeting that 'this question you are called upon to decide today – the willingness to take any action to win world peace – transcends any claim in connection with wages or hours of labour'.[24] Lloyd George assured the Labour movement that its fears were exaggerated. In October, an armistice between Russia and Poland was arranged and the threat of British armed action subsided.

The extent to which the Polish crisis indicated British trade union support for the Bolsheviks should not be overstated. Some union leaders, notably J. R. Clynes of the National Union of General Workers, deprecated direct action for political ends; they thought it might lead to civil war. Ranged against these were John Bromley, General Secretary of ASLEF, the railway drivers' union, and Robert Smillie, president of the miners' federation. They believed that strikes were justified to bring about international peace. Moreover, trade union action over Allied intervention in Russia and arms for Poland was motivated by considerations besides sympathy for the Bolsheviks: trade unionists wanted no more involvement in foreign wars, they wanted an end to conscription, and they wanted the government to get on with the more important tasks of full employment and making a land 'fit for heroes'.[25]

Nevertheless, these events seemed to inspire the Russians with the idea that they could direct British trade unionism into revolutionary courses, and they tried to do so, though with little to show for their pains. In 1920, the 'Red' International of Labour Unions (Profintern) was established in Moscow with international revolutionary objectives like those of Comintern, created in the previous year. A British communist, J. T. Murphy, formed a British branch of Profintern with the aid of subsidies from Moscow, but it made little headway. Accordingly, it was decided in Moscow to change tactics and, instead of forming independent communist trade unions, to penetrate the existing unions. The British communist trade union organisation therefore changed its name to the 'Minority Movement', which might sound less subversive, and also less offensive to the Labour party, with which the communists were now seeking affiliation.[26]

The Soviet Union provided the Minority Movement with directives and subsidies, and with the latter it published two general journals, *All Power* and *The Worker*, together with periodicals for particular workers such as the seamen and miners. Miners' unions were always fertile soil for communist tendencies. The poverty and harsh working conditions of miners serve to arouse antagonism to the 'system' and in the communist philosophy the mines were a vital source of power through which capitalism could be paralysed. Seamen were important, too, because strike action by them could interrupt war supplies to Russia's enemies, as the dockers' action had done in 1920.

Penetration of the unions at first seemed to go well. In 1924, the TUC at its meeting in Hull received a fraternal visit from Soviet trade unionists and decided to send a party to the Soviet Union in return. British delegates to the Vienna Congress of the International

Federation of Trade Unions (the Amsterdam International) tried to negotiate a reconciliation with Pronfintern. In the following year ten British communists attended the TUC conference in Scarborough and helped inspire a resolution which aimed at struggle 'in conjunction with the party of the workers for the overthrow of capitalism'.[27] Shortly after the Scarborough conference, however, the TUC General Secretary, Fred Bramley, died: he had worked for reconciliation with the communists and had urged the IFTU to 'get rid of the panicky fear that seems to invade and dominate your minds in dealing with Russia'.[28] He was succeeded by Walter Citrine, a sympathiser with Russia, like Bramley, but one who changed his mind later.[29] In October 1925 British trade unions were urged by MacDonald and Bevin at the annual Labour party conference not to elect communist delegates to the party conference.

Further strains between the trade unions and the communists came with the General Strike in sympathetic support of the miners, called in May 1926 and lasting for nine days. Soviet trade unions offered £26,000 in support of the strike, but the TUC rejected it, though the miners, whose strike lasted until November, had most of their strike costs paid from Soviet sources: they expressed their gratitude for this by flocking to join the communist party.[30] The Soviet trade unions could not understand the TUC's action in refusing the money, in allegedly letting down the miners and in failing to use this great crisis to overthrow the system. But there seems little doubt that TUC leaders feared the Conservative charge that the strike had been engineered and paid for by Moscow. At an excited meeting at the Albert Hall, the Conservative MP, Sir Henry Page-Croft, said that the miners' leader, A. J. Cook, 'has declared he is a Bolshevik and is proud to be a humble disciple of Lenin . . . treating the miners of this country, whom we all respect and honour, as cannon fodder'.[31] The audience responded by calling for Cook's lynching. Such incidents disturbed respectable union leaders, as did also the invective dealt out by Moscow. Citrine later recalled that 'we resented the use of such terms as "traitor" and "lick-spittle", although we had been told that these expressions were commonplace in the Russian movement and nobody took any notice of them'.[32]

Relations between trade unions and the communist worsened. In July 1926, the Labour party, jointly with the TUC, circulated a pamphlet based on a government blue-book consisting of evidence of subversion allegedly seized in a police raid on communist party offices shared with the Minority Movement: it was intended to show how the communists and the Minority Movement sought to infiltrate working-class bodies and then bring them under Soviet control. One consequence was that a year later the TUC abandoned its policy of co-operation with Soviet trade unions and an advisory committee set up to promote it was abolished.

Although British trade unions, like all who considered themselves socialists, opposed the Conservative government's breach of diplomatic relations with Russia in 1927, coolness grew between them and the communists. In 1928, the Labour party banned communists from its conferences even when they came as trade union delegates, and this further curbed the Minority Movement's power to penetrate the unions. The Russians therefore decided that the Movement should now start to form unions strictly under its own control, and as part of this strategy, two break-away organisations were formed, the United Mineworkers of Scotland and the United Clothing Workers in the East End of London. The Russians also hoped to use the Minority Movement to turn the National Unemployed Workers' Movement into a revolutionary body. But the TUC disaffiliated that organisation in 1928 on the ground that it was subversive and this may have persuaded the majority of the unemployed to have nothing further to do with it.

Despite the TUC's inclination to favour an alliance with the Soviet Union in the struggle against fascism, the breach between the unions and the communists seemed to widen in the thirties. The Minority Movement was disbanded owing to its lack of success and the Russians advised the communist party to recruit union members directly to it. The TUC countered in 1934 by issuing its famous 'Black Circular', which recommended member unions to exclude known communists from office and ban them from trades councils. Citrine visited Russia in the following year and concluded that Soviet trade unions, like the government itself, were completely under the communist party's control. There could therefore be no effective co-operation with British trade unions. Bevin's dominating influence in the trade union movement was thrown on the same side of the argument.

Bevin declared that 'the philosophy of the Red International cannot mix with our form of democracy'.[33] He considered that the Russians had destroyed their chances of co-operating with British trade unions by trying to infiltrate them through the communist party. If Russia 'had never supported the communist party in England, but allowed the British trade union movement to help Russia', Bevin thought, 'she would have been in a much better position than today'.[34] It was through Bevin's battles against communist infiltration in the unions that the basis for his antagonism towards Russia as Foreign Secretary after 1945 was laid. He told Soviet ambassador Maisky in 1937, 'you have built up the Soviet Union and you have the right to defend it. I have built up the Transport Union and if you try to break it, I'll fight you – and fight to the death'.[35]

The Nazi–Soviet pact of 1939 had its expected effect of deepening the gulf between the communist world and the trade unions, but the zeal which communists devoted to the war effort after Hitler's attack on Russia in 1941 did much to remove the old estrangement. In 1943, the TUC withdrew its 'Black Circular' and as a result the communist party greatly extended its union membership. By 1941, Citrine had so far put aside his suspicions of Russia as to join in forming a Joint Committee of British and Soviet Trade Unions for mutual assistance, but the Committee's history was by no means smooth. In 1943, for instance, Citrine was involved with resolutions in the Committee, for which the Russians pressed, urging the government to open a Second Front. Citrine had doubts: he argued that if a Second Front were opened in Europe, it would mean diverting shipping, then used to take food and other supplies to Russia's hard-pressed forces. He pointed out defensively that Britain was the only country involved in the war, apart from Germany, which had entered it voluntarily, to which the Russians retorted that Britain had egged on Hitler by making a pact with him at Munich. Then Citrine came back with the reply that it was Stalin's pact with Hitler which made war inevitable. Nevertheless, despite this wrangling, the Anglo-Soviet Committee transformed itself into the World Federation of Trade Unions (WFTU) in 1945. It now represented some 150 communist and non-communist unions, and, by 1945, the trade union movement in Britain had so widened its ranks to communists that they held key posts in many of the major unions.

It was not long, however, before all this was swept away by the opening phases of the Cold War. The fact that communists, and fellow-travellers generally, had risen so high in public esteem owing to Russia's resistance to Nazi invasion, meant that they were in a vulnerable position when the tide of feeling swept in the opposite direction. Russia was now the enemy, and all the enemy's friends in Britain were anathematised. In 1948, an attempt by Arthur Horner, the communist General Secretary of the National Union of Mineworkers, to pledge the union's support for a French miners' strike against the Marshall Plan misfired and an anti-communist backlash followed in British trade unions. In 1949, the TUC once more advised unions against electing communists to vital posts; it was back to the Black Circular. The Transport and General Workers' Union decided in 1950 to ban communists from holding office and nine communist officials were dismissed. The Clerical and Administrative Workers' Union endorsed the ban. The Amalgamated Engineering Workers' President campaigned against subversive communist activity, although he failed to persuade his union to impose the ban. At the international level, non-communist trade unions decided at a meeting in London in 1949 to break away from the WFTU, which now became a communist organisation exclusively, and formed the International Confederation of Free Trade Unions. At its birth the ICFTU embraced some 70 unions in 53 countries with an estimated membership of 50 million.

In some British trade unions, such as the Fire Brigades' Union and the Electrical Trades Union, communists had secured such a hold that they were not easily ousted. Nevertheless, Soviet actions in 1956, especially Khrushchev's revelations of Stalin's reign of terror and the Soviet invasion of Hungary, led indirectly to the ETU finally purging itself of communists. Two members of the union, Frank Chapple and Les Cannon, decided to leave the communist party and wrest control of the union from communist hands. At length, in 1960 Chapple and another union member, John Byrne, who believed himself cheated of the secretaryship of the union by communist intrigue, issued writs against the union for rigging the elections in 1959. In 1961, judgment was given in favour of the plaintiffs. The judge, Mr Justice Winn, observed that the posts of President, General Secretary and Assistant Secretary, and five seats on the executive council, were held by communists, though communists formed only about one per cent of the union's membership.

The ETU was a good example of how successful communists could be, despite Russia's unpopularity with the public in general, in levering themselves into power in the unions. Just as Lenin had seized power in Russia in 1917 with a small group of highly disciplined party workers, so other communists, despite small numbers, captured power in the unions through self-discipline and well-planned strategies. The communist technique was to insist that party members join trade unions, when they were eligible, and work hard in them, attending every meeting, unlike the general body of union members.

The ETU affair, and the growing awareness of communist methods, led to the suspicion that they were, and are, behind every form of industrial unrest. Harold Wilson's phrase about 'tightly knit groups of politically motivated men' caught on. In 1975, possibly because of a miners' strike which brought down Edward Heath's Conservative government, subversive influences in trade unions came under particularly heavy fire. Ross McWhirter published an advertisement in the *Spectator* (he said it was the only journal with the courage to print it) claiming that the unions were being manipulated by 'politically motivated men' who were now 'virtually in control of the country'.[36] He asked for funds to establish a free press in the event that the unions tried to black out other sources of information.

One Conservative MP, Eldon Griffiths, contended that the most vital sectors of the economy were being penetrated by communists. Another, Jill Knight, declared that, thanks to the work of the KGB, 'British trade unions were falling wholly into the communists' grip'. However, Lenin would no doubt have felt most proud of Lord Chalfont's statistics, though their source was not particularised. He maintained in a speech in the Upper House that ten per cent of officials in the majority of the unions were card-carrying communists, though they accounted for only 0.30 per cent of the total trade union force. 'A small, cohesive and vigorous organisation like the communist party', he said, 'can exert enormous and disproportionate influence as a pressure group in the trade union movement'.[37]

Whatever the actual percentage of communists in British trade unions (it would be almost impossible to compile accurate satistics), the outcry against them is itself evidence that their impact is out of proportion to their numbers. Fears of communist power in the unions were aroused again in April 1975, when Shelepin, formerly head of the KGB, visited Britain as part of a Soviet trade union delegation which was returning a visit to Russia by a British trade union group two years before. He was greeted by protests from Soviet exiles and groups concerned about human rights in the Soviet Union. An agreement nevertheless emerged from the visit to hold further exchanges and to discuss the possibility of resurrecting the Anglo–Soviet Trade Union Committee formed during the war. No-one could doubt that British and Soviet trade unions are entirely different kinds of entities, British unions being agencies for maintaining and improving wages and working conditions of their members, Soviet unions being channels for conveying government policy to the workers. Nevertheless, British union leaders showed no strong support for the Soviet group which in 1977 tried to establish themselves as an independent trade union. Nor has the TUC been especially active on behalf of human rights in Soviet bloc countries.

In general, British trade unions in the 1980s seem indifferent to the Soviet Union, being neither very critical nor very approving. Perhaps their attitude is best described as defensive, suspicious of Western campaigns against Soviet repressiveness, but still far from trustful in regard to Soviet intentions. Nevertheless, the influence of the Soviet Union on their twentieth-century development has been considerable. It has harmed them as national institutions by stimulating an active, though small minority – the communists – to seek control of them, not in the direct interests of their members, but, it seems, for the purpose of undermining the social system. On the positive side, the existence of the Soviet state has probably heightened the morale and self-confidence of the unions: it has shown how working-class conditions can be improved by organisation and persistence. It remains to be seen to what extent these improvements could be pushed to the detriment of the community as a whole.

III

The British Communist party, unlike some others in continental Europe, has never been a major force in national politics. Its importance has been that of an irritant to the rest of the Labour movement. The Labour party's success in capturing working-class support and engineering social reform in Britain has robbed the Communist party of backing it might otherwise have won. Moreover, the Marxist–Leninist ideology, or indeed any abstract political doctrine, jars with the pragmatic strand in the British tradition. Marx himself wrote that the British lacked 'the spirit of generalisation and revolutionary fervour'. The atheism and totalitarian associations of communism also weakened sympathy for the party in Britain, and it never acquired the popularity which

French and Italian communists acquired through their part in the Resistance during the Second World War.

The fact that the British party has until recently undeviatingly followed the Soviet line and seemed to most people little more than a conduit for Soviet influence was a severe handicap. Joining such a party could not but seem like signing on as the agent for a foreign state. Moreover, without the influence of the Soviet Union, it is doubtful whether there would have been a communist party in Britain, or whether it would have taken the course it did. It was Moscow that brought together the disparate Marxist groups that existed in Britain and helped to form a party out of them. It was Moscow which decided the political strategy it was to follow.

In 1919, when the Moscow-controlled Communist International invited foreign delegates to a conference, there existed several British Marxist groups, none with a membership of more than 10,000. The largest was the British Socialist party (BSP), which had grown out of the Social Democratic Federation and sought socialism through the parliamentary system. A smaller, but more revolutionary, group was the Socialist Labour party (SLP), centred upon Clydeside and much influenced by the American Marxist De Leon, who believed in revolution through industrial action. Two other Marxist groups were the Workers' Socialist Federation, led by Sylvia Pankhurst, daughter of the suffragette leader, Emmeline Pankhurst, and the Shop Stewards' and Workers' Committee: both stressed revolutionary action and, like the rank and file of the SLP, opposed affiliation to the Labour party.

Attempts to unite the four groups foundered on the two issues of the means to achieve the socialist future and relations with the Labour party. When Lenin's advice on these questions was sought, he pronounced, curiously, in favour of parliamentary methods and co-operation with the Labour party. Naturally, the time he could afford to devote to study of British affairs in 1919 must have been short. It seems, too, that much of the information he received about the position in Britain came through the BSP, and that group was already affiliated to the Labour party and considered that they could attain their ends through it. The editor of *The Worker*, the journal of the Scottish Workers' Committee, wrote that, on making inquiries in Petrograd and Moscow, he found that 'most (if not all) of the information of the British rebel movement landed in Russia through the medium of the BSP'.[38]

Lenin opposed Sylvia Pankhurst's advocacy of revolutionary tactics and advised a Unity Convention called by the leaders of the BSP and the SLP in July 1920 that he personally was 'in favour of participation in Parliament and of adhesion to the Labour party on condition of free and independent communist activity'.[39] In a pamphlet published just before the meeting called *Left Wing Communism – an infantile disorder*, Lenin again advocated affiliation to the Labour party. Owing to his immense influence, the Convention adopted a resolution in favour of affiliation, but when the application was made to the Labour party, it was rejected for the first of many times.

Conceivably, the Soviet leader believed that the Labour party could be appropriated by the communists and used as a tool for their, and his, purposes. But the effect was to condemn British communists to years of fruitless effort. It was an example, at the beginning of the new party's life, of the price of basing its efforts on the experience and advice of another country. When the Marxist groups united at a meeting in Leeds in January 1921 to become the British communist party, delegates rose to their feet and spontaneously broke into the Internationale. William Paul, lately returned from Russia, exclaimed that, from that moment, there was 'a breath of Moscow, a breath from the East, where there is wisdom'.[40] But the price the new party paid for the doubtful wisdom it received from Moscow was high: excluded from the Labour party, it was to spend its life in the shadows.

The party began with a small membership, which remained small: in 1922 it had only 5116 members, of whom only 2300 were paid-up. It was therefore from the start dependent upon Comintern funds, which brought it under Moscow's control. At the beginning, the party did not seem to appreciate this. The Second Congress of Comintern had decreed that communist parties were to be organised on the principle of 'democratic centralism', which meant that decisions of the Congress and of the Executive Committee of the Communist International (ECCI) were binding on all members. An ex-member of the British party wrote that until about 1927 the party did not follow this rule:

Differences of opinion up to the deciding vote were what most party members took for granted, and most of us assumed it was so in Russia. Before long, such doubts and abstentions, let alone votes against, would become violent heresy, bringing expulsion, denunciation, victimisation.[41]

There was also a distinct lack of interest in ideological problems in the party, reflecting British pragmatism. The Soviet campaign against Trotsky, for example, initiated by Stalin in 1924, did not cause turmoil in the British party as it had in others. In 1925, ECCI criticised British communists for not giving enough attention to theoretical questions. The independence of the British communists from Moscow, such as it was, did not, however, have the effect of making them more acceptable to the Labour party.

At the Labour party's annual conference in 1922, Frank Hodges, of the Miners' Federation, voiced an opinion shared by many delegates when he described British communists as:

> the intellectual slaves of Moscow, unthinking, unheeding, accepting decrees and decisions without criticisms or comment, taking orders from the Asiatic mind.[42]

In fact, the communists were in a cleft stick. On the one hand, the more persistently they applied for affiliation to the Labour party, as they did annually from 1920 until 1924, the more they were rejected. In the years of the Zinoviev letter and the General Strike, the Labour party dared not be seen accepting affiliation proposals from communists. On the other hand, as Moscow changed its tune towards the end of 1927 and began to denounce parliamentary socialists as 'social fascists', pressure on foreign communist parties to toe the ideological line mounted.

The latter development was symbolised in the British party's case by a change in its leadership, which may have been engineered from Moscow, when Harry Pollitt, the Comintern's man, replaced Albert Inkpin as General Secretary. At the same time, party membership was falling: in 1926, when the party was supporting the miners' strike, membership rose over the 10,000 mark, but in the following year, with the collapse of the strike, it fell to 7377. In the general election in November 1931 which voted the National government into power and almost obliterated the Labour party, Labour still managed to poll six and a half million votes and the communists only 74,000. The communist party fell still further under Moscow's grip and became still further alienated from the ordinary worker through its supine adoption of Soviet-inspired slogans which seemed without relevance to conditions in Britain. In 1930, the party stipulated that the *Daily Worker*, the communist newspaper, should not include sports reports or racing tips, though this ban was later relaxed, and this ensured that it would never become a popular newspaper. Partly in reaction against domination from Moscow, dissident splinter groups began to appear in a party which was hardly more than a splinter movement itself. In 1932, one such formation, the Balham Group, led by Reginald Groves and Harry Wicks, was expelled from the party and later formed the first British Trotskyist party.[43]

The trend was somewhat reversed when Moscow changed its strategy in the 1930s and adopted the Popular Front campaign as part of the struggle against fascism. As related in the previous chapter, some of the country's leading intellectuals either joined the party or came out in support of its stand against fascism, mass unemployment and war, though not nearly to the extent as happened in continental Europe. But such gains were more than eclipsed by the depressing effects of the justificatory contortions enforced on the party by the Nazi-Soviet pact of August 1939 and by Russia's subsequent invasions of eastern Poland and Finland. The *Daily Worker* hailed the Nazi-Soviet agreement as:

> a shattering blow to the policy of the anti-comintern pact on which past aggressions, particularly in Spain and in the Far East, were based; a thunderbolt for the Chamberlain Cabinet, which has for long months been sabotaging the conversations for an Anglo–Soviet Pact in the hope of reaching another 'Munich' with Hitler.[44]

When Stalin received his reward for the pact with Hitler with the annexation of eastern Poland, the *Daily Worker* explained that the Soviet action was aimed at saving the people living there from 'the ruthless terror of the Nazi oppressions'.

This did not prevent the communist party from finding its way back into public favour once Russia entered the war, this time on the right side, in June 1941. The party sunned itself in the warmth of the alliance. Its membership climbed to 56,000 in 1942, though, when the question of a pact with the communists was raised once more at annual Labour party conferences in 1944 and 1945, the vote was still negative. In the general election in 1945, which swept Labour to victory, the communists won only two seats and their stock fell further with the onset of the Cold War. Comintern had been disbanded by Stalin in 1943 and the British party was not invited to join its post-war replacement, Cominform, when it was founded in 1947. Nevertheless, the party continued to follow closely Moscow's line.

In doing so, it inevitably suffered still further losses of support. In 1948, when Stalin quarrelled with Tito of Yugoslavia, British communists took Stalin's side and won disfavour as a result. Further shocks were sustained in 1956, with Khrushchev's disclosure of the horrors of Stalinist times and his own crushing of Hungary's dash for freedom. By 1958 the party had lost a third of its members. And with this began a gradual movement which culminated in 1968, when the party committed its first major act of dissent from the Soviet Union. On 24 August, the party's National Executive Committee stated that it:

> deeply deplores the military intervention in Czechoslovakia on Tuesday, August 20th, by troops of the Soviet Union, Hungary, Poland, Bulgaria and the German Democratic Republic . . . . The military intervention which took place [the statement went on] had no support from any leading body in the Czechoslovak communist party or state, and is opposed by them. No grounds have been brought forward that can justify this violation of the national sovereignty of the Czechoslovak people and Government.

The statement asserted that the party would continue the closest fraternal relations with the Soviet communist party, but that 'interference by a socialist country in the internal affairs of another socialist country cannot be justified'.[45]

In December 1979, the British party further demonstrated its independent spirit by criticising the USSR for its intervention in Afghanistan. At the same time, the party indicated its support for the Afghan 'anti-imperialist revolution' and denounced 'anti-Soviet hysteria' in Britain.[46]

The policy of independence from Moscow, however, really came to maturity with the party's programme, called 'The British road to socialism', overwhelmingly approved by the 35th National Congress in November 1977. The Congress laid down the general principle that 'Britain's road to socialism will be different from the Soviet road because of its different conditions'.[47] Socialism in Britain was to be achieved gradually by a series of Left-wing governments, which were at first to be Left-wing Labour governments aided by an influential and stronger communist party. Parliamentary democracy and the pluralist society would be maintained. Even parties hostile to socialism would be tolerated. At the Congress the USSR was criticised for being a one-party state and for its harsh treatment of dissidents. Nevertheless, an address of friendship from the Soviet communist party was applauded with enthusiasm.

There is a temptation to describe the British Communist party as 'Eurocommunist', though its General Secretary, Gordon McLennan, has dismissed that expression as 'neither accurate nor useful'. Like the Eurocommunist parties of France, Italy and Spain, the British party now evidently wishes to gloss over its totalitarian associations and emphasise the differences between its own sort of socialism and the Soviet variety. If proportional representation were to be introduced into Britain, the party might win a few seats in Parliament – at present it has none, and its membership of 25,000 is not impressive. But the British people apparently have no warm regard for communists, and prefer a middle road even between the two existing major parties. The failure of the communists to find a place for themselves within the main party of the Left is undoubtedly one reason for their low standing, and the communists have their traditional, though now weaker, links with the Soviet Union to thank for this. It is a curious fact that Moscow, once the headquarters of a faith which seemed likely to sweep the board, is now such a handicap for its adherents around the world that merely to acknowledge any connection with it is a form of political suicide.

9. Economic Relations

THE most striking features of Anglo-Soviet economic relations since the 1917 Revolution have been three. First, those relations have been few, despite the interests both sides have had in increasing them. Secondly, they have been peculiarly sensitive to the state of political relations between the two countries, and, thirdly, they have made little or no contribution in themselves to creating a better political climate between the two. The mutual affairs of Britain and Russia have been overwhelmingly determined by political factors, though, with encouragement, more substantial economic relations could have improved them.

From the first contacts between Britain and Russia through the English Muscovy Company in the sixteenth century, trade took on the typical pattern between a developed and a developing country, the former exchanging its industrial products with the food and raw materials of the latter. From the earliest times Russia sent to Britain timber and rigging for its ships, together with furs, oil, salt and wax, and received in return cloth, sugar, herrings and, in the nineteenth century, manufactured goods. The distinctive feature of this trade, even with the vast expansion of commerce over the past hundred years, was its paucity. Russia, with its huge territorial extent, including almost all the climatic zones of the world, had little need of imports. It accounted for only 4 per cent of world trade before 1914, as compared with Britain's 13 per cent.

Even so, by 1870 Britain was being overtaken by Germany as Russia's most important trading partner, and the competition with Germany has remained strong ever since. In 1870 Russia took 39.5 per cent of its imports from Germany and 31 per cent from Britain. Britain was still Russia's most important customer, however, taking 47.2 per cent of Russia's exports, while Germany took 21.1 per cent. But by 1913 Germany was both sending most exports to Russia and receiving most imports from there. In that year, Russia bought 52.6

per cent of its imports from Germany and only 13.9 per cent from Britain. It sold 31.8 per cent of its exports to Germany and 18.8 per cent to Britain.[1]

Germany's common border with Russia at that time, of course, facilitated trade, and German goods were on the whole cheaper than British, though not always of better quality, and the range of products tended to be wider.[2] German traders also went to greater lengths to sell their goods, a familiar story, and took more trouble to please their customers, as for instance by using the purchaser's own language to a greater extent than British exporters.

The British were also relatively sluggish in investing money in pre-1914 Russia. In the period 1907 to 1913, for instance, British capital invested in Brazil, where the risks were greater and the profits higher, was twice as much as that invested in Russia. British capital invested in Argentina was two and a half times as much.[3] There was some improvement after the Anglo-Russian Convention of 1907, but there remained significant omissions in the British investment programme. British businessmen almost totally ignored investment in Russian railways, even though they were at that time building railways in many other countries which supplied Britain with food and raw materials. Even the Russian timber industry, unlike that of Scandinavia, did not much attract British capital in the decade before 1914, important though Russia was at that time becoming as a source of timber for Britain.

According to a report by the Russian Supreme Economic Soviet in 1922, of the total foreign capital invested in Russian joint stock companies between 1856 and 1913, Franco-Belgian capital accounted for 46.3 per cent, German for 27.4 per cent and British for only 16.8 per cent. The French were particularly encouraged to invest in Russia by the favourable political climate created by the Franco-Russian alliance of the 1890s.[4] Of course, after the Revolution British financiers could congratulate themselves that they had not lost money through the confiscation of foreign capital on the scale of French and German losses. But it does not seem that anticipation of the Revolution played much part in their investment policy.

The First World War and the Revolution, followed by civil war and Allied intervention, temporarily put an end to all economic relations between Russia and the West, and, after the Bolshevik seizure of power, the territory occupied by the Leninists was subjected to an Allied blockade which was not lifted until June 1920.

There followed the extraordinary spectacle of the two countries, Britain and Russia, having the greatest interest in developing their economic relations to the fullest extent, yet prevented from doing so by a thick tangle of mainly political difficulties. The Russians needed industrial equipment to help them overcome the ravages of the war and civil war. The Bolsheviks were bent on rapid industrialisation, which began in earnest in 1928, and their appetite for industrial equipment was almost insatiable. Britain had a massive unemployment problem, topping the three-million mark in 1933, with a permanent core of a million jobless concentrated in the old areas of heavy industry which produced precisely the goods Russia wanted for its industrialisation. Rakovsky, the head of the Soviet delegation to the trade and financial talks in London in 1924, summed up the position by saying that:

> The economic structure of Great Britain and that of the USSR are mutually complementary. On the one hand, a country possessing the most important industry, financing and shipping in the world, on the other, a state with a population of 130 millions and in possession of enormous potential riches, which requires for its development large quantities of industrial products and credits.[5]

Of course, the Bolshevik authorities lacked the means to pay on the nail for the imports they needed for their industrialisation. They needed credits from the rest of the world, and that is the normal process when a country undergoes industrialisation. The basic capital equipment of a community cannot be produced unless those producing it are maintained until such time as the new wealth produced by the capital equipment can be used to repay those who lent money or sacrificed consumption to make it possible. To the great damage of relations between Soviet Russia and the West, its industrialisation in the inter-war period was not achieved by Western states, including Britain, investing in it and receiving their reward later on. It was achieved by the Russian people being forced to pay for it themselves, as a charge against their living standards. The complementary needs of Britain and Russia were not matched and the Russian people suffered more in the way of dictatorship as a result than they need have done. No substantial links of an economic kind were formed, which might have had beneficial political effects. Instead, Russia's leaders were obliged to build up an export surplus, the opposite of normal industrialisation, in order to acquire foreign currency to buy capital equipment, and this further exacerbated relations with the West.

Admittedly, the reasons for this failure to marry British and Soviet economic needs in the years following the Revolution were by no means all the result of hostility of the British business world towards the Bolsheviks. Some were due to circumstances over which the British had no control. In the first place, foreign trade in the new Russia was no longer left to private initiative, except to a limited extent under the New Economic Policy (NEP) introduced by Lenin as a stop-gap in 1921. It was controlled by state agencies which ensured that it accorded with national economic policy and had no justification outside that policy. For them, the purpose of exports was nothing beyond the earning of foreign currency to pay for essential imports, and the purpose of imports was solely to fill deficiencies in the country's needs. Or that was the theory. This was not always easy for foreign dealers to understand, and doing business with pathologically suspicious, politically self-conscious Soviet officials made it no easier. British traders were happier getting along with parts of the world where old-fashioned methods were still in vogue. The Germans, who in any case knew more about bureaucracy and state intervention, could be left to deal with the Russians if they wanted to.

Besides, before trade and investment could be resumed, the whole tangle of financial claims and counter-claims arising out of the Revolution had to be resolved, or at least a start made on resolving it. The Anglo-Soviet commercial agreement of March 1921 was a small step towards normalisation, though it did not amount to de iure recognition of the new state, which did not come until 1924.[6] But the financial problem seemed to defy solution. At inter-Allied conferences from 1920 until 1922, delightful in location–Cannes, The Hague, Genoa–but barren of result, British, Belgian, French and Italian statesmen and the new Russian spokesmen wrestled with utterly incompatible forms of logic and got nowhere. The Allies wanted compensation from the Bolsheviks for their confiscation of foreign investments in Tsarist Russia. The Bosheviks said they could not talk about compensation unless they first had foreign economic help to enable them to get their people back to work. In any case, they said, they wanted compensation, too, for the loss and damage inflicted on their country during the period of Allied intervention. The Allies replied that they could not extend or guarantee a loan to

Russia for reconstruction without some security that the communist economic system would not collapse and take their investments with it, or that the communists would not do the same as they had done in 1918, that is, take all they could lay their hands on, including any new loans. The talks went on in a circle.

How hard these disagreements over the credit-worthiness of the new regime made the revival of foreign trade for Russia was shown in the controversy about oil. The Russians were highly dependent upon the export of oil to the West to help pay for foreign technology. But the world oil companies refused to buy what they called 'stolen' Russian oil, that is, oil from wells belonging to foreign concerns which the Bolsheviks had appropriated. No doubt the campaign was intensified by world oil companies having to compete with cheaper Russian oil, allegedly resulting from state subsidies. The head of one of the companies most affected, Sir Henri Deterding of Shell, is said to have been active in applying pressure on the British Conservative government in 1927 to break off diplomatic relations with Russia.[7] In the same year, the *Daily Mail* launched a campaign to dissuade motorists from buying 'stolen' Soviet oil. The newspaper issued posters for garages to display announcing that they were not selling 'Red' oil.

As it happened, however, the campaign enjoyed little success. Certain Western oil concerns broke through the boycott and the Soviet authorities made it worth their while to do so. They were greatly helped by an agreement made with the British firm Sale and Company for the disposal of Soviet oil in 1923. It was the first major penetration of the united front of the world oil companies against the purchase of Soviet oil.[8] It was followed in the same year by an agreement between Royal Dutch Shell and the Soviets for the purchase of Russian oil. In 1923, too, an agreement was signed between the British Gouria Petroleum Corporation and the Soviet Chief Concessions Committee, intended to last for 40 years, for the exploitation of 1100 square miles in Gouria, near the Black Sea. As the 1920s went on, British imports of Soviet oil increased, despite the boycott, with the Soviets intensifying their efforts to obtain the badly needed foreign currency. Soviet oil was undoubtedly cheap, and the authorities did their best to keep it so, fuelling Western complaints of Soviet 'dumping'. In 1926 Britain imported 381,270 tons of Soviet oil; in 1927 the figure rose to 714,014 tons.[9] Nevertheless, the Soviets had to fight for trade, and the endless disputes over compensation for property confiscated during the Revolution made the fight all the harder. At the same time, the more the Soviet authorities succeeded in their efforts to establish themselves in world markets, the more foreign firms affected by Soviet competition determined to prevent them, and their complaints against the legitimacy of Soviet trade was of some assistance in their efforts.

The whole question might have been resolved in 1924, when, as we have seen in a previous chapter, the first Labour government under MacDonald (though without MacDonald's help) laboriously worked out with Rakovsky a formula for the settlement of the bondholders' claims, which, had Parliament accepted it, might have made possible a loan for Russian reconstruction, raised in the City and guaranteed by the government.[10]. But that was not to be. The MacDonald government fell and the Conservatives, on returning to office, almost at once plunged into the miasma of accusations against Soviet misdemeanours which culminated in the diplomatic breach in May 1927. That event, involving the closure of the Soviet trade agency in London, Arcos, was a serious setback to Anglo-Soviet trade and to the Soviet struggle to build up reserves of foreign exchange just at the time when intense industrialisation under the first five-year plan was about to start. The fact that the late 1920s and the period of the Great Slump (1929–33) were marked by relatively greater falls in the prices of food and raw materials, which Russia mainly exported, as against those of manufactured products, which it mainly imported, was an additional handicap for the Soviet state. The breach did no good to Britain either; among its other drawbacks was the fact that, during the breach, the Russians were encouraged to send their technicians to the United States and Germany for their training, and this meant that, when diplomatic relations were restored, they were less willing to buy machinery from Britain which their technicians could not use.

No sooner had Anglo-Soviet relations been restored by the second labour government under MacDonald in October 1929 than a new development occurred to further depress the outlook for trade between the two countries. This was the fiercely protective spirit injected into British trade policy by the Great Slump. If foreign competitors were going to be affected by this protective spirit, it was inevitable that competition in the form of Soviet exports would be concerned as much as any. The Soviet state was notorious for its vitriolic campaigns against the capitalist system. Its record for using the criminal law, in the most dubious manner, against foreigners foolhardy enough to do business with it was well-known, and the trial in Moscow of British Metropolitan-Vickers engineers in 1933 was merely one example.[11] Moreover, if the Soviet authorities sought to give their exporting agencies the benefits of unfair competition with British and other foreign traders, they had the whole resources of virtually unchallenged state authority to use for that purpose. It was right that they should have the taste of their own medicine.

As it happened, before this new campaign began, Anglo-Soviet trade looked set for an appreciable increase. A temporary commercial agreement concluded between the two countries after the diplomatic resumption in 1929 included a 'commercial and financial consideration clause' which attempted to eliminate all forms of discrimination in economic relations and which carried with it the added inducement of the grant to Russia of most-favoured-nation treatment (MFN). It was the first time a private enterprise economy had sought to end the use by a planned economy of discriminatory practices. For some time and on the basis of this agreement, Anglo-Soviet trade flourished. The Soviet Union became for a time the most important market outside the United States for British machine tools. A number of important technical assistance agreements were concluded between the Soviets and British firms. In 1930, for instance, Imperial Chemical Industries Ltd agreed to provide technical assistance for Soviet chemical industries and to sell 30 million roubles' worth of chemicals to Russia on a credit basis. A technical assistance agreement was also made with Metropolitan-Vickers, one of the few British firms to continue to do business with the Russians during the diplomatic breach, for the production of electrical apparatus. A similar agreement with the Birmingham Small Arms Company enabled the Soviets to develop their bicycle industry so that it became for a time the sector with the highest growth rate.[12]

In the same period, a number of British firms secured large orders from the Soviets, showing that the potential was there, despite all the regular difficulties. The Soviet Union, for example, ordered rolling-mill equipment from David Brown and Sons and large forgery manipulators from Davy Brothers, Ltd. Similar equipment for steel works was supplied by Craven Brothers (Manchester) Ltd and 100 marine diesel engines for fishing boats were ordered in 1932 from Ruston and Hornsby. In the following year, Appleyard of England built a dry-cleaning plant for coal in the USSR. Altogether, British manufacturers supplied £15 million worth of goods for the first Soviet five-year plan, by no means a massive contribution to the employment problem, but achieved at a time when almost any business of this kind was welcome.[13]

But, as so often tended to happen in Anglo-Soviet relations, promising developments began only to have to suffer a setback, and in this case it was the bitter conflict between the two countries over 'unfair' trading practices, or 'dumping'. The Great Depression of the early thirties forced all prices down, and especially the prices of the agricultural produce which comprised Russia's principal exports. It meant that the Soviets had to export all the more in order to acquire the same amount of foreign exchange. From 1930 to 1931, the peak years of Soviet trade, the volume of exports had to be increased roughly two and a half times that of 1927–8 in order to secure approximately the same financial return.[14]

The clamour against Soviet exports actually reached a climax in Britain in 1930, the campaign being mainly levelled against imports of Russian grain, barley, timber, eggs, butter, fruit pulp and some manufactured products, such as soap. All the time-honoured prejudices against and fears of the communist state were resurrected to stoke up the campaign, together with allegations that Soviet exports were able to dominate foreign markets because they were produced by slave labour and at minimum cost: in the case of timber, there was probably not a little truth in the charge. The 1930s, of course, was a period when, for the first time in its modern history, Britain was opting for protection of its foreign trade, with the Import Duties Act and the Ottawa system of imperial preference in 1932. The fact that Canada produced, and had a valuable market in Britain for, the same sort of agricultural and forestry products as Russia meant that the drive against Soviet 'dumping' would receive special encouragement in that country.

At the conference in the Canadian capital in 1932 which established imperial preference Britain reached an agreement with the Canadian government to prohibit the import of commodities which had been aided by state subsidies in the form of underpaid labour organised by public authorities. Accordingly, on 17 October 1932, the British government denounced the Anglo-Soviet commercial agreement of 1930, to the tune of outcries about the likely effect on the unemployment figures. The President of the Machine Tool Trade Association, for which Russia was a customer of crucial importance, declared that:

Russia is the only country in the world which is engaged on a wide scheme of industrialisation and consequently it is from Russia alone that large-scale orders for industrial plant are available.[15]

The *Spectator*, not noted for its friendliness towards Russia, said that the denunciation of the trade agreement was 'profoundly unfortunate'. Germany and America, the newspaper considered, were 'eager enough to snatch Russia's orders that might be keeping British workmen employed'.[16] Of the Ottawa agreements as a whole, the *Manchester Guardian*, with its strong interest in foreign trade, remarked:

> Everyone knows that the allegations about Russian 'dumping' are largely nonsense and only another way of saying that after some years' absence from the world markets, Russian exports have returned, and, because of the already demoralised conditions, have helped to force world prices lower. Everyone knows also that the motives which led to the drafting of the Ottawa formula were crude and mercenary to the last degree.[17]

Along with the Ottawa restrictiveness went a tougher British attitude towards credits for financing Anglo-Soviet trade. Stanley Baldwin, then the Conservative leader, argued on one occasion in March 1931 that British credits for Russia were financing 'the very weapon that is going to run us through the vitals'.[18] It was established policy of the Board of Trade in those years to 'consider sympathetically' applications for guarantees in respect of the export of heavy engineering equipment, but, strangely, the depressed ship-building industry was excluded from this undertaking, and it was in that field that British trade prospects were promising. In the entire period from the Revolution until the Nazi invasion of Russia in 1941, Britain supplied more equipment to the Soviet merchant marine than any other country, contributing in excess of 28 per cent of Soviet hulls and almost 32 per cent of marine engines.[19] A more liberal credit policy would have helped Anglo-Soviet trade considerably.

The allegations against Soviet 'dumping' were wildly exaggerated and reflected accumulated political prejudice. The Minister for Agriculture in the second Labour government, Dr C. Addison, pointed out in October 1930 that the depression was due to the 'enormous surplus in the world's stocks', to which Russia's contribution was minute.[20] The surplus was estimated by the government at 633 million cwt, of which Russia's contribution was only 30 million. During the first nine months of 1930, when the campaign against Soviet 'dumping' was at its height, wheat imports from the Soviet Union amounted to only just under 5 per cent of total British wheat imports.[21] Throughout the 1920s and 1930s, Soviet trade accounted for no more than 2.5 per cent of total world trade and Britain's imports from Russia were never more than 2 per cent of its total imports. The British Chamber of Commerce, which could not be charged with partiality for communism, adopted a report from a special committee on trade with Russia which was published on 8 December 1931 and stated that, with regard to timber, imports from Russia had increased, bringing the figures up to pre-1914 levels, and that, a few years previously, they had been marketed at 'cut prices' and 'thus brought down the general market value', but that this seemed to be no longer the case.

The beneficiaries from the British anti-dumping campaign and the accompanying restriction of British credit for trade with Russia were Britain's trade rivals, especially Germany. Germany concluded the so-called Pyatakov trade agreement with the Soviets in April 1931 for increasing credits for trade with Russia, and under this German exports to that country greatly increased. In the entire year 1931 Germany provided as many as 37 per cent of Soviet imports, when the proportion for Britain had fallen to 6 per cent; Germany's share in 1932 was 46 per cent, Britain's falling even more to 5 per cent. Yet in these two years Britain imported twice as much as Germany from the USSR, showing the impact of the restrictions on British credit policy. On 12 April 1932, the Secretary of the Overseas Trade Department was asked in the Commons to extend the British credit system so as to win more orders from Russia in view of the increasing trade between Germany and Russia. His reply was that the Russians wanted too long to pay.[22]

Pressure nevertheless continued to be exerted on the National government to expand trade with the Soviets and negotiations were opened with Moscow on new commercial arrangements which would deal with the 'dumping' question and also with the way in which MFN agreements were working in trade with Russia. The British contention was that MFN treatment had been extended to Russia as a concession, but no private enterprise country could count on the Russians not to switch their foreign trade to a third country as an act of policy, since all Soviet trade, after all, was a state monopoly. The negotiations nevertheless opened in July 1932, then were interrupted owing to the Metropolitan-Vickers trial in April 1933, when both countries placed embargoes on trade with the other, and eventually issued in a new temporary commercial agreement signed on 16 February 1934. It included the MFN clause from the 1930 agreement, but permitted derogations from it in respect of certain commodities at certain times. Provision was also made for complaints about 'dumping' to be submitted to negotiation.

Prospects for Anglo-Soviet trade accordingly revived once more, especially with the deterioration of Soviet-German relations during the Nazi era in the thirties. It showed how responsive trade with the Soviet state was to the ups and downs of political conditions. Signs of improvement appeared in 1934, a notable achievement in November of that year being the settlement of the long-standing dispute between the Russians and British shareholders in the Lena goldfields. In 1934, Britain even surpassed Germany as the leading exporter to Russia, supplying 19.9 per cent of Soviet imports, as compared with the 12.4 per cent provided by Germany. In 1935 Britain replaced Germany as Russia's foremost foreign market. Britain continued to have a large adverse balance in visible trade with Russia, though this was offset to some extent by Britain's sizeable trade in such invisibles as shipping and insurance. In the technological field, Britain had the distinction of providing the model for Moscow's much-vaunted Underground, opened in 1935. It was copied, with improvements, from the London system, and the British method of shield tunnelling was used in its construction.

Arguments for a British loan to Russia to offset competition from Germany were invariably met with the old complaints about the dispossession of property-owners during the Revolution. On the other hand, the advocates of more trade pointed to the benefits in terms of jobs. One of the most articulate of these was the Conservative MP, Robert Boothby, who argued that Germany had used its credit position with Russia to build up its trade during the 1930s:

It is no exaggeration to say [Boothby contended in November 1935] that Germany owes the entire modern structure of her industries, and therefore her present capacity for armament production, to her export trade with Russia during these critical years. A trade which we literally threw away. After the crisis of

1931 Germany defaulted widely on her foreign commitments. Russia, on the other hand, has repaid in full.

'Today', Boothby went on, 'a fresh opportunity presents itself, owing to the inevitable estrangement between Soviet Russia and Nazi Germany, and the need of the former for a long-term loan which we alone are capable of financing'.[23]

Spurred on by a new credit agreeement between Russia and Germany signed in April 1936, the British authorities concluded a fresh pact with Moscow on 30 July of that year, and this made provision for credits up to a total of £10 million of British exports to Russia during the period ending 30 September 1937. The rate of interest was fixed at 5½ per cent, one half per cent lower than that charged by Germany. As a result, Britain's sales to Russia rose from just under £13 million in value in 1936 to £19½ million in 1937, though there was a decline to slightly less than £17½ million in 1938. Britain provided 14.3 per cent of total Soviet imports in 1937 and 16.9 per cent in 1938. Germany's exports to Russia, on the other hand, fell, owing to political tension between the two countries, from 15 per cent of total Soviet imports in 1937 to only 4.7 per cent in 1938.

Again, as so often before in Anglo-Soviet relations, with the improvement in the political climate following the wartime alliance from 1941, trade followed suit and, for a time, things looked brighter than they had ever done before. In April 1941 a new Anglo-Soviet commercial agreement was signed which was to reverse dramatically the old pattern under which Britain generally imported more from Russia than it exported to that country. Britain granted a five-year credit to Russia of £10 million, and when that was exhausted, another, this time for £25 million was agreed to. The interest charged was three per cent, and in return for the credit the Soviet Union was to make available to Britain its surplus of raw materials, especially timber and hemp. In September 1942, a Soviet trade delegation arrived in Britain to arrange for the purchase of large quantities of machinery, including machine tools, electrical equipment, medical instruments and supplies, and certain raw materials, such as non-ferrous metals. At the same time, interest developed in Britain in the possibilities of raising the level of economic dealings with Russia once the war was over. *The Economist*, for instance, argued in April 1943 that Russia's outstanding role in the war showed how anomalous was her small share of pre-war international trade.[24] Efforts should be made, the newspaper contended, to bring the Russians more fully into the Western trading system. Indeed, after the war Russia would be so devastated that it would have to import more than it had previously done. In order to do so, the Russians would stand in need of far more long-term credits.[25]

II

That hope was not realised. Once the war against the Axis ended, Anglo-Soviet economic relations slumped back to the marginal level for both countries at which they always had been. There were two reasons for this, both arising from the ideological division, first of Europe, then of a large part of the rest of the world, which followed the onset of the Cold War. The first of these was the split between the Soviet economic system, which the Russians forcibly extended to their new allies in eastern Europe, and the system which grew up in the non-communist world; the second was the strategic embargoes enforced against economic relations with the Soviet bloc by the newly formed NATO collective defence system.

As for the first of these developments, the Soviet Union decided to form no part of the world monetary and trading arrangements which the rest of the world created in the mid-1940s, chiefly under American inspiration, to avoid a return to the financial and economic chaos of the inter-war period. The Russians took an active part in the Bretton Woods (New Hampshire) conference in 1944 which led to the formation of the International Monetary Fund (IMF) and the International Bank for Reconstruction and Development (IBRD), but they did not ratify or consider themselves bound by the agreements of the conference. Nor did they take any part subsequently in those organisations, or in the abortive discussions on the creation of a World Trade Organisation (WTO) at Havana in 1946, or in the setting up of the General Agreement on Tariffs and Trade (GATT) in 1947, through which the rest of the world has sought to reduce obstacles to international trade by successive rounds of negotiations.

After all, the Soviet economic system was fundamentally different from that of the rest of the world: it was a managed system through and through, and all decisions, except for the most trivial, as to what was to be produced in the different sectors, and how much, who to trade and do business with in the outside world, and in what sorts of products, were taken by the central authorities as part of their over-all plan. There could be economic dealings with the market-economy and mixed-economy countries in the world outside, but this would have to be on an entirely *ad hoc* basis, the purpose being strictly to fill deficiencies in the Soviet system and to dispose of its surplus products. In fact, most of the international negotiations about economic questions between the non-communist countries in the post-1945 period were concerned with eliminating the weaknesses of the world capitalist system. In the nature of things, the Soviet authorities had no interest in such activities; if anything, they wanted them to fail.

The gulf between the Soviet economy and that of the rest of the world was dug even deeper as a result of the Marshall Plan under which most of western Europe recovered from the war with American dollar aid between 1948 and 1952. The Soviet authorities not only refused to participate in the Marshall Plan on the terms which the states taking the leading role in west European recovery, Britain and America, demanded; they also denied the east European states which fell under their control at the end of the war the right to participate in the Plan, too, and formed their own recovery plan based on their own international organisation, the Council for Mutual Economic Assistance, or Comecon. The Marshall Plan was ostensibly no more than a recovery operation, but it had important long-term consequences. The west European democracies participating in the Plan, 16 in number, formed a co-operative body, the Organisation for European Economic Co-operation (OEEC), which in the 1960s, with the admission of Japan and the United States, became the OECD, or Organisation for Economic Co-operation and Development, and this body is today by far the most important agency for economic co-operation in the developed non-communist world. Moreover, within the framework of the OEEC originated the movement towards the closer integration of, first, six and then, in 1973, nine of its members, resulting in the formation of a supranational authority for coal and steel, and later, by the Rome treaty signed in March 1957, a European economic community. In none of these developments did the Soviet Union or its east European allies have any share. This did not in itself prevent any amount of trade or other economic transactions between Russia and the Atlantic nations, including Britain; but it did mean that East–West economic relations would receive little encouragement. If they did thrive, it would have to be in spite of the lack of formal channels and of any on-going dialogue between the two worlds about economic questions.

The blow to economic relations with Russia caused by the post-war system of strategic embargoes was less fundamental, but more irritating. If anyone had set out at the end of the Second World War to devise a scheme to give Britain trouble, and not only in its relations with the Soviets, he could hardly have framed a more effective one than the system of embargoes on trade with the communist world. In 1949, as soon as the North Atlantic treaty was signed, the Western Powers set up a Co-ordinating Committee for Multilateral Export Controls (known as Cocom) to draw up a list of goods to be embargoed which might be useful to the Soviet bloc in a military sense. Cocom represented 15 countries, all NATO states except Iceland and Japan. The Cocom list was not binding on the states among which it was operative, but by the Battle Act of 1951, the United States made observance of the embargo a condition of the receipt of American military and financial assistance.

The Cocom arrangement had obvious commonsense about it. It was absurd to supply Russia (and China, for which a similar, though even more severe, system was introduced) with military equipment and technology when the Western Powers were feverishly improving their defences against possible Soviet and Chinese aggression. It is hard to know to what extent, after 30 years, the strategic controls have in fact affected communist military strength. But those effects would have had to be considerable to offset the problems the controls created for Britain and its NATO allies and the strains it placed on relations between them. In the first place, though this had no direct bearing on Anglo-Soviet relations, Britain objected to the greater severity of the Chincom list as compared with the Cocom list, which British Ministers said reflected American feelings about China rather than the objective needs of the situation; in 1957 they unilaterally equalised the two lists for British trade.[26] But the very existence of the lists, at a time when Britain needed all the foreign trade it could get, could not but be an irritant in Anglo-American relations.

The United States could hardly be expected to understand British grievances about the embargoes: it was not an important trading nation like Britain, and even if it had been, it was immeasurably wealthier than Britain and better able to afford the loss of trade with the communist world. It was notorious, too, that Americans were more than slightly hysterical about communism, and Britain and the other west European allies were expected to pay for American fears. The anger of British Labour MPs against capitalist America which dictated to an impoverished Britain with whom it could trade was equalled by the contempt of American Congressmen for British appeasers. In January 1952, Arthur Bottomley, the Labour MP, declared that 'the most natural markets for ourselves and the Commonwealth countries are in the East' and that 'we must not allow political expediency to damage our long-term interests'.[27] Labour politicians repeatedly complained that Britain was observing the embargo too stringently; it was a theme well-suited for the expression of hurt national pride stimulated by a military alliance with a rich super-Power. Harold Wilson argued in a letter to *The Times* in September 1953 that the Soviet Union was not inhibited in sending to the West such strategic materials as platinum, manganese, chrome and oil, to say nothing of grain and timber, and Britain would have to spend precious dollars to get such goods from America. The strategic controls, Mr Wilson said, were clearly out of date and were probably more harmful to Britain than to Russia.[28] At the TUC conference in September 1953, pleas were made for reducing the embargo list. British dockers, it was stated, went short of work because of the ban on rubber exports to Russia, although rubber was reaching the Soviet Union through Amsterdam, Antwerp and Rotterdam.[29]

The Cocom system provided the Soviet authorities with an excellent instrument for stirring up bad blood between British politicians and businessmen on one side, and the United States on the other, by harping on the limitless possibilities of trade if the embargo system were done away with. In April 1952, a world economic conference was held in Moscow, and although Britain was not officially invited, a delegation of British businessmen led by Lord Boyd-Orr went to the conference and returned with several commercial agreements calculated to whet the appetite. Moreover, by proposing contracts for the supply of goods likely to be affected by the embargo, the Russians skilfully drew attention to the disabilities Britain laboured under as a result of its NATO connections. In August 1953, for instance, the Soviets placed orders in Britain for millions of pounds' worth of trawlers and fish-factory ships, but the embargo intervened.[30] In September of the same year, they attempted to buy in Britain five grain- and ore-carrying ships at

£700,000 each, but, again, export licences were refused. At a meeting in London in November, the Soviet chargé d'affaires rammed the point home by stating that 'the expansion of British-Soviet trade could result in great advantages to both countries'.[31]

This Soviet pressure, and the positive British response to it, had some effect. In May 1954, the British government refused export licences for three more fish-factory ships worth £4 million on the ground that the vessels could be converted into submarine depot ships. In August, however, the regular NATO talks on the embargo list came round and British representatives pressed strongly for the list to be scaled down, Soviet orders for machine tools and other equipment being held up pending a decision. As a result of the talks, the embargo list was reduced from 270 to 170 items. Goods on the list not entirely banned but subject to quantitative restrictions were scaled down from 90 to 70. These changes were estimated to have the effect of releasing some £5 million worth of British exports to Russia and her allies. Orders for £15 million were still reported to be held up by the strategic controls and ships remained subject to the same restrictions as before.

The strategic control system was in fact becoming a handy lever for the Russians to press for all kinds of concessions by dangling the mirage of increased trade before the British if it were not for the NATO system. In 1956, when he visited Britain with Soviet Prime Minister Bulganin, Mr Khrushchev had a field day denouncing the NATO embargoes, which he said had done nothing to prevent his country making great strides forward in aircraft design, hydrogen bombs and guided missiles. At the same time, he offered Soviet purchases of British goods worth between £800 and £1000 million during the following five years. About two thirds of this shopping list were not affected by the strategic controls, but the third which was served to excite resentment in Britain against the embargo system, especially when it became known that the entire proposal might be dependent on the abolition of the system. One striking gain from the Khrushchev–Bulganin visit in 1956 was a contract for the British to build a rubber-tyre factory in Russia, the biggest in the world outside the United States.[32] No single firm was large enough to handle the deal and a consortium of British manufacturers, Rustyfa Ltd, was formed to execute the order. It was the first time the Russians had agreed to a package deal of this kind for more than twenty years.

But it soon became clear that the promises of the Khrushchev–

Bulganin visit were not going to be fulfilled. In June of the following year, Prime Minister Harold Macmillan expressed his concern to Soviet leaders, saying that it would be helpful if the Russians placed more orders for consumer goods and vehicles in Britain and allowed British businessmen direct access to Soviet enterprises interested in their products.[33] He received the unsurprising reply from Bulganin that the Soviet suggestion of an increase of trade to between £800 and £1000 million was dependent upon the removal of the strategic embargo.[34]

Nevertheless, this exchange had effects. By January 1958, workers in the British ship-building industry were protesting against the strategic controls, which they charged with damaging employment prospects. Their arguments were echoed by Harold Wilson in a debate in the Commons that month on East–West trade. He contended that, with the advent of 'push-button' warfare, many of the strategic controls were out of date. Full employment in certain British industries positively depended on more trade with the Soviet bloc. He believed that orders totalling £150 million in value were available to Britain if chemical plant could be exported to Russia, but in nearly every case some part of the plant depended on an American patent. The American government, according to Mr Wilson, would not let the relevant firms co-operate. The American belief that these restrictions retarded Soviet development was ridiculous, he said: even during the maximum restrictions, Soviet industry developed far more rapidly than anything seen in the West.[35]

The campaign against the embargoes once more made progress, underlining the theory that perhaps they had never done much good, except to Soviet propagandists against the Western alliance. In August 1958, Cocom agreed to reduce the strategic list once more. A wide range of items was freed for export, including civil aircraft and aero-engines, many machine tools, ships (with certain restrictions on speed), all civil vehicles and all electrical motors. A list consisting of quotas on 25 items was abolished and the remaining items on the list were reduced from 170 to 118. Russia's technological progress was a factor encouraging this process: the previous year, 1957, was the year of Sputnik. *The Times* commented that one reason which sustained the embargo in the minds of some but had now been 'dusted away' was the 'exaggerated belief in western technological superiority'.[36]

But the embargo had yet another drawback for Britain. It created tensions with allies, who were suspected of ignoring the embargo in everything but the letter, while Britain was handicapped by its strict fidelity to the alliance. The theme was well-suited to angry debates in the House of Commons in which the alliance and allies came in for a full share of blame without Anglo-Soviet trade benefiting much as a result. In March 1954, the inexhaustible Harold Wilson cited the case of copper wire, which the Russians wanted for trolley bus and tramcar cables. They preferred it without insulation but the embargo restrictions prohibited its export in this form. Foreign manufacturers had evidently circumvented the embargo by covering the wire with false insulation which was easily stripped off. In one case cited by Wilson, a paper-insulated wire was produced with a kind of zip-fastener attachment for easy stripping. By stringently applying the strategic controls, he said, Britain was losing good business.[37]

A more serious argument with allies over the controls, this time with West Germany, sprang up in 1963 concerning the export of oil pipes to Russia. In March of that year, the Americans objected to West Germany selling such pipes to Russia and the West German government prevailed on the Bundestag to discontinue the sales. In May, however, the Russians offered a British company, the South Durham Steel Company, a contract for the supply of large diameter steel pipes. The West German Foreign Minister, Dr Schröder, pointed out that to allow the sale would be to break the NATO embargo. To which the British government replied that when the NATO authorities had issued a ruling on the pipes in the previous November, Britain had asserted that it had no binding force: in any case, there was no legislation in Britain to prevent such a sale if the firm in question wished to proceed with it.[38] Occasions for irritation between the allies on questions of this kind were never lacking, and it would have been remiss of the Russians not to wring as much political profit as they could from them. Their aim was to create all the friction within NATO that they could and the strategic embargo fell into their hands as a means of doing so.

In the last twenty years–until the worsening of East–West relations resulting from the Soviet intervention in Afghanistan in December 1979–the impact of the embargo on Anglo-Soviet trade has been so whittled down that it has not contributed much to the generally low level of that trade. Although Britain has remained one of Russia's most important customers, trade between the two states has never risen much above two per cent of total British trade. The reasons for this have been stated earlier in this chapter, and to them must be added, as before 1914, the well-known tendencies of Britain's trade competitors to take more trouble over the marketing of their products. British firms, for instance, are notorious for their neglect of specialist trade journals in the USSR as advertising agencies, on the ground that trade in the Soviet Union is a state monopoly and hence there is no need for advertising. Britain's competitors, on the other hand, believe that managers of Soviet enterprises do read the journals and advise the purchase of foreign goods on that basis. If all such complaints about the lack of British enterprise in Russia are true, it is remarkable that British exporters have done as well as they have.

Another factor militating against the expansion of trade with the Soviets in the last two decades has been the shortage of Soviet purchasing power, intensified by inflation in Britain and the rise in the value of the pound. This is perhaps surprising in view of the persistent deficit which Britain has had in her trade with Russia, and which has been a constant subject of complaint to Moscow. The Russians first replied, after the formation of the European Free Trade Association (EFTA) in 1960, and then, after Britain joined the European Economic Community (EEC) in 1973, that these trading blocs were an obstacle to Anglo-Soviet trade, though they could not in themselves have prevented the Russians buying more British goods. The Soviet campaign against British membership of the EEC seemed more politically inspired than otherwise. Perhaps a more important factor in the sluggish rate of growth in the Soviet demand for British goods was the Soviet expenditure of foreign currency on grain and other food imports, chiefly from the United States, which was necessitated by the poor Russian harvests in the second half of the 1970s. The exploitation of British North Sea oil was another drawback for Anglo-Soviet trade, since it meant a fall in demand for Soviet crude oil; on the other hand, the resulting improvement in the technology of oil production in Britain provided the basis for a new British market in Russia.

In 1973, Britain's trade deficit with the Soviet Union increased by 70 per cent. Exports to Russia increased from £89 million in 1971 to £97 million in 1973, but imports from Russia mounted in the same years from £199 million to £327 million. The increased deficit was partly due to the rise in price of Soviet exports, especially diamonds, which Britain re-exported, and which accounted for as much as one third of British imports from the Soviet Union.[39] To encourage more trade, the British Labour government concluded an agreement with the USSR for the development of economic, scientific, technological and industrial co-operation. The hope was that this might facilitate British firms winning more Soviet contracts. Prime Minister Wilson followed up this agreement by visiting Moscow in February 1975 and opening a £950 million line of credit at an estimated rate of interest of 7 to 7 ½ per cent, lower, many Conservative critics pointed out, than Britain itself had to pay on credit it received from other countries.[40]

For some time the agreement acted as a boost to British sales to Russia. During the period 1974–5, British exports to that country more than doubled in value, and had doubled again by 1978. A number of major contracts had been signed by the Soviet authorities with British firms by the end of the first year of the agreement. These included contracts for the delivery of British-made equipment for the Mogilyov synthetic fibre mill, technological equipment for the second stage of the Nizhnekamski factory, and for a number of sparking-plug factories, two large-capacity forge complexes and diverse machine-tool equipment.[41] The Soviet Union also concluded two 'compensation' agreements with British companies for the production of low-pressure polyethylene and toys.[42] By such agreements, the Soviets pay for the equipment by exporting the goods it produces, thus saving foreign currency. Another important area of co-operation, this time involving Soviet sales, was established in 1975, when Russia signed a contract with the British Central Electricity Generating Board and the South of Scotland Electricity Board for the enrichment of British uranium in Soviet plants for use in British nuclear power stations. The £17.5 million contract was to be effective in 1980 and to run for ten years.

Similar deals followed. In October 1977, a multi-million pound agreement was announced between the British firm Dunlop and the Soviet licensing body, Licensingtorg, for the supply of technology to assist the Russians to build a latex-foam factory to make mattresses and other forms of cushioning, and to train the personnel to work in it. During the period 1977–8 orders were signed with British companies for £7.8 million worth of cigarette-making machines, £87.4 million worth of gas compressor pumps and station equipment, a high-density polyethylene plant valued at £46.2 million, two methanol plants valued at £147 million, and equipment for two tyre factories valued at £23.8 million and £54.1 million respectively. In October 1978, Rank Xerox won the contract to be sole supplier of xerographic copying services to the 1980 Moscow Olympic games, a deal worth £1.29 million.

All this showed that there was useful business to be done with the Soviet state, despite the worsening international climate towards the end of the 1970s. British exports rose to £455 million by 1970, imports from Russia, at £786 million, showing the same tendency to run ahead. Nevertheless, the 1975 credit agreement did not serve as the turning point in Anglo-Soviet relations which had been hoped for. The British export figures were in fact somewhat misleading, since between 10 and 20 per cent of export proceeds represented shipments of uranium through Britain to the Soviet Union by third countries. By February 1980, when the credit agreement expired, the Soviet Union had used up only £550 million of the £950 million available. During the last twenty months of the credit's duration, Britain secured only two major contracts: a £50 million deal signed by Davy International for the construction of an alpha-olefins plant at Nizhnekamski and a £36 million contract signed by Woodhall–Duckham for a glass-fibre plant near Polatsk.

III

There is certainly room for expansion in Anglo-Soviet trade, which is unlikely for years to come to reach a level of actual dependency of one country on the other, and therefore to be open to political objections. For Britain, Russia is an important source of supply for timber, oil and oil products, textiles, furs and diamonds: it is conceivable that the last of these could become more important if trade with South Africa declined because of the application of sanctions in which Britain joined. The Soviet Union also wishes to increase its exports of manufactured goods, such as watches, cars and cameras, for which there is a growing market in Britain. In 1978, Britain was Russia's biggest Western market for automobiles, sales reaching 19,420 vehicles in that year.[43]

On the side of British sales to Russia, there are great potentialities in the field of technology, in which the Russians have shown particular interest. British knowledge of the technology of oil extraction is now considerable and British firms could win contracts for energy projects in the Caspian and Barents Seas. There are also prospects for Britain to participate in the Soviet timber industry, the products of which have always been important to it. Another substantial opportunity for British enterprise is in chemicals. The

Russians particularly need fertilisers, pesticides and herbicides to improve their agricultural yields, and Britain lags behind France, Italy, Japan, the United States and West Germany in trading in chemicals with the USSR. The sphere of microprocessing technology is also one in which Britain could take the lead, and in which the Soviet Union tends to be inferior to the West. It could be argued that Britain and its allies should not go out of their way to help the technological progress of a hostile or potentially hostile Power. But the Soviet Union's scientific and technological advance since the war has been such that it may soon draw abreast of the West in many such fields, and there may be some advantage in ensuring that it does so in collaboration with the West and drawing upon Western human and material resources.

Whatever the future for economic relations between Britain and Russia, however, it seems unlikely that these will ever become so substantial as materially to affect their general relations in either a positive or a negative sense. For both countries, but especially for Britain, trade and other economic contacts between them have been marginal since 1917, and though there have been fluctuations, these have generally been within a narrow range. Moreover, even these exiguous relations have been from time to time subjected to interruptions and restrictions, chiefly on the British side, the most important being the breach of diplomatic relations in 1927 and the strategic embargo since the Second World War. Although these interruptions and restrictions no doubt seemed well justified at the time, it is doubtful whether, on balance, they did more good than harm to Britain. They reinforced the Soviet obsession with the implacable enmity of the capitalist world. They probably stiffened central government controls in Russia by giving the men in power more excuses to tighten their grip on the country. And they represented a missed opportunity to use economic contacts to help break down the wall of mistrust between the two peoples.

On the other hand, if economic relations were not allowed to develop far enough to serve as a solvent of political differences, neither did they act as sources of those differences. Whatever else may be said about the alarming divide which sprang up between Russia and the West as soon as the Second World War ended, it cannot be argued that economic conflicts were responsible for it. But this is not to say that, over a long period, more commercial and economic dealings between Britain and its allies, on one side, and Russia and its friends, on the other, could not alleviate the alarming political conflicts between them. Britain, of all countries, has everything to gain from doing more business with the Soviet bloc, and very little to lose.

10. Summing Up

THE time has not yet come–perhaps it never will–for a definitive account to be written of Anglo-Soviet relations since the revolution, seen from the standpoint of both countries, for the simple reason that the Soviet side of the story is practically unknown to us. We know almost nothing of the course of debate in Soviet governmental quarters about their dealings with this, or any other, country, or about the considerations on which the decisions they make about these dealings are based. We know hardly any more about such arguments as go on (if any do) among ordinary Russian people about Britain and its problems; in any case, the real knowledge of this country and contact with its people which the ordinary Russian has must be so slight as hardly to form a basis for genuine formation of opinion. It is an extraordinary fact that within the next few years the British and Russian people could find themselves destroying each other, and no doubt with a sense of right on both sides, without having much more personal knowledge of each other than if they inhabited different planets.

The physical distance between Britain and Russia, even in these days of high-speed travel, is certainly one factor in this lack of mutual contact, and there are language and cultural differences. But a vastly more important cause is the Soviet government's policy, sedulously pursued, with few interruptions, since 1917, of sealing off their country from the world outside, making unrestricted travel for foreigners within the Soviet Union difficult, if not impossible, and hampering the freedom of their own people to move freely in and out of their own country. The warnings issued by the Soviet authorities to their people against mixing with foreign visitors during the Olympic Games in Moscow in 1980, for fear of their subversive activities, form an incident in a continuing story. The unrelenting claustrophilia of Soviet officialdom has, of course, a venerable ancestry, connected no doubt with the historical vulnerability of the country to invasion and the insecurity neurosis this has bred in the Russian mind. On this has been grafted the Marxist *ideé fixe* of the Soviet state as a besieged island of socialism in a threatening bourgeois sea, an image now obsolete but still retaining its compulsive force. To which should be added the insecurity mania seemingly inherent in the ruling communist elite in Russia itself, and their determination to keep their heavily indoctrinated people insulated against foreign allurements. The Soviet leader resembles a religious fundamentalist fiercely defending his flock against the devil's temptation.

As Soviet self-confidence in their world power grows, as new recruits join the dissidents in labour camps and psychiatric hospitals, and if and when Soviet living standards rise comparably with those in Western Europe and North America, the policy of the closed society may relax. But of that we cannot be sure, and in any case the process will be painfully slow. And yet Soviet leaders, or at least some of them, are almost bound to ask in the course of time whether the closed society any longer serves Russia's national interest, if it ever did, and whether it can be permanently maintained. The more the Soviet Union becomes a world power, the more it expects other nations to come and admire its achievements, as at the Olympic Games, the harder must it be to keep the country a sealed chamber to outsiders. But it must also be asked whether it is safe, even for Russia herself, to keep the door shut, or almost shut, against the outside world. It is a curious fact that, in the military sphere, Moscow pursues a policy, if not of openness, at least of relative openness, and that where it would not be expected. It trundles out its monstrous weapons on public view in Red Square on May Day and other occasions, flexing its muscles before the windows of the world, no doubt because it wants other nations to know about its strength. It has persistently advocated the exchange of information between the bourgeois and communist worlds on military manoeuvres and pressed for the inclusion of this in the Final Act of the Helsinki conference of 35 nations in 1975. It presumably did so on the sensible ground that the better informed each side is of the hardware possessed by the other, and of the other's intentions in regard to it, the less likely will it be tempted into military adventures or misread the signals of mutual deterrence.

But the same could be said of the political realm. So long as Russia's policies and objectives remain a 'riddle wrapped inside an enigma', so long will the outside world have an incentive to place the worst possible interpretation on them. All the more is this so after the long experience the non-communist world has had of the fatal consequences of accepting at their face value the blandishments of dictators in the past. It may be that the democracies are today as gullible as they always were, as prone to think the best of the totalitarians. But, judging from their reactions to Soviet policies during the Cold War, it seems unlikely. Their inclination seems rather to put the worst construction on totalitarian behaviour, even though in the event they may not have been willing to do much about it. Yet, as we have seen repeatedly in this book, the Soviet Union, in its policy towards the outside world, has been much more realistic, circumspect and restrained than most other states have been willing to concede. To be sure, Soviet policy has been unhesitatingly self-interested, but this has not excused the way in which other countries, including Britain, have lost opportunities to benefit themselves by developing common interests with the Soviet state, and they have often done so through sheer distaste for the Soviet system, to which their ignorance of it has contributed. It may be, in short, that Soviet leaders will one day discover that they can improve their national security, about which they worry so much, by somewhat lifting the veils hanging over the making of their policies.

From the hermetically sealed character of the Soviet state derives the greatest paradox of the British experience of that state since its foundation in 1917, which is the subject of this book: namely, the fact that British politics, internal and external, and much of our thought on other matters, too, have been profoundly affected by our encounter with Soviet communism, and yet our actual knowledge of that system, not mainly through any fault of our own, has been minimal, and as a result our assessments of the Soviet phenomenon have wildly fluctuated from one extreme to another. These three basic elements in the paradox are worth some further elaboration.

First there is the dominant place occupied by the Soviet Union in the life and thought of the British people since the First World War. On the whole, Russia has not been one of Britain's intimate partners in world affairs, except during the quite exceptional period of the alliance in the Second World War, and even then the partnership did not run very deep. We think of the Commonwealth, especially the old, white Dominions, of France and other west European countries, and of the United States, as Britain's particular friends and allies, comrades-in-arms in two world wars and linked to Britain by a thousand and more ties of race and kinship, religion and language, and shared moral and political principles. We are all formally

Christian states; we understand what democratic usages and the
Atlantic Charter are and, at the Cenotaph on Armistice Day, stand in
silence for the men who died for them. Yet there are senses in which
the British connection with Russia, displeasing though some of its
aspects may seem to us now, runs even deeper in our experience than
any of these.

For one thing, it is much older than some of our associations with
Western countries, as for instance the United States and most of the
Commonwealth countries. Britain has been a leading participant in
the international system, or rather the classical European
international system, in close partnership with Russia for at least two
centuries; the relationship goes back to a time before the United
States existed, before Britain acquired a world-wide empire. Over
these centuries, the governments of Britain and Russia attained some
degree of knowledge about each other's policies and diplomatic styles:
they learned how each other played the diplomatic game. To this
system, the Americans, until the last 30 or 40 years, were strangers,
and remain to a large extent unversed in it. The idea of peaceful
coexistence, for instance, which for European Powers is the normal
rule and *raison d'être* of diplomacy, has generally had for Americans
the overtones of cohabitation with the devil. This is not to say that
British and Russian interests necessarily coincide today more than
they conflict, or that they ever have done so. But it does mean that
both countries probably know more than do most of their newer
friends about how to live with their conflicting interests without
blowing themselves up.

In the second place, fundamental as is Britain's commitment to the
democratic values which she shares with her Western partners, and
profound as is the gulf between these values and those of Russia's
present leaders, it is nevertheless true that the Russian revolution of
1917 raised questions about Western society and politics as massive as
any of those raised by the Great French Revolution of 1789. There
are ways in which British life has been more affected by the former of
these two cataclysms than by the latter. Britain is undoubtedly a
democratic society in the sense that its roots lie in the idea of the
sanctity of the individual personality and its right to such forms of
self-expression as freedom of speech, writing and association,
freedom of religion and belief, freedom from discrimination on
grounds of race, sex, age, class or faith. In the twentieth century,
however, democratic society faced challenges which shook it to its

foundation, and on its ability to deal with which its future depended. These challenges to a large extent arose from the tendency of the democratic society to deny the very human rights it professed to satisfy.

One of these challenges was total war, now perhaps an obsolete, or at least obsolescent, phenomenon, in the sense of the complete mobilisation of a nation and all its resources and equipment for armed conflict with another nation or group of nations. The First World War demonstrated that the mass of the people in the different countries would not in future fight wars on such a scale without some assurance that the governments would do all they could to make them impossible, and that the war's objectives must include, if not be wholly dedicated to, the welfare of ordinary people. The second challenge, following on from the first, was the demand that government should expressly commit itself to the promotion of public welfare and that should in fact become a virtual condition of government, in the sense in which the Rights of Man were advertised as a condition of government in Europe after 1789.

These two themes, the purposes and justification of total war, and the relation of the state to the well-being of the masses, have been the dominant ideas of our own times, the issues of our politics, the legitimate basis of state activity. That is why, in Britain and perhaps for most other Western countries, too, the person we have called the intellectual, that is, the man or woman with a sense of calling to thought and writing about the human condition, has had his or her mind dominated since at least 1914 by the problem of war and the problem of welfare. Whatever the consequences for the quality of its intellectual or artistic work, the mentally creative community in Britain could not, after the First World War, disinterest itself in the problem of the good society, understood as a society free from war and free from want. The same has been true, to a very considerable extent, of the Church in Britain, too. What about war? What about want?—were questions no intelligent person after 1900 or 1914 could ignore. And he could not ponder them without concluding that they portended something fundamentally at fault with the capitalist system he and his forebears had previously taken for granted. The mere fact that such a slogan-like expression could be used was a measure of how far the language of the iconoclasts had taken over.

Now, in the 1980s, the age of social commitment has lost its savour, the river even runs in the opposite direction. The socialist writer or poet is *passé*; in politics, the pendulum, after the Labour governments of 1950–51, swung to the Right, or at least towards 'consensus' and the fudging of the old ideological divisions; attempts to revive the radical Left convinced nobody but the converted. Perhaps this was inevitable. It is the fashion of the intellectual, perhaps the political, community to switch to the other extreme when one position has held the field for a time. Moreover, the peculiarly stubborn character of Britain's problems after the Second World War seemed not to yield to any prescription–Left, Right or Centre–and, with people in a state of sceptical puzzlement, the Promised Land of social democracy was soon perceived to have its weeds and droughts, like any other human experience. As for the erstwhile Soviet paradise on earth, it was seen on closer inspection to have, not only feet of clay, but boots firmly planted on the necks of nations which the Great Patriotic War was supposed to have liberated. George Orwell's *1984* became the required reading of all the best people and the year of its publication, 1949, followed the year of Marshal Tito's defection from the Soviet camp, an act of defiance greeted all over Britain as a dash for freedom from the road to serfdom, even though Tito's system remained a one-party dictatorship.

The standing of the Soviet Union in British eyes bore the brunt of this post-war disenchantment with socialism and the planned society, and this because the Soviet Union was deeply involved in the two great challenges to capitalist democracy which we mentioned earlier. In the first place, the Russian army in 1917 staged the first major popular revolt against the institution of total war: the soldiers on the Eastern front voted for 'bread, land, peace and freedom' with their feet, and in so doing formulated the basis on which governments must later secure the co-operation of ordinary people in making the social system work and fighting its wars. In Britain, Viscount Cecil recalled in his memoirs how, shortly after the Russian revolution, he asked some workmen on his estate whether they had any sympathy with the Bolsheviks, and how they told him that, unless something was done to make another war like the First World War impossible, the Bolshevik system would spread. Cecil wrote that his experience helped to make him a life-long champion of the League of Nations.[1] The Russian revolution seemed to show that the sort of war which machine-industry had made possible in the twentieth century, that is, total war, could only be fought if it was made to accord with the ideas of ordinary men and women on what they could expect from it when it was all over. It was not that the revolution as a matter of history made policies thereafter decided in Moscow relevant to the needs of the masses. But that is what it seemed to do, and this changed the character of war, both for those who declared it and those who fought it.

In addition, the Russian revolution and the regime which emerged from it helped–we claim no more than that–to establish as a basic rule in the twentieth century that the condition of government and the state is their ability to satisfy the mass of the people that their welfare is the primary object of policy. It is not that the Soviet government after 1917 in fact made public welfare its primary object, or even that it tried to. Nor is it that, in any country in which communists later achieved power, public welfare was in fact elevated to the supreme objective. But, after the revolution in Russia, though by no means because of it alone, the purpose of government began to be universally thought of as the promotion of public welfare. As far as Britain is concerned, this was symbolised, after years of resistance, by the wartime coalition government's acceptance in 1944 'as one of their primary aims and responsibilities the maintenance of a high and stable level of employment';[2] by the overwhelming victory of the Labour party with its egalitarian and welfare policies in 1945; and by the conversion of the Conservative party to the welfare state under Mr R. A. Butler's guidance in the 1950s. This great shift in the conception of government in Britain was not effected by admirers of Soviet Russia, nor was it in any way an adoption of the Soviet model. Its architects, as we have explained in an earlier chapter, were men and women deeply distrustful of Russia, even afraid of it. But there can be no question that the advent of Soviet communism in 1917 raised the question of what political power is for, on what basis it can rest, and demonstrated that unless it rested, or appeared to rest, on the widest possible basis of public welfare, its foundations would be as shaky as those of the Romanovs. The people who, for better or worse, achieved a social revolution in Britain after 1945 were products of an intellectual climate in which the Soviet model, however misunderstood, played a major part. That they were able to do so without apparent damage to the parliamentary system testifies to a high order of political skill.

A country which has played such a large part in our thinking about the state and society in the past 60 or 70 years, larger perhaps than that of any other major country with which Britain has had to do, should surely be well-known to our politicians and people. The reverse is the case. Our ignorance of Russian history, Tsarist and communist, of the Russian land and its people, is perhaps not greater than that of other people, but it is extraordinary considering both the way in which the fates of Britain and Russia have been intertwined and the dangerous states into which Anglo-Soviet relations have slipped since 1945, and in which they are today. The ignorance exists on the Russian side, too, perhaps to an even greater extent, but at least we are thankfully more free than they to do something about it.

The ignorance reveals itself equally on the side of Russophiles and Russophobes. Nothing is more striking about many of the British intellectuals who adulated the Soviet Union in the 1930s than the way they shut their eyes to the totalitarian features of the country they depicted as a paradise: the denial of personal freedom, the state trials and purges, the decimation, and more than decimation, of high-ranking Soviet politicans and officials disclosed by Mr Khrushchev in his speech at the 20th Congress of the Soviet communist party in Moscow in February 1956, the cruel repression of dissent and a thousand other offences against human rights which are still everyday practice in the Soviet Union. It might be said in defence of the Russophiles in Britain that the facts were kept from them by the Soviet authorities, but it seems more likely that they did not see what they did not want to see. But if it is asked why Russophiles in particular, during the 1930s and the Second World War, were blind to the dark side of the Soviet moon, the answers may lie in the strength of the emotions aroused in them by the two challenges to Western side we have discussed.

The revulsion aroused in sensitive minds in the West by these two problems was such that the Soviet Union became for them, for two decades or so, a cynosure because it seemed to have placed war and the social problem of capitalist society on the agenda of politics, and that is where thoughtful men and women in the West wanted them. Just as the French Revolution of 1789 and the Spanish civil war in the 1930s called to socially conscious people of their time, not so much because of what they actually were, or because they represented social models worthy of adoption, but because they stood against, or seemed to stand against, the palpitating evils of the times, so for British Russophiles it has been revolt against their own society that turned them towards Russia and encouraged them to seek there answers to problems which horrified them at home. The Burgesses,

Macleans, Philbys, Blunts–the brightest and best of British society–succumbed to Soviet allurements because of disgust, however merited, of the society they knew at home, though that was no doubt mixed with personal psychological problems of which we know little. It is significant that, since that society has become, if not more efficient in the management of its affairs, at least more fair and equal, and certainly more compassionate in its treatment of the deprived, the incentive to idolise the Soviet state has diminished.

But ignorance has, of course, characterised British Russophobes, too, both in the last century and in this. As with the Russophiles, ignorance is both a cause of strong feelings about Russia in those who fear it, and also a consequence in the sense that rooted objection to Russia, like rooted partiality towards it, stimulates and encourages the closed mind: if ignorance strengthens comfortable prejudices, there is no inducement to dispel it. Undoubtedly, the British Russophobe, or, more correctly, Sovietophobe, has been actuated, as well as by ignorance, by fear of the implications for his own wealth and social power of the sort of dispossessing revolution which the Bolsheviks mounted in 1917. But perhaps it is the effects of Sovietophobia on our perceptions of Russia which are more interesting and have greater practical relevance. One of these is to make us think that the Russians, or rather their present-day leaders, are for some reason more wicked than other people, more imperialistic, expansionist, dominating. The possibility that this may represent the behaviour of all powerful states at the summit of their strength tends to be overlooked, though examples from British history are not hard to find. The Russians are sometimes thought to have been awarded more than their fair share of the 'Old Adam' in man when they were made.

A second assumption which our ignorance fosters, especially if we are already unfavourably disposed towards the Russian phenomenon, is that Russian leaders are united in the pursuit of some single, unwavering 'design' or 'strategy', and this is variously represented as 'to conquer the world', or 'to communise the world'. The fact that revolutionaries, or any people who wish to change the world, tend to be far more schismatic than conservatives, that every revolution of which we have record seems to have ended with the revolutionaries falling out among themselves, and that Soviet policy, for instance, over such important issues as Germany or the Middle East, has followed a far from consistent course, is disregarded. Moreover, policies and actions which are regarded as normal in other great Powers tend to be looked upon as evidence of the 'grand design' when they are Russia's. It is regarded as somehow reprehensible for the Russians to pursue their national interest, as they perceive it, in Afghanistan, while it was not so for the British, who did not very different things in that country a century or more ago. Again, although the Western Powers spent 20 or 30 years after the Second World War keeping firmly ahead of the Soviet bloc states in force levels and every type of armament in Europe, Western critics of Soviet policy are now indignant because Russia takes a leaf out of the West's book and pulls ahead in the arms field, which they represent as certain indications of aggressive designs. The only recourse for the West, it is said, is to increase its arms spending so as to keep a 'step ahead' of the Russians. There is no possible danger to peace in this because the West's being a 'step ahead' has no aggressive connotations whereas if Russia gets a lead over the West it will at once be used for sinister ends.

We must remember, however, not merely this bipolar character of British attitudes to Russia, both the 'antis' and the 'pros' having substantial ingredients of ignorance within them, but that the bipolar pattern has always been subject to violent oscillation, so that, at one moment, the Russophiles seem entirely to disappear from the picture, while at another they have it wholly their own way and leave the Russophobes with no place in which to have their say. A chart showing the different intensities of British feelings for and against Russia since 1917 would follow a zig-zag course, the depths of the negative periods (say, 1925 to 1930) matching in their extent and unreality the high peaks of general adulation (say, from 1941 until 1945). The sheer extent of this oscillation of feelings is in itself evidence for the fact that we are indeed talking about feelings, rather than about rational thought processes and of this we have given many examples in this book. It is a wise rule, in all our dealings with Russia, not to be carried away either by too much hostility or too much love. Nor should we be too sure that our state of mind on the subject today will necessarily be the same as our state of mind tomorrow.

It is because of the volatility of our feelings towards Russia that actions which seem to us normal in a great Power, however regrettable, become intolerable when Russia does them. 'Imperialism', for example, meaning the spread of a great Power's presence in the world such that it encroaches upon the rights of other states, was excusable, even laudable, in European states in their prime, but is inexcusable in Russia: the rules have changed, we say, the world is now a nobler place. The drive of a great Power for 'spheres of influence' adjacent to its border in order to buttress its security has been visible in the United States in relation to Latin America since the Monroe Doctrine was announced in 1823. But in Russia's case it is an unmistakable sign of a plan to conquer the world. 'Intervention' in other states, or 'meddling', in Africa or South West Asia, is one of the worst aspects of Russian behaviour in Western eyes these last ten years. But few other countries in their prime have 'meddled' more abroad than the United Kingdom: the list of countries with which Britain has been in armed conflict at one time or another is incomparably longer than Russia's. The United States, with its famed doctrine of national self-determination, ravaged, plundered and pillaged a small Oriental country, Vietnam, for nine years with the full force of half a million soldiers and the sophisticated equipment of the world's greatest military Power: then, when defeat stared it in the face, it packed up and left, with no word of remorse ever uttered by any of its public men to the innocent people who suffered the American invasion. Yet, when such things, inexcusable as they all are, are done by Russians, they seem to take on in Western eyes an extra dimension of depravity. Perhaps it is that the Russophile elements in British minds, which still linger, and which have led us in the past to think of Russians as unnaturally virtuous, compel us, when they act disappointingly like any other great Power, to think of them as unnaturally vicious.

Russia's international conduct takes on additional criminality in British eyes at present because it is the behaviour of a state whose internal social system we have grown to reject, though many of us once admired it. What is instrumental here is the British, or perhaps Anglo-Saxon, idea that the international behaviour of a state is all of a piece with its internal set-up, that 'states which violate human rights at home will also do abroad', that foreign policy is merely the projection into the international arena of domestic policy. We seem to object, not so much to Soviet power, but to the social causes which that power is used to promote. From this springs the West's preoccupation (not eternal, but certainly in force since Mr Carter entered the White House in January 1977) with making Soviet conformity with Western standards in the matter of human rights a condition of the West's coexistence with the Soviet state.

However morally laudable this aim may be, it is important to recognise the pitfalls which surround it as practical policy, and it may be because of these that East–West relations deteriorated during Mr Carter's presidency to a point comparable with the worst days of the Cold War. We must acknowledge, first, that it has never been in the tradition of European diplomacy to make the issue of human rights central to relations with another state. It is not unknown, but traditional European practice has been based on the acceptance of internal affairs as part of the reserved domain of states. The American tradition is different, having long been associated with political instability in Latin America and problems of diplomatic recognition arising therefrom. It may be that, under present conditions, there are not, and cannot be, any longer matters within the exclusive jurisdiction of states. At the same time, it cannot be denied that, to go beyond the quiet urging of another state to mend its ways and pay regard to human rights, and to make its performance over human rights a condition of agreement on all other matters is to plunge international relations into a cauldron of anger, hurt pride and fears for domestic peace. Especially is this so in relations between countries with such historical differences as Russia and the West. The Soviet government cannot but feel that the human rights campaign is nothing less than yet another attempt to unseat the communist regime in Russia, comparable with Allied intervention which followed the Bolshevik seizure of power in 1917. Some Westerners may not object to that because they consider that the destruction of communism should be the first object of their policy. Western governments, however, are bound to give the first priority to the security and survival of their people, and circumstances can easily be envisaged in which these take precedence even over human rights.

It is also questionable whether another country, especially a powerful one like the United States or the Soviet Union, can really be expected to undertake to change, or rather try to change, its whole way of life, which it might have pursued for centuries, as part of a diplomatic agreement negotiated at the conference table, and in return for which it may expect concessions from the other side. To ask a British government, for example, as part of an arms control deal, to undertake to implement the economic right of everyone in the country to have a paid job as from a certain date, would be trafficking with impossibilities. A government might sign such an undertaking, but to try to implement it would be to fly in the face of all the ingrained habits of the community. Similarly, to say to the Russians that they must act in their internal affairs as they would have acted had they had the same history as the United States, otherwise there can be no agreements between them and the West to stabilise the peace, is to place aspirations before practical politics. What the West wants to know from Russia is whether her conception of her national interests is roughly congruent with the Western states' conception of theirs. Will Russia respect the West's definition of its vital interests in return for a pledge that the West will respect hers? Unless questions of this kind are asked and answered, the precarious peace which now exists is in danger, and on that peace the whole prospect of influencing Russia's internal affairs, which is the most that can be expected in the field of human rights, depends.

Perhaps there are some general rules for the conduct of affairs with the Soviets which emerge from all this. It should be stressed above all that nothing can come from attempts to belittle or ignore the Soviet Union (we have done that, with disastrous results before) or to deny it what Soviet leaders seem most to want, that is, recognition as a super-Power, the equal of the United States. Associated with this is the necessity to maintain diplomatic contact with the Soviet state as a means of ascertaining (though in the end that may not be possible) the motives and objectives of Soviet policy. The idea, of which many highly placed Americans seem so fond, that difficulties created by another state are best dealt with by not talking to it–as married couples sometimes sustain their quarrels by tactics of silence, or 'talking through the dog'–is not only childish: it is a dangerous form of childishness. President Carter's decision not to attend Marshal Tito's funeral in Belgrade in May 1980, because he wished to punish Mr Brezhnev for his invasion of Afghanistan by not speaking to him, is a text-book example.

It is unfortunately true that all Western efforts to penetrate Soviet thinking on Afghanistan, Poland and other issues may end in failure. But this in no way absolves the West from exerting itself to the uttermost, using every possible channel, to try to discover whether coexistence with the Soviet Union is practicable, and on what terms. Most Western opinion on Soviet policy, official and unofficial, often has the appearance of being not much more than guesswork, sometimes intelligent, sometimes not. We should recall that the Atlantic pact nations, Britain included, have in effect, by article 5 of that treaty, pledged themselves to commit suicide if relations between Russia and the West deteriorate to a point where an armed attack on one of the treaty's signatories occurs. Most people would agree that such an act of mass suicide would be justified only on one condition, namely, that the Atlantic pact nations had done everything in their power to find out, by patient inquiry and negotiation, whether there was any other way of living with the Soviet Union than that of fighting it out. It is impossible to say that, at present, even a beginning is being made on satisfying that condition.

In the post-Afghanistan era, anyone who tries to see some reason in Russia's international position is apt to be written off as an 'appeaser', and charged with wanting to run down Western defences and thus create conditions for the 'finlandisation' of the non-communist world. It cannot be stated too strongly that this is not the conclusion to which this book is intended to lead. We recognise that the Russians, on the test of their past behaviour, will tend to force their power into areas of weakness facing them, though more perhaps because such areas are threats to their own security than because of any acquisitive instinct. Hence, there is no doubt that if the Western nations are to remain secure and pursue their lives without forceful interruption, the deterrent structure of the NATO pact is a necessity. It has proved its value over the past thirty years by helping to give Europe more stability than it has enjoyed since 1914. NATO's political cohesion and military effectiveness must be a prime concern to Britain, though there is no sense in wasting resources in matching and countering every Soviet attempt to gain a symbolic lead in arms when existing weapon strength is adequate for deterrence.

But it should never be forgotten that the Soviet Union has as strong an interest in peace as Britain or any other Western Power. The Russians have had a devastating experience of war and have no wish to renew it. Whatever interpretation we may place on the Soviet interest in *détente*, the fact remains that it was from Moscow that the initiative for it originally came. Mr Khrushchev, for all his faults, could be described as the first world statesman to recognise the implications of nuclear weapons for international relations and to show willingness to revise long-held political dogmas to take account of them. We may be sure that the Soviets, while insisting on their own interests, especially in security, will accept Western interests when they realise that to disregard them involves the definite risk of war. The West and the Soviet Union, as Mr Khruschev was fond of saying, are like animals in Noah's ark: they can only protect themselves against the nothingness outside by accepting the fact that each will fight for its life if it thinks its existence is threatened, but that in respect for each other's existence lies the most effective guarantee of its own.

Source Material

The following is a selection of source material used in writing this book. Other references are given in the Notes to each chapter.

The place of publication is London unless otherwise stated.

I DOCUMENTS

J. Degras (ed.), *Soviet Documents on Foreign Policy, 1917–1941,* 3 vols (R.I.I.A. 1951–53).

HMSO, *Documents on British Foreign Policy, 1919–1939* (1947) continuing. (Cited in this book as D.B.F.P.)

―――――, *Documents on German Foreign Policy, 1918–1945* (1957) continuing. (Cited in this book as D.G.F.P.)

UK, Public Record Office, Cabinet Minutes, Cabinet Conclusions, Cabinet Office Papers, Foreign Office Files.

USA, Department of State, *Foreign Relations of the United States,* Washington, DC. (Cited in this book as F.R.U.S.)

II MEMOIRS AND BIOGRAPHIES

The Earl of Avon (Sir Anthony Eden), *Facing the Dictators* (Cassell, 1962).

―――――, *Full Circle* (Cassell, 1962).

Sir W. S. L. Churchill, *The Second World War,* 6 vols (Cassell, 1948–54).

Sir W. M. Citrine, *Two Careers* (Hutchinson, 1962).

―――――, *Men and Work* (Hutchinson, 1964).

M. Cole (ed.), *Beatrice Webb's Diaries, 1913–1924* (Longman, 1952).

――――― (ed.), *The Webbs and Their Work* (The Harvester Press, 1974).

A. D. Cooper (Lord Norwich), *Old Men Forget* (Hart-Davis, 1953).

H. Dalton (Lord Dalton), *The Fateful Years. Memoirs, 1931–1945* (Muller, 1957).

―――――, *High Tide and After, Memoirs* (Muller, 1962).

C. H. Darke, *The Communist Technique in Britain* (Collins, 1953).

I. Deutscher, *Stalin. A Political Biography* (OUP, 2nd edn., 1967).

E. Dicey, *A Month in Russia during the Marriage of the Czarevitch* (Macmillan, 1867).

M. A. Hamilton, *Arthur Henderson* (Heinemann, 1938).

W. A. Harriman and E. Abel, *Special Envoy to Churchill and Stalin, 1941–1946* (Hutchinson, 1976).

J. Heenan, *Not the Whole Truth* (Hodder and Stoughton, 1971).

C. Hull, *The Memoirs of Cordell Hull,* 2 vols (New York: Macmillan, 1948; Hodder and Stoughton, 1971).

Sir R. H. B. Lockhart, *Memoirs of a British Agent* (Putnam, 1936).

I. N. Macleod, *Neville Chamberlain* (Muller, 1961).

H. Macmillan, *Memoirs, 1914–1963*, 6 vols (Macmillan, 1966–73).

I. Maisky, *Who Helped Hitler?* (Hutchinson, 1964).

————, *Memoirs of a Soviet Ambassador, The War, 1939–1943* (Hutchinson, 1967).

D. Marquand, *Ramsay MacDonald* (Jonathan Cape, 1977).

K. Martin, *Harold Laski. A Biographical Memoir* (Gollancz, 1953).

A. Monkhouse, *Moscow, 1911–1933* (Gollancz, 1933).

K. Muggeridge and R. Adam, *Beatrice Webb. A Life (1858–1943)* (Secker and Warburg, 1967).

M. Muggeridge, *Winter in Moscow* (Eyre and Spottiswoode, 1934).

M. Paléologue, *An Ambassador's Memoirs,* tr. by F. A. Holt, 3 vols (Hutchinson, 1923–25).

A. Ransome, *Six Weeks in Russia in 1919* (Allen and Unwin, 1919).

J. von Ribbentrop, *Zwischen London und Moskau* (Leoni am Starnberger See: Druffel-Verlag, 1953).

P. (Viscount) Snowden, *An Autobiography,* 2 vols (Nicholson and Watson, 1934).

S. H. Spender, *World Within World. The Autobiography of Stephen Spender* (Hamish Hamilton, 1951).

Lord Strang, *Home and Abroad* (Deutsch, 1956).

Lord Templewood, *Nine Troubled Years* (Collins, 1954).

Sir R. G. (Lord) Vansittart, *The Mist Procession* (Hutchinson, 1958).

H. G. Wells, *Russia in the Shadows* (Hodder and Stoughton, 1920).

F. Williams, *Ernest Bevin* (Hutchinson, 1952).

———— (ed.), *A Prime Minister Remembers. The War and Post-War Memoirs of the Rt. Hon Earl Attlee* (Heinemann, 1961).

Sir H. Wilson, *The Labour Government, 1964–1970* (Weidenfeld and Nicolson and Michael Joseph, 1971).

B. F. Wootton (Baroness Wootton), *In a World I Never Made* (Allen and Unwin, 1967).

III SECONDARY STUDIES

P. Addison, *The Road to 1945* (Jonathan Cape, 1975).

M. S. Anderson, *Britain's Discovery of Russia, 1553–1815* (Macmillan, 1958).

————, *The Eastern Question, 1774–1923* (Macmillan, 1966).

A. B. Atkinson, *Unequal Shares* (Allen Lane, Penguin Press, 1972).

B. Barker, *Ramsay MacDonald's Political Writings* (St. Martin's, 1962).

M. Beloff, *The Foreign Policy of Soviet Russia, 1929–1941,* 2 vols (OUP, 1947).

P. M. S. Blackett, *Atomic Weapons and East–West Relations* (Cambridge: CUP, 1956).

A. Boyle, *The Climate of Treason* (Hutchinson, 1979).

J. F. Byrnes, *Speaking Frankly* (New York: Harper, 1947).

D. F. Calhoun, *The United Front* (Cambridge: CUP, 1976).

E. H. Carr, *A History of Soviet Russia,* 4 vols and 7 parts (In progress. Macmillan, 1950–).

————, *The Soviet Impact on the Western World* (Macmillan, 1946).

C. Caudwell, *Illusion and Reality* (Macmillan, 1937).

D. Caute, *The Fellow-Travellers* (Weidenfeld and Nicolson, 1973).

R. Challinor, *The Origins of British Bolshevism* (Rowman, 1977).

W. H. Chamberlin, *The Russian Revolution,* 2 vols (New York and London: Macmillan, 1935).

L. G. Churchward, *Contemporary Soviet Government* (Routledge and Kegan Paul, 1968).

A. M. Cienciala, *Poland and the Western Powers* (Routledge and Kegan Paul, 1968).

J. Clark, et al. (ed.), *Culture and Crisis in Britain in the Thirties* (Lawrence and Wishart, 1979).

L. D. Clay, *Decision in Germany* (Heinemann, 1950).

W. P. and Z. Coates, *A History of Anglo-Soviet Relations,* 2 vols (Lawrence and Wishart, London, 1953–58).

R. Cobden, *Political Writings,* vols 1 and 2 (Ridgeway, 1867).

G. D. H. Cole, *History of the Labour Party from 1914* (Routledge and Kegan Paul, 1948).

I. Colvin, *The Chamberlain Cabinet* (Gollancz, 1971).

R. Conquest, *The Soviet Political System* (The Bodley Head, 1968).

————, *The Great Terror* (Macmillan, 1973).

A. A. Cooke, *A Generation on Trial* (Hart-Davis, 1950).

E. Crankshaw, *Russia and Britain* (Collins, n.d.).

B. Crick, *George Orwell: A Life* (Secker and Warburg, 1980).

C. A. R. Crosland, *The Future of Socialism* (Jonathan Cape, 1956).

R. H. S. Crossman, *Planning for Freedom* (Hamish Hamilton, 1965).

R. H. S. Crossman, M. Foot and I. Mikardo, *Keep Left* (New Statesman, 1947).

D. J. Dallin, *Soviet Russia's Foreign Policy, 1939–1942* (New Haven, Conn.: Yale University Press, 1943).

H. A. Deane, *The Political Ideas of Harold J. Laski* (New York: Columbia University Press, 1953).

I. Deutscher, *Russia after Stalin* (Hamish Hamilton, 1953).

————, *The Great Contest. Russia and the West* (OUP, 1960).

G. Dimitrov, *The United Front* (Lawrence and Wishart, 1938).

M. Dobb, *Soviet Economic Development since 1917* (Routledge and Kegan Paul, 1948).

D. Donnelly, *Struggle for the World. The Cold War, 1917–1965* (New York: St. Martin's, 1965).

E. F. M. Durbin, *The Politics of Democratic Socialism* (Routledge, 1940).

W. K. Eubank, *Munich* (Norman: University of Oklahoma, 1963).

————, *The Summit Conferences, 1919–1960* (Norman: University of Oklahoma, 1966).

X. J. Eudin and H. H. Fisher (eds), *Soviet Russia and the West, 1920–1927* (Stanford, Cal.: Stanford University Press, 1957).

Z. Fallenbuchl and C. McMillan (eds.), *Partners in East-West Economic Relations* (New York: Pergamon Press, 1980).

H. Feis, *Churchill, Roosevelt, Stalin. The War They Waged and the Peace They Sought* (Princeton, N.J.: Princeton University Press, 1957).

————, *Between War and Peace. The Potsdam Conference* (Princeton, N.J. Princeton University Press, 1960).

————, *From Trust to Terror. The Onset of the Cold War, 1945–1950* (Anthony Blond, 1970).

R. F. Fenno, Jr., (ed.), *The Yalta Conference* (Boston, Mass.: D. C. Heath and Co., 1955).

P. Ferris, *The New Militants* (Penguin, 1972).

L. Fischer, *The Soviets in World Affairs,* 2 vols (Princeton, N.J.: Princeton University Press, 1951).

D. F. Fleming, *The Cold War and its Origins, 1917–1960,* 2 vols (New York: Doubleday, Allen and Unwin, 1961).

H. Fontaine, *History of the Cold War. From the October Revolution to the Korean War, 1917–1950,* tr. by D. D. Paige (New York: Pantheon, 1968).

M. Frankland, *Khrushchev* (Harmondsworth: Penguin, 1966).

H. Gaitskell, *The Challenge of Coexistence* (Methuen, 1957).

M. P. Gehlen, *The Politics of Coexistence. Soviet Methods and Motives* (Bloomington, Ind.: Indiana University Press, 1967).

G. Gerschuni, *Die Konzessions Politik Sowjetrusslands* (Doctoral thesis submitted to Basle University, 1926, Berlin 1927).

M. Gilbert, *The Roots of Appeasement* (Weidenfeld and Nicolson, 1966).

J. H. Gleason, *The Genesis of Russophobia in Great Britain* (Cambridge, Mass.: Harvard University Press, 1950).

G. Gorodetsky, *The Precarious Truce. Anglo-Soviet Relations, 1924–27* (Cambridge: CUP, 1977).

S. R. Graubard, *British Labour and the Russian Revolution, 1917–1924* (Cambridge, Mass.: Harvard University Press, 1956).

R. Groves, *The Balham Group* (Pluto Press, 1974).

L. J. Halle, *The Cold War as History* (Chatto and Windus, 1967).

M. F. Hertz, *Beginnings of the Cold War* (Bloomington, Ind.: Indiana University Press, 1966).

E. Hinterhoff, *Disengagement* (Stevens, 1959).

D. Horowitz, *From Yalta to Vietnam* (Penguin, 1967).

G. Hosking, *Beyond Socialist Realism* (Granada Publishing, 1980).

A. Hutt, *British Trade Unionism* (Lawrence and Wishart, 1975).

M. Jakobson, *The Diplomacy of the Winter War. An Account of the Russo-Finnish War, 1939–1940* (Cambridge, Mass.: Harvard University Press, 1961).

H. Johnson, *The Soviet Power* (New York: International Publishers, 1940).

B. Jones, *The Russia Complex* (Manchester: Manchester University Press, 1977).

D. Joravsky, *Soviet Marxism and Natural Science, 1917–1932* (Routledge and Kegan Paul, 1961).

W. Kendall, *The Revolutionary Movement in Britain, 1900–21; the origins of British communism* (Weidenfeld and Nicolson, 1969).

G. F. Kennan, 'The Sources of Soviet Conduct', *Foreign Affairs* (New York: The Council on Foreign Relations, July 1947).

————, *Russia, the Atom and the West* (OUP, 1958).

————, *Russia and the West under Lenin and Stalin* (Hutchinson, 1961).

F. P. King, *The New Internationalism. Allied Policy and the European Peace, 1939–1945* (Newton Abbot: David and Charles, 1973).

L. Kochan, *The Making of Modern Russia* (Cape, 1962).

A. Koestler and others, *The God That Failed* (Hamish Hamilton, 1950).

J. Korbel, *Détente in Europe* (Princeton, N.J.: Princeton University Press, 1972).

H. J. Laski, *Trade Unions in the New Society* (G. Allen, 1950).

V. I. Lenin, *Lenin on Britain,* 2nd impression (Moscow: Foreign Languages Publishing House, 1965).

J. Lewis, *The Left Book Club* (Gollancz, 1970).

W. Lippmann, *The Communist World and Ours* (Hamish Hamilton, 1959).

E. Luard (ed.), *The Cold War* (Thames and Hudson, 1964).

R. W. Lyman, *The First Labour Government, 1924* (Chapman and Hall, 1957).

L. J. Macfarlane, *The British Communist Party* (MacGibbon, 1966).

S. Macintyre, *Little Moscows* (Croom Helm, 1980).

————, *A Proletarian Science* (Cambridge: CUP, 1980).

R. Martin, *Communism and the British Trade Unions, 1924–1933* (Oxford: The Clarendon Press, 1969).

W. McElwee, *Britain's Locust Years, 1918–1940* (Faber, 1962).

W. H. McNeill, *America, Britain and Russia. Their Co-operation and Conflict, 1941–1945* (OUP, 1953).

W. N. Medlicott, *British Foreign Policy since Versailles, 1919–1963* (Methuen, 1968).

K. Middlemas, *Diplomacy of Illusion* (Weidenfeld and Nicolson, 1972).

V. M. Molotov, *Problems of Foreign Policy* (Moscow: Foreign Languages Publishing House, 1949).

C. L. Mowat, *Britain Between the Wars* (Methuen, 1962).

N. J. T. M. Needham, *Time: the Refreshing River* (Allen and Unwin, 1943).

J. P. Nettl, *The Eastern Zone and Soviet Policy in Germany, 1945–1950* (OUP, 1951).

W. L. Neumann, *Making the Peace, 1941–1945* (Washington, D.C.: Foundation for Foreign Affairs, 1950).

K. Newton, *The Sociology of British Communism* (Allen Lane, Penguin Press, 1969).

H. Noguères, *Munich or the Phony Peace* (Weidenfeld and Nicolson, 1965).

F. S. Northedge, *The Troubled Giant. Britain among the Great Powers, 1916–1939* (London School of Economics and Bell, 1966).

————, *Descent from Power. British Foreign Policy, 1945–1973* (Allen and Unwin, 1974).

A. Nove, *Stalinism and After* (Allen and Unwin, 1975).

B. R. von Oppen, *Documents on Germany under Occupation, 1945–1954* (The Royal Institute of International Affairs, 1955).

Sir B. Pares, *The Fall of the Russian Monarchy* (Cape, 1939).

H. M. Pelling, *The British Communist Party* (Black, 1958).

————, *A Short History of the Labour Party* (St Martin's, 1977).

————, *A History of British Trade Unionism* (St Martin's, 1977).

D. Pennington and K. Thomas (eds), *Puritans and Revolutionaries* (OUP, 1978).

C. Pincher, *Their Trade is Treachery* (Sidgwick, 1981).

H. B. Price, *The Marshall Plan and its Meaning* (Ithaca, N.Y.: Cornell University Press, 1955).

K. Robbins, *Munich, 1938* (Cassell, 1968).

B. A. W. Russell (Earl Russell), *The Practice and Theory of Bolshevism* (Allen and Unwin, 1920).

F. L. Schuman, *Russia since 1917* (New York: Knopf, 1957).

P. Seabury, *The Rise and Decline of the Cold War* (New York, London: Basic Books, 1957).

M. Seton, *Sergei M. Eisenstein* (The Bodley Head, 1952).

H. Seton-Watson, *The East European Revolution* (Methuen, 1950).

————, *The Pattern of Communist Revolution* (Methuen, 1960).

S. H. Spender, *Forward from Liberalism* (Gollancz, 1937).

J. Stevenson and C. Cook, *The Slump. Society and Politics during the Depression* (Jonathan Cape, 1977).

E. J. St L. Strachey, *The Coming Struggle for Power* (Gollancz, 1932).

B. H. Sumner, *Survey of Russian History* (Duckworth, 1944).

————, *Russia and the Balkans, 1870–1880* (Hamden, Conn., and London: Archon Books, 1962).

A. C. Sutton, *Western Technology and Soviet Economic Development, 1917–1930* 3 vols (Hoover Inst., Stanford, Calif.: 1968, 1971, 1973).

A. J. P. Taylor, *English History, 1914–1945* (Oxford: The Clarendon Press, 1965).

————, *The Trouble Makers* (Panther, 1969).

H. Thomas, *The Spanish Civil War* (Eyre and Spottiswoode, 1961).

A. J. Toynbee, *The Impact of the Russian Revolution, 1917–1967* (OUP, 1967).

J. F. Triska and D. D. Finley, *Soviet Foreign Policy* (New York: Collier-Macmillan, 1968).

A. Tudor, *Theories of Film* (Secker and Warburg, 1974).

A. B. Ulam, *Expansion and Coexistence. The History of Soviet Foreign Policy, 1917–1967* (Secker and Warburg, 1968).

D. Urquhart, *Expositions of Transactions in Central Asia* (Longman, 1841).

S. J. and B. Webb, *Soviet Communism,* 3rd edn, new impression (Longmans Green, 1947).

A. Werth, *Russia at War, 1941–1945* (Barrie and Rockliff, 1964).

G. Werskey, *The Visible College* (Allen Lane, 1978).

Sir J. W. Wheeler-Bennett, *Brest-Litovsk. The Forgotten Peace* (Macmillan, 1938).

S. White, *Britain and the Bolshevik Revolution* (Macmillan, 1980).

C. Wilmot, *The Struggle for Europe* (Collins, 1952).

J. Wilczynski, *The Economics and Politics of East–West Trade* (Macmillan, 1969).

T. H. Wolfe, *Soviet Power and Europe, 1945–1970* (Baltimore: Johns Hopkins Press, 1970).

N. Wood, *Communism and British Intellectuals* (Gollancz, 1959).

Sir E. L. Woodward, *British Foreign Policy in the Second World War,* 5 vols (HMSO, 1970–76).

B. F. Wootton (Baroness Wootton), *Plan or No Plan* (The Camelot Press, 1934).

Notes

1. CONTACT AND CONFLICT

1. See ch. 2, p. 30.

2. Arthur Koestler and other, *The God That Failed: Six Studies in Communism,* with an introduction by Richard Crossman (Hamish Hamilton, 1950).

3. B. H. Sumner, *Survey of Russian History* (Duckworth, 1944) pp. 318–9.

4. Nicholas V. Riasanovsky, *A History of Russia* (OUP, 1963 and 1969) p. 471 ff.

5. Sumner, *Russian History,* pp. 324–5.

6. A contemporary account is given in Richard Hakluyt, *The Principall Navigations, Voiages and Discoveries of the English Nation, etc.* (G. Bishop and R. Newberie, 1589).

7. An account of the Metro-Vickers trial is given in Lord Strang, *Home and Abroad* (Deutsch, 1956) ch. 3.

8. See ch. 2, p. 40.

9. See ch. 9.

10. D.B.F.P., First Series, IV, pp. 635–8.

2. LIVING WITH A REVOLUTION

1. A Duff Cooper, *Haig* (Faber and Faber, 1936) vol. II, p. 114; CAB 23/16, 159 A.

2. 91 H.C. Deb. 5s. Col 1421.

3. Sir G. W. Buchanan, *My Mission to Russia and Other Diplomatic Memories* (Cassell, 1923) vol. II, pp. 4, 5, 43–9.

4. G 131, CAB 21/42.

5. Misc. No 10 (1917), Cd. 8387, p. 5.

6. D.B.F.P., First Series, III, pp. 362–4.

7. J. W. Wheeler-Bennett, *Brest-Litovsk: The Forgotten Peace* (Macmillan, 1938) p. 260.

8. C. K. Cumming and W. W. Pettit, *Russian-American Relations, 1917–1920* (New York: Harcourt, Brace and Howe, 1920) pp. 65–7

9. *The World Crisis. The Aftermath 1911–1918* (Butterworth, 1929) pp. 24–5.

10. Quoted in Stephen White, *Britain and the Bolshevik Revolution* (Macmillan, 1980) p. 49.

11. 114 H.C. Deb. 5s. Cols 2939–46.

12. Published by Macmillan, p. 211.

13. F.R.U.S., *1919, Russia,* pp. 10–14.

14. Louis Fischer, *The Soviets in World Affairs* (Princeton, N.J.: Princeton University Press, 2nd. edn., 1951) vol. II, p. 167.

15. 139 H.C. Deb. 5s. Col 2511 (22 March 1921).

16. 150 H.C. Deb. 5s. Col 1265 (16 February 1922); ibid, 135, Col 1719 (6 December 1920).

17. FO 371/6855/N11337; 11 October 1921.

18. Cmd. 1207 (1921).

19. Russia No 3 (1927), Cmd. 2895, p. 13.

20. E. H. Carr, *A History of Soviet Russia,* vol. IV, The Interregnum, 1923–1924 (Macmillan, 1954) p. 245.

21. Quoted in White, *Britain and the Bolshevik Revolution,* p. 233.

22. MacDonald, *The Foreign Policy of the Labour Party* (Cecil Palmer, 1923) pp. 49–50.

23. Sir Harold Nicolson, *King George the Fifth* (Pan Books, 1967) p. 499.

24. *Socialist Review,* June 1923.

25. Labour Party Annual Conference, *Report,* 1923.

26. 159 H.C. Deb. 5s. Cols 1084–5 (1 December 1922).

27. The Labour men included George Lansbury, E. D. Morel, A. A. Purcell and R. C. Wallhead. See Morel's account of the episode in *Forward,* 23 August 1924.

28. 176 H.C. Deb. 5s. Col 3138 (7 August 1924).

29. Ibid, Col 3034.

30. Cmd. 2895, pp. 24–5.

31. See ch. 3, pp. 49–50.

32. Quoted in White, *Britain and the Bolshevik Revolution,* p. 52.

3. OUR FATAL CHOICES

1. David Carlton, *MacDonald versus Henderson. The Foreign Policy of the Second Labour Government,* (Macmillan, 1970) p. 148.

2. D.B.F.P., Second Series, VII, pp. 62–4.

3. Carlton, *MacDonald versus Henderson,* p. 162.

4. *Statistical Abstract for the United Kingdom,* Cmd. 4233 (1934), pp. 318–21.

5. Max Beloff, *The Foreign Policy of Soviet Russia 1929–1941,* (OUP, 1947–49) vol. I, p. 35.

6. Treaty Series No 11 (1934), Cmd. 4567.

7. Beloff, *Foreign Policy of Soviet Russia,* vol. I, p. 111.

8. *The Times,* 17 June 1933.

9. Beloff, *Foreign Policy of Soviet Russia,* vol. II, p. 16.

10. Ivan Maisky, *Who Helped Hitler?* (Hutchinson, 1964).

11. Norman Rose, *Vansittart. Study of a Diplomat,* (Heinemann, 1978) p. 113; FO 371/18299; N 4718/1/38.

12. D.B.F.P., Second Series, VII, pp. 567–76; Strang, *Home and Abroad,* Ch. 3. Also see above, Ch. 1, p. 16.

13. The Earl of Avon, *The Eden Memoirs. Facing the Dictators* (Cassell, 1962) p. 162.

14. 299 H.C. Deb. 5s. Col 1409.

15. CP 24 (38); CAB 24/274 (8 February 1938).

16. Winston Churchill, *The Second World War,* vol. I, *The Gathering Storm* (Cassell, 1948) p. 132.

17. See Beloff, *Foreign Policy of Soviet Russia,* vol. I, p. 97.

18. *The Speeches of Adolf Hitler,* ed. by H. N. Baynes (The Royal Institute of International Affairs, 1942) vol. II, pp. 1404–6.

19. D.B.F.P., Third Series, II, p. 266.

20. League of Nations Official Journal, Special Supplement 189, pp. 34–5.

21. D.B.F.P., Third Series, II, pp. 255–6. Also Georges Bonnet, *Défense de la Paix*, vol. I, *De Washington au Quai D'Orsay* (Geneva: Bourquin, 1946) pp. 198–200.

22. Boothby, *I Fight to Live* (Gollancz, 1947) p. 161.

23. S. Morrell, *I Saw the Crucifixion* (Davies, 1939) p. 291.

24. *Documents and Materials Relating to the Eve of the Second World War, I* (Moscow: Foreign Language Publishing House, 1948) p. 240; Zdeněk Fierlinger, *Ve Sluzbach CSR*, part I (Prague: Orbis, 1951) Appendix 3.

25. *Izvestia*, 26 September 1938; Czechoslovak Republic and USSR, *New Documents on the History of Munich* (Prague: Orbis, 1958) p. 118.

26. Keith Middlemas, *Diplomacy of Illusion* (Weidenfeld and Nicolson, 1972) p. 445.

27. CAB 23/95.

28. Ibid.

29. CAB 27/646.

30. Lord Dalton, *The Fateful Years. Memoirs, 1931–1945* (Muller, 1957) p. 188.

31. David Dilks (ed.), *The Diaries of Sir Alexander Cadogan, 1938–1945* (Cassell, 1971) p. 117.

32. D.B.F.P., Third Series, IV, pp. 123–4.

33. D.G.F.P., Series D, II, p. 327.

34. D.B.F.P., Third Series, I, pp. 496–7.

35. C 14471/41/18; FO 371/21659.

36. Middlemas, *Diplomacy of Illusion*, p. 432.

37. D.B.F.P., Third Series, I, pp. 161–5.

38. C.O.S. 772.

39. C.O.S. 887 (FP 36/82).

40. Chamberlain's letters, 20 March 1938.

41. C 1935/95/62 (FO 371/21626).

42. FP 36/56.

43. 333 H.C. Deb. 5s. Col 1400.

44. Ian Colvin, *The Chamberlain Cabinet* (Gollancz, 1971) pp. 190–1.

45. 345 H.C. Deb. 5s. Col 509.

46. D.B.F.P., Third Series, V, pp. 17–18.

47. Ibid, Third Series, IV, pp. 526–30.

48. Ibid, Third Series, V, pp. 216–9.

49. Jane Degras (ed.), *Soviet Documents on Foreign Policy 1917–41* (The Royal Institute of International Affairs, vol. III, 1953) pp. 315–22.

50. Quoted in Sidney Aster, *The Making of the Second World War* (Deutsch, 1973) p. 273.

51. CAB 23/99. See also C. J. Hill's *The decision-making process in relation to British foreign policy, 1938–1941*, an unpublished thesis submitted for the D. Phil., Oxford, in 1978.

52. Rose, *Vansittart*, p. 236.

53. *The Diplomatic Diaries of Oliver Harvey, 1937–1940* (Collins, 1970) p. 291.

54. Minute by Vansittart, 16 June 1939; FO 371/23009, C 8923/53/18. See also Erich Kordt, *Nicht aus den Akten* (Stuttgart: Union Deutsche Verlagsgesellschaft, 1950).

55. Maurice Cowling, *The Impact of Hitler. British Politics and British Policies, 1933–1940* (London: Cambridge University Press, 1975) p. 355.

56. D.B.F.P., Third Series, VII, pp. 1–2.

57. Ibid, pp. 85–6.

58. Ibid, p. 225.

59. *The Diaries of Sir Alexander Cadogan,* p. 166.

4. THE WARTIME ALLIANCE

1. Sir W. L. S. Churchill, *The Second World War,* vol. II, *Their Finest Hour* (Cassell, 1949) p. 511.

2. Sir Llewellyn Woodward, *British Foreign Policy in the Second World War* (HMSO, vol. I, 1970) p. 604.

3. Ibid, p. 621; Churchill, *The Second World War,* vol. III, *The Grand Alliance* (1950) p. 320.

4. (Muller, London, 1945.)

5. Churchill, *The Second World War,* vol. I, *The Gathering Storm* (1948) p. 300.

6. Ibid, vol. III, p. 337.

7. A. J. P. Taylor, *English History, 1914–1945* (Oxford: The Clarendon Press, 1965) p. 469, n.1.

8. R. J. Sontag and J. S. Beddie (eds), *Nazi-Soviet Relations, 1939–1941* (Washington: Department of State, 1948) p. 222.

9. Woodward, *British Foreign Policy,* vol. I, p. 615, n.2.

10. Churchill, *The Second World War,* vol. III, pp. 332. 402, 587–8, 594.

11. Woodward, *British Foreign Policy,* vol. II (HMSO, 1971) pp. 15–16.

12. Ibid, p. 40.

13. Ibid, p. 266.

14. Churchill, *The Second World War,* vol. III, p. 586.

15. Herbert Feis, *Churchill, Roosevelt, Stalin. The War They Waged and the Peace They Sought* (Princeton, N.J.: Princeton University Press, 1957) p. 114.

16. Ibid, p. 116.

17. Woodward, *British Foreign Policy,* vol. II, pp. 276–9.

18. F.R.U.S., 1943, vol. I, p. 782.

19. Churchill, *The Second World War,* vol. VI, *Triumph and Tragedy* (Cassell, 1954) p. 198.

20. Ibid, p. 255 and Appendix C, p. 617. See also CAB 80/90. WP (43) 522.

21. 542 H.C. Deb. 5s. Col 228 (30 June 1948).

22. Churchill, *The Second World War,* vol. VI, p. 439.

23. CAB 81/45; PHP (44) 14 (0) (Final), Occupation of Germany. Allotment of Zones.

24. 449 H.C. Deb. 5s. Cols 34–5 (6 April 1948).

25. Churchill, *The Second World War,* vol. VI, p. 138.

26. Feis, *Churchill,* p. 637.

27. See above, pp. 106–7.

28. p. 103 and Misc. No 1 (1947); Treaties of Peace with Italy, Rumania, Bulgaria, Hungary and Finland, Cmd. 7022, p. 79.

29. Woodward, *British Foreign Policy,* vol. II, p. 232.

30. Ibid, p. 228.

31. Churchill, *The Second World War,* vol. III, p. 616.

32. Feis, *Churchill,* p. 58.

33. CAB 65/47; WM (44) 111; Confidential Annex, Minute 7, 28/8/44.

34. Protocol of the Proceedings of the Crimea Conference, Cmd. 7088 (1947).

35. Feis, *Churchill*, p. 123.

36. Ibid, pp. 291–2.

37. General Sikorski Institute (eds), *Documents on Polish-Soviet Relations, 1939–1945*, vol. II, 1967, p. 419.

38. Cordell Hull, *The Memoirs of Cordell Hull* (Hodder and Stoughton, 1948) vol. II, pp. 1447–8.

39. Churchill, *The Second World War*, vol. VI, p. 400.

40. Admiral W. D. Leahy, *I Was There* (Gollancz, 1950) p. 442.

5. COLD WAR AND DÉTENTE

1. Mayhew, *Party Games* (Hutchinson, 1969) pp. 84, 86.

2. See Ch. 3, p. 50.

3. *Statistical Material Presented During the Washington Negotiations*, Cmd. 6707 (1945).

4. French Yellow Book, Documents of the Conference of Foreign Ministers of France, the United Kingdom and the USSR held in Paris from 27 June to 3 July 1947, Imprimerie National.

5. 438 H.C. Deb. 5s Col 2239 (19 June 1947).

6. Ibid, 446 Col 405 (22 January 1948).

7. F.R.U.S., *The Conferences at Cairo and Teheran, 1943* (Washington: US Government Printing Office, 1961).

8. 423 H.C. Deb. 5s. Col 2036 (5 June).

9. Cmd. 6984 (1946).

10. Cmd. 7301 (1947).

11. 427 H.C. Deb. 5s. Col 1516.

12. Ibid, 437 Col 1737.

13. Ibid, 446, Col 404.

14. Ibid, Col 418.

15. Ibid, Col 404.

16. Misc. No 14 (1955), Cmd. 9543.

17. Misc. No 28, Cmd. 9289 (1954); Misc. No 32, Cmd. 9304 (1954).

18. For the text of the Western Powers' security proposals, see Misc. No 21 (1955), Geneva Conference, Cmd. 9633, Annex I, pp. 99–101.

19. 557 H.C. Deb. 5s. Col 248 (24 July 1955).

20. For the Soviet proposals, see Cmd. 9543, pp. 21–3.

21. For the text of the Khrushchev note, see Germany No 1 (1959), Cmnd. 634, pp. 7–21.

22. The original 12 signatories were: Belgium, Canada, Denmark, France, Iceland, Italy, Luxemburg, the Netherlands, Norway, Portugal, the United Kingdom, the United States. Cmd. 7883 (1950).

23. Misc. No 2 (1948), Cmd. 7367.

24. *The Times*, 12 December 1979.

25. This is discussed in R. E. Hunter, *The Brussels Treaty and the Origins of the North Atlantic Treaty Organisation* (an unpublished PhD thesis, University of London, April 1969).

26. Quoted in David Horowitz, *From Yalta to Vietnam, American Foreign Policy in the Cold War* (Harmondsworth: Penguin Books, 1967) p. 80.

27. Attlee's account of his visit to Washington in December 1950 is given in his statement in the Commons on 14 December: 482 H.C. Deb. 5s. Cols 1350–62.

28. *The Times,* 15 February 1950.

29. 515 H.C. Deb. 5s. Cols 896, 897.

30. Cmd. 9418 (1955).

31. 596 H.C. Deb. 5s. Col 1376.

32. Cmnd. 634 (1959).

33. 601 H.C. Deb. 5s. Col 449 (4 March 1959). For communiqué on Mr Macmillan's visit to Moscow, see Soviet Union No 1 (1959), Cmnd. 689, pp. 2–3.

34. Misc. No 5 (1960), Cmnd. 1052.

35. *Pointing the Way, 1956–1961* (Macmillan, 1972) p. 213.

36. See ch. XXXIII, entitled 'The Double Line', in Viscount Templewood's memoirs, *Nine Troubled Years,* (Collins, 1954).

6. RUSSOPHOBIA AND RUSSOPHILIA

1. Hansard, *The Parliamentary History of England,* vol. XXIX, 29 March 1791, pp. 52–7, 70–4.

2. 21 May 1793.

3. 24 October 1817, quoted in J. H. Gleason, *The Genesis of Russophobia in Great Britain* (Cambridge, Mass.: Harvard University Press, 1950) p. 43.

4. Published by Ridgeway, London, 1817. See p. vii.

5. Gleason, *Russophobia,* p. 1.

6. Hansard's Parliamentary Debates, 3rd Series, vol. CXXX, Col 1035 (February 20, 1854).

7. Ibid, Col 885.

8. *The Triumph of Lord Palmerston* (Allen and Unwin, 1924) p. 183.

9. Gleason, *Russophobia,* p. 1.

10. Published by Nelson, London. See pp. v, 301, 322.

11. See above, ch. 2, pp. 38–40, 47–8.

12. See Harold Nicolson, *Curzon. The Last Phase* (Constable, 1934).

13. See above, ch. 2, pp. 34–5.

14. Russia No 3 (1927), Cmd. 2895.

15. See above, ch. 2, pp. 42–3, 44–5.

16. Douglas Hyde, *I Believed* (Kingswood and Melbourne: 1948) The World's Work (1919), Ltd, p. 67.

17. Quoted in David Caute, *The Fellow-Travellers* (Weidenfeld and Nicolson, 1973) p. 66.

18. See above, ch. 3, p. 53.

19. Allan Monkhouse, *Moscow, 1911–33* (Gollancz, 1933) p. 347.

20. Quoted in Emrys Hughes, *Pilgrim's Progress in Russia* (Houseman's, 1959) p. 68.

21. *The Daily Mirror,* 7 October 1957.

22. 13 April 1961.

23. *The Nation,* July 1934.

24. H. J. Laski, *London, Washington, Moscow. Partners in Peace?* (National Peace Council, 1943) p. 18.

25. A. J. P. Taylor, *Beaverbrook* (Hamish Hamilton, 1972) p. 528.

26. Paul Addison, *The Road to 1945* (Jonathan Cape, 1975) p. 135.

27. Published by Macmillan, 1946. See pp. 59–60, 84–5, 114.

28. See Bill Jones, *The Russia Complex. The British Labour Party and the Soviet Union* (Manchester: Manchester University Press, 1977) esp. chapters 9–11.

29. 28 December 1979.

30. 2 January 1980.

31. 29 December 1979.

32. Hyde, *I Believed,* p. 218.

33. 'Public opinion about Russia', *Political Quarterly,* October–December 1941, vol. XII, no 4.

34. H. D. Willock, 'Attitudes towards America and Russia', *Political Quarterly,* January–March 1948, vol. XIX, no 1.

7. RUSSIA AND THE INTELLECTUALS

1. Bertrand Russell, *The Practice and Theory of Bolshevism* (Allen and Unwin, 1920) p. 5.

2. *Russia in the Shadows* (Hodder and Stoughton, 1920) p. 88.

3. Ibid, p. 150.

4. Koestler and others, *The God that Failed,* p. 25.

5. Russell, *Bolshevism,* pp. 9, 15, 17.

6. Ibid, p. 19.

7. Allen and Unwin, 1919, p. 63.

8. *The Thirties, 1930–1940, in Britain* (Hamish Hamilton, 1940) p. 68. Writings by British and other academic visitors to Russia in the 1930s are listed in H. W. Nerhood, *To Russia and Return,* (Columbus: Ohio State University Press, 1968).

9. Koestler, *The God that Failed,* p. 28.

10. Stephen Spender, *World Within World* (Hamish Hamilton, 1951). p. 139.

11. An account of British writers not appreciably influenced by the Soviet Union is found in Arnold Kettle, 'W. H. Auden: Poetry and Politics in the Thirties', in Jon Clark and others (eds), *Culture and Crisis in Britain in the Thirties* (Lawrence and Wishart, 1979) p. 87.

12. Spender, *World within World,* p. 167.

13. Ibid, pp. 306–7.

14. Kitty Muggeridge and Ruth Adam, *Beatrice Webb. A Life, 1858–1943* (Secker and Warburg, 1967) p. 238.

15. Ibid, p. 241.

16. Ibid, p. 245.

17. (Longmans Green, 1935) vol. II, pp. 1127–8.

18. Quoted in *The Webbs and Their Work,* ed. by Margaret Cole (The Harvester Press, 1974) p. 223.

19. Kitty Muggeridge and Ruth Adam, *Beatrice Webb,* p. 243.

20. Princeton University Press, Princeton N.J., 1954, chs 1 and 4.

21. (Gollancz, 1937) p. 71.

22. Ibid, p. 288.

23. 'To Christopher Isherwood' (August 1935), in *The English Auden,* ed. by Edward Mendelson (Faber and Faber, 1977) p. 155.

24. 'The Magnetic Mountain', in *Collected Poems, 1929–33,* (The Hogarth Press, 1935) p. 139.

25. Gollancz, London, p. 116.

26. Frank Cass, London, pp. 45, 48.

27. The Hogarth Press, London.

28. 'The crisis in our civilisation', *Foreign Affairs,* vol. XXVI, no 1.

29. John Lewis, *The Left Book Club* (Gollancz, 1970) pp. 13–14.

30. Ibid, p. 132.

31. Ibid, p. 114.

32. For a detailed account of British scientists and communism, see Gary Werskey, *The Visible College* (Allen Lane, 1978).

33. Joseph Needham, *Time: the refreshing river* (Allen and Unwin, 1943) p. 48.

34. Ibid, p. 272.

35. Andrew Boyle, *The Climate of Treason* (Hutchinson, 1979); Chapman Pincher, *Their Trade is Treachery* (Sidgwick, 1981).

36. See Z. A. Medvedev, *The Rise and Fall of T. D. Lysenko* (New York: Columbia University Press, 1969).

37. See above, ch. 6, p. 146.

38. *Lost Illusion* (Allen and Unwin, 1949).

39. Needham, *Time: the refreshing river,* p. 71.

40. Ibid, p. 74.

41. *Searching for Light* (Michael Joseph, 1968) p. 156.

42. *Christians and Communism* (Putnam, 1956) p. 45.

43. John Middleton Murry, *The Necessity of Communism* (Jonathan Cape, 1932).

44. John Heenan, *Not the Whole Truth* (Hodder and Stoughton, 1971) p. 133.

45. Ibid, p. 136.

46. Kitty Muggeridge and Ruth Adam, *Beatrice Webb,* p. 237.

47. Barbara Wootton, *In a World I Never Made* (Allen and Unwin, 1967) p. 79.

48. In Koestler and others, *The God that Failed,* pp. 270–1.

49. Ibid, p. 8.

50. Spender, pp. 290–1.

51. From Orwell's preface to the translation into Ukrainian of *Animal Farm, Kolgasp Tuarin Kazka,* by Ivan Chernyatinskiy (Paris: Sabine, 1946).

52. For the rejection of *Animal Farm* by Gollancz, see Bernard Crick, *George Orwell. A Life* (Secker and Warburg, 1980) p. 310.

53. A general account of the influence of communism on British intellectuals is given in Neal Wood *Communism and British Intellectuals* (Gollancz, 1959).

8. THE IMPACT ON THE LEFT

1. A detailed account of the Labour party's reaction to the Russian revolution is given in Stuart Macintyre, *A Proletarian Science* (Cambridge: CUP, 1980).

2. Maurice Orbach, quoted in Jones, *The Russia Complex,* p. 4.

3. See above, ch. 2, p. 29.

4. B. Barker, *Ramsay MacDonald's Political Writings* (St Martin's, 1962) p. 237.

5. *Forward,* 31 July 1920.

6. See above, ch. 2, pp. 37, 38, 40, 41.

7. Aneurin Bevan, John Strachey and George Strauss, *What we saw in Russia* (The Hogarth Press, 1931) p. 29.

8. See above, ch. 2, pp. 36, 37, 42, 43.

9. *The Secret Battalion. An examination of the Communist attitude to the Labour party* (The Labour Party 1946).

10. *The Times,* 24 April 1956.

11. C. R. Attlee, *Problems of a Socialist Government,* ed. by Sir Stafford Cripps (Gollancz, 1933) p. 203.

12. *Finland. The criminal conspiracy of Stalin and Hitler* (The Labour party, 1940).

13. Wootton, *In a World I Never Made,* p. 184.

14. Routledge, 1940, 1965, p. 61.

15. C. A. R. Crosland, *The Future of Socialism* (Jonathan Cape, 1956) p. 77.

16. Approved by the Labour party conference in 1943.

17. *The Times,* 7 November 1977.

18. *New Left Review,* November–December 1967, p. 15.

19. 'Protest and Disturbance in the Trade Union Movement', *Political Quarterly,* 1969, p. 453.

20. Paul Ferris, *The New Militants* (Penguin Books, 1972). p. 77.

21. *Trade Unions in the New Society* (G. Allen, 1950) p. 29.

22. Quoted by Allen Hutt, *British Trade Unionism* (Lawrence and Wishart, 1975) p. 89.

23. 132 H.C. Deb. 5s. Cols 2628–30 (5 August 1920); ibid, 133, Cols 253–63 (10 August 1920). For a full discussion of the incident, see L. J. Macfarlane, 'Hands off Russia in 1920', *Past and Present,* no 38 (December 1967), Past and Present Society, Oxford.

24. Allen Hutt. *British Trade Unionism,* p. 89.

25. See above, ch. 2. p. 29.

26. See Roderick Martin, *Communism and the British Trade Unions, 1924–33* (Oxford: Clarendon Press, 1969) for a detailed study of the Minority Movement.

27. Allen Hutt, *British Trade Unionism,* p. 105.

28. Ibid, p. 103.

29. See Daniel F. Calhoun, *The United Front* (Cambridge: CUP, 1976) p. 166.

30. In some Welsh and Scottish mining villages, Communist and Labour militants, inspired by the Soviet example, for a time assumed control of the communities, which became known as 'Little Moscows'. See Stuart Macintyre, *Little Moscows* (Croom Helm, 1980).

31. *The Morning Post,* 10 July 1926.

32. W. M. Citrine, *Men and Work* (Hutchinson, 1964) p. 95.

33. Quoted by Alan Bullock, *The Life and Times of Ernest Bevin,* vol. I (Heinemann, 1967) p. 559.

34. Ibid.

35. Francis Williams, *Ernest Bevin* (Hutchinson, 1952) p. 203.

36. The *Spectator,* 26 April 1975.

37. 357 H. L. Deb. 5s. Col 825 (26 February 1975).

38. John S. Clarke, *The Worker,* 2 October 1920.

39. V. Lenin, *Lenin on Britain* (Moscow: Foreign Languages Publishing House, 1965) p. 504.

40. *The Worker,* 5 February 1921.

41. Reginald Groves, *The Balham Group* (Pluto Press, 1974) p. 16.

42. Labour Party Annual Conference, *Report,* 1922, p. 198.

43. Groves, *The Balham Group.*

44. 23 August 1939.

45. *Comment,* vol. 6, no 36, 7 September 1968.

46. Report by Jack Woddis to the Communist Party National Executive Committee

Meeting on Afghanistan, 12/13 January 1980.

47. *The British Road to Socialism* (Communist Party of Great Britain, 1977) p. 28.

9. ECONOMIC RELATIONS

1. Jules Gay, 'Anglo-Russian Economic Relations', *The Economic Journal,* June 1917.

2. Ibid.

3. *The Statist,* 25 November 1916.

4. *The Economist,* 18 November 1922.

5. The *Manchester Guardian,* 15 April 1924.

6. See above, ch. 2, p. 38.

7. L. Denny, *America Conquers Britain: a record of economic war* (New York, London: Knopf/Allen, 1930) pp. 291–2.

8. A. C. Sutton, *Western Technology and Soviet Economic Development, 1917–1930,* vol. I (Stanford, Calif.: Hoover Inst., 1968) p. 41.

9. *The Economist,* 25 January 1930.

10. See above, ch. 2, pp. 40–2.

11. See above, ch. 3, p. 53.

12. A. C. Sutton, *Western Technology,* vol. II, p. 334.

13. Monkhouse, *Moscow, 1911–1933,* p. 245.

14. *The Economist,* 10 April 1943.

15. The *Manchester Guardian,* 28 October 1932.

16. 22 October 1932.

17. 8 October 1932.

18. The *Manchester Guardian,* 7 March 1931.

19. A. C. Sutton, *Western Technology,* vol. II, p. 79.

20. 244 H.C. Deb. 5s. Col 266 (30 October 1930).

21. Ibid, Col 676 (4 November 1930).

22. 264 H.C. Deb. 5s. Col 652.

23. *The Times,* 20 November 1935.

24. 10 April 1943.

25. *The Spectator,* 24 April 1943.

26. Statement by Mr Selwyn Lloyd, 571 H.C. Deb. 5s. Cols 618–20 (30 May 1957).

27. *The Times,* 7 January 1952.

28. Ibid, 8 September 1953.

29. *The Times,* 11 September 1953.

30. Ibid, 20 August 1953.

31. Ibid, 9 November 1953.

32. Ibid, 8 April 1957.

33. Ibid, 17 June 1957.

34. Ibid, 25 July 1957.

35. Ibid, 10 January 1958.

36. 14 June 1958.

37. *The Times,* 23 March 1954.

38. Ibid, 19 March 1963.

39. 886 H.C. Deb. 5s. Col 1118 (18 February 1975).

40. Soviet Union No 1 (1975); Visit of Prime Minister and Secretary of State for

Foreign and Commonwealth Affairs to Soviet Union, Cmnd. 5924; 886 H.C. Deb. 5s. Cols 1111–20 (18 February 1975). Report on Prime Minister's visit to Soviet Union.

41. *The Times,* 21 October 1976.
42. Ibid.
43. *The Financial Times,* 2 November 1979.

10. SUMMING UP

1. *All The Way* (Hodder and Stoughton, 1949), p. 159.
2. Cmd. 6527 (May 1944).

Index

References to Britain and Russia/USSR are not included since these countries are mentioned on almost every page.